BANKERS

Q&A

Questions & Answers

Practice of Banking 2

GW00717054

BANKERS

Q&A

Questions & Answers

Practice of Banking 2

Brian Anderton & Tony Sawyer

Financial Training

First published in Great Britain 1985 by Financial Training Publications Limited,
Avenue House, 131 Holland Park Avenue, London W11 4UT

ISBN: 0 906322 62 6

Typeset by LKM Typesetting Ltd, Paddock Wood, Nr Tonbridge
Printed by The Pitman Press, Bath

Contents

Acknowledgement

The authors and publisher wish to thank the Institute of Bankers for their kind permission to include selected past examination questions in this publication.

About the authors

Brian Anderton, BSc (Economics) Hons, AIB is a senior lecturer in banking and finance at the City of Birmingham Polytechnic. After working in banking he became a lecturer at Derby Lonsdale College of Higher Education and joined the City of Birmingham Polytechnic in 1981. He is a member of the Council of the Association of Banking Teachers. He is also involved in running Law and Practice of Banking 1 revision courses for a major bank and for students in the West Midlands.

Tony Sawyer is an Associate of the Institute of Bankers and also holds a Certificate of Education. After 12 years of experience with Lloyds Bank, he joined the accounting department of a West Midlands public company. He then trained as a teacher and has spent the last 6 years at City of Birmingham Polytechnic where he is a Senior Lecturer.

He is primiarily responsible for Banking Courses but has also taught on degree and non-professional courses. He specialises in Financial Accounting and Practice of Banking, being involved in running Accountancy and Practice of Banking 2 revision courses for a major bank and local students also.

Introduction

This book contains 90 questions, most of which are taken from or based on past examination questions set by the Institute of Bankers. The authors have in some instances written questions to cover topics where suitable questions were not available.

The answers have been written in a style indicated to be desirable by the Chief Examiner. They are based on:

(a) an appreciation of the significance of the question;
(b) a reasoned practical approach to the problem;
(c) use of tabulation rather than an essay.

The book is divided into two sections; firstly Advances with six chapters, and secondly Bank Services with three chapters. The introduction to each chapter identifies the main topics for that particular part of the syllabus.

When considering questions it is most important that you actually attempt the question *before* reading the suggested answer. In this way you will develop your question answering skills. It is not intended that you try to memorise the answers, but rather that you learn the principles upon which each answer is based. This is very important, as the examiner often puts in a similar question, but presented from a different viewpoint.

The examination is also divided into the same two sections, i.e., Section A, Advances and Section B, Bank Services. From April 1985 students will be required to answer any three questions out of four in Section A, and any two questions out of three in Section B. All now carry 20 marks.

The marks awarded for questions in the book are a guide for you, as to how detailed an answer is required for the question under consideration. A question which carries 30 marks is considered equivalent in detail to one and a half questions, in the new examination structure, a question which carries 20 marks to one question, a question which carries 10 marks to half a question and so on.

Also, from April 1985, students will be able to use the 15 minutes' reading time to write on or mark the examination paper, though not to write anything on their scripts. This is a very useful facility indeed as, in the case, say, of an advances question, it allows you to underline main points, making notes as necessary. Also you can calculate ratios, and even commence budgets for a selected question, which gives you a very good start.

Remember that it is far more important to complete five questions fairly well, rather than four to a higher standard.

SUGGESTED METHOD FOR ANSWERING SECTION A QUESTIONS

Lending questions may take any format and are impossible to predict. The section is very practical by nature, as the examiner seeks to place you in a position of management responsibility, with requests by third parties to borrow your depositors' funds. The questions in the examination are all rather long.

Have some plan of attack, based on the examiner's preference for numbered points and short sentences — *never* write an essay. The following is a suggested planned layout for your consideration:

(a)   the proposition and annual cost thereof;
(b)   background of customer;
(c)   analysis of historical accounts (if in business);
(d)   budgeted accounts (or income less expenditure if non-business);
     and finally amalgamating (a)-(d) into:
(e)   a decision whether or not to lend, *and* security available if you go ahead.

In conclusion, a successful approach to Section A will be the ability to have an overview of the situation. This is only developed by considerable practice, based on the application and knowledge of ratios and budgeting techniques. Remember that in many questions you will need to make up figures for items not shown, e.g., overheads, living expenses, even sales. In this way you will be able to complete your customers' budgets.

SUGGESTED METHOD FOR ANSWERING SECTION B QUESTIONS

The questions here normally require students to follow the procedure shown below in constructing their answers:

(a)   Identify the problem or problems which confront the customer.
(b)   Identify a bank service or services which might solve these problems.
(c)   Explain to the customer the advantages of adopting the bank service or services identified.

The above formats for both Section A and Section B have been used in the answers to questions in this book.

SECTION A — ADVANCES

PART ONE FINAL ACCOUNTS AND BUDGETING TECHNIQUES

1 Scanning final accounts (historical)

INTRODUCTION

The aim of this chapter is to establish whether you can look across a series of balance sheets, together with supporting information from the income and expenditure accounts, and identify those questions you may need to ask, in the case of each named item. Two or more possibilities usually exist, for example:

Balance sheets	1982	1983	1984
Freehold land and factory	£80,000	£80,000	£170,000

Initial thoughts:

(a) Could be £90,000 spent on new premises.
(b) Could be a £90,000 revaluation where a capital reserve is evident.
(c) Could be a mixture of (a) and (b) and even a sale of a part.

Take each named item one at a time, e.g., 'plant and machinery' may well come next.

Furthermore, as you consider each 'set' of figures, you should attempt to identify other figures which have a relationship with those you are examining. Thus when you arrive at balance sheet debtors, you must automatically consider sales, from which they are derived. In this chapter please avoid the temptation of using the calculator to work out ratios — this work will be done in Chapter 2. Set your mind, rather, to what should be happening in a well run business. Consider the following:

Balance sheets	1982	1983	1984
Debtors	£40,000	£50,000	£75,000

'Scanning' the above we find a 25% increase in the year 1983, and a 50% increase in 1984. Our dominating thought is: are sales increasing (at least) by similar amounts each year? If not, debtor recovery is worsening.

To be able to scan, understand and question accounts presented to us, as lending managers, is of paramount importance — after all it is not the best idea to use a calculator with one's customer present!

(The suggested answers in this chapter are not necessarily exhaustive.)

1 MANUFACTURES LTD
(Question set in 1981)

	1979		1980		Draft balance sheet as at 28 February 1981	
	£	£	£	£	£	£
Current assets:						
Debtors	320,000		400,000		370,000	
Stock	150,000		190,000		120,000	
Work in progress	80,000	550,000	85,000	675,000	90,000	580,000
Current liabilities:						
Bank	40,000		30,000		60,000	
Creditors	180,000		200,000		240,000	
Tax	60,000		79,000		80,000	
Dividend	10,000	290,000	11,000	320,000	–	380,000
Net current assets		260,000		355,000		200,000
Fixed assets:						
Freehold premises		100,000		105,000		105,000
Plant and machinery		60,000		50,000		50,000
		420,000		510,000		355,000
Capital authorised and issued		80,000		80,000		80,000
Reserves		200,000		200,000		200,000
Profit and loss account		140,000		230,000		75,000
		420,000		510,000		355,000
Sales		1,200,000		1,500,000		800,000
Purchases		700,000		850,000		600,000
Bad debts		2,000		1,500		75,000
Tax		90,000		100,000		–
Depreciation		10,000		10,000		–
Net profit (loss)		75,000		90,000		(155,000)

The top of the column reads: Balance sheets as at 31 August 1979, 1980, and Draft balance sheet as at 28 February 1981.

Required:

Consider the historical accounts presented, and write notes to describe what has happened over the past three years, together with any other thoughts which may prompt questions of the company's directors.

Do not work ratios/percentages but you should highlight any other figures which may have a relationship with those you are considering.

20 marks

2   A LTD
(Question set in 1981)

Balance sheets as at 31 August

	1980 £	1981 £		1980 £	1981 £
Current liabilities:			Current assets:		
Creditors	115,800	157,000	Debtors	42,000	40,000
Bank	39,000	63,000	Stock	92,000	156,000
Directors' loans	2,000	2,000			
				134,000	196,000
	156,800	222,000	Fixed assets:		
Share capital	1,000	1,000	Land and buildings:		
Capital reserve	65,000	65,000	leases	74,400	74,400
Profit and loss			Shop improvements	28,000	23,000
account	39,800	38,800	Fixtures and fittings	22,800	29,000
			Motor vehicles	3,400	4,400
	262,600	326,800		262,600	326,800

	1980	1981
Sales	556,000	640,000
Purchases	343,000	446,000
Gross profit	243,000	261,000

Required:

Consider the historical accounts presented, and write short notes to describe your thoughts on the past two years' operations of the company, and of the near future. Highlight questions you would need answering.

Do not work ratios/percentages but you should highlight any other figures which may have a relationship with those you are considering.

15 marks

3   SENTINEL LTD
(Question set in 1981)

The summarised balance sheets of Sentinel Ltd at 31 December 1979 and 31 December 1980 (unaudited) were as follows:

	1979 £000	1980 £000		1979 £000	1980 £000
Ordinary shares £1			Goodwill	260	260
each	1,200	1,200	Freeholds at cost	420	420
Profit and loss			Plant and machinery		
account	400	780	cost less deprecia-		
Bank overdraft	–	180	tion	60	20
Trade creditors	280	840	Motor vehicles at cost		
			less depreciation	–	120
			Stocks:		
			Raw materials	260	220
			Work in progress	60	40
			Finished goods	400	1,140
			Debtors and prepay-		
			ments	300	780
			Cash at bank	120	–
	1,880	3,000		1,880	3,000

The following additional information is available:

(a)   Extracts from manufacturing, trading and profit and loss accounts:

	1979	1980
	£000	£000
Sales	4,640	7,740
Net profit	200	380
Depreciation: Plant and machinery	40	40
Motor vehicles	–	20
Cost of materials consumed	2,400	5,200

(b)   It is the company's policy to give cash discounts for prompt payments. An analysis of debtors at 31 December produces the following figures:

	1979	1980
	£000	£000
Botterill Ltd	20	22
Norton Ltd	180	620
Newbould Ltd	35	34
Parker Ltd	27	31
Other customers	38	53
20% deposit on purchase of additional freehold property	–	20
	300	780

(c)   Analysis of sales:

	1979	1980
	£000	£000
1 Jan to 30 June: Botterill Ltd	224	240
Norton Ltd	–	2,480
Newbould Ltd	275	290
Parker Ltd	306	300
Other customers	1,155	1,270
1 July to 31 Dec: Botterill Ltd	207	210
Norton Ltd	580	1,240
Newbould Ltd	281	296
Parker Ltd	240	250
Other customers	1,372	1,164
	4,640	7,740

(d)   No sales have been made to Norton Ltd since 1 September 1980.

Required:

Consider the historical accounts and data provided, making notes on items presented and questions you would need answering. Do not work ratios/percentages, but highlight other figures which may have a relationship with those you are considering.

15 marks

4

ANSWERS

1 MANUFACTURES LTD

Draft as at 28.2.81

Last column – how reliable if unaudited? Six month figures can give anomolies in ratio analysis for 'time' calculations particularly, e.g., debtors recovery, creditor repayment, stock turnover, especially if trade is seasonal.

Debtors

25% increase during 1980, so we would hope sales have moved by the same proportion *at least* to prevent extension of debtor recovery time – looks spot on, £300,000 extra being ¼ of last year's £1.2 million.

Debtors in draft accounts show little change from 1980 – expect same turnover for full year to 31.8.81 – £800,000 doubled near enough; but consider seasonal savings by taking debtors out of the '31 August' sequence, i.e., 28 February. Ask directors.

Does the debtor figure represent trade debts only? We would wish to extract any debts for capital items, e.g., machinery sold *and* prepayments must also be deducted.

Raw material stocks

Tend to vary with sales targets. So that a £40,000 increase in 1980, almost ¼, is in line with sales increases (see above).

Considerably less raw material stock held in draft accounts, i.e., looks great, a much faster stock turnover, but can £120,000 service sales of £1.6 million (2 × £800,000) *or* are sales about to fall dramatically so as not to reach this figure, *or* has stock been over-valued in previous years?

Work in progress

Consists of raw material stocks passing through machinery. To the amount is added direct labour (£) (at least), if a marginal costing system is in force; more if other costing systems are used, e.g., factory overheads (£) apportioned.

The figure will not dramatically alter with sales, as machinery can only cope with so much production, unless new plant is bought. The latter does not look to be evident here (plant machinery constant).

Bank overdraft

Taken from the company's cash book, not the bank statement. Thus the total rarely agrees with the bank balance at 31 August annually. Often the cash book overdraft is considerably more than the bank account overdraft due to the three days it takes to clear cheques. Many companies 'live' on this three day period, knowing that cheques received and banked on a *daily* basis will not allow the bank overdraft at their branch to go 'over the top'.

Is the account secured or not?

The figure, although part of the current liabilities, will be added into loans, when bankers calculate gearing.

Creditors

May also be related to sales trends, although again any accruals, or fixed asset purchases will have to be extracted from them. Assuming they all represent trade purchases, there is only a 10% plus, say, increase in 1980 against 1979 (£20,000), yet sales are up ¼. We are fortunate to have a purchases figure each year, showing a £150,000 rise in 1980 which is about 20% more. Thus Manufactures Ltd must be paying its creditors more quickly.

Corporation tax

Always an accrual, each figure relating to the previous year's taxable profits. We can rarely confirm the total, as we cannot reconstruct the tax computation, since we do not have information on capital allowances (originating from *most* fixed assets bought, and stock relief).

Tax computation:	£
Net profit for year	X
Add: Depreciation for year	X
Less: Capital allowance	(X)
Taxable	X

Note: Capital allowances are being phased out over the next few years and will be 'balanced' by falls in the rate of corporation tax.

Corporation tax falls into two sections: (i) mainstream corporation tax (MCT) which is paid nine months after the year end — unless the company was established before April 1965 when between nine and 21 months before payment could prevail; (ii) advanced corporation tax (ACT) which is an earlier tax and relates to the amount of dividends paid — a type of penalty for paying them. It is paid 14 days after the end of the 'standard' quarters (31 March, 30 June, 30 September and 31 December), depending on the quarter within which the dividend was paid.

Thus the banker needs an ACT and MCT split of the tax bill, and *when* each is to be paid. Ask directors.

Dividends

Those shown in the balance sheet are current liabilities at the year end, and invariably represent the final dividend. Thus if an interim has been paid it would be in addition to the item shown. It would seem that excessive dividends are not being paid, however, as retained profit is considerable (draft accounts excepted).

Net current assets

These are the amount of working capital, and the current ratio is essential before we can comment on it.

Freehold premises

These show little movement; even so, a purchase *and* sale *and* revaluation could have taken place in any one year. Doubtful here though. Bankers would wish to know whether the asset is at cost price *or* revaluation value (which would create a revaluation (capital) reserve which could be within the reserves figure. Also ask as to when the premises were bought — £5,000 (net) addition recently perhaps?

Plant and machinery

This item creates exactly the same question as all fixed assets, i.e., purchases less sales less depreciation for the year so changing the opening net total. We also wonder how old machinery is? Does the company attempt to update it regularly? It should strive for the best machinery possible by keeping as little in working capital funds as it can manage with.

Issued capital

Shows no movement, and we can assume no transactions. When shares do increase we must consider whether they are 'rights' issues for cash *or* 'scrip' issues which are bonus issues from capitalisation of reserves, the latter being reduced.

Reserves

These are of two groups: revenue reserves made out of trading profit retentions; and capital reserves out of windfall profits usually 'across' the balance sheet, e.g., revaluation reserves, share premium on rights issues. The latter may only be capitalised (as new shares), *not* paid out as dividend. We need to know the origins of the £200,000.

Profit and loss account

This is definitely revenue reserves retained, and can often be balanced with retained profit in the profit and loss (appropriation) account, i.e., balance £140,000 at 31.8.79, add £90,000 retention 1980 = balance £230,000 at 31.8.80. Likewise between 1980 and 1981, when losses are deducted.

Sales

Increases must be examined to see whether they represent *real* growth or merely inflationary price rises. The 25% rise in 1980 represents *real progress*, well over prevailing inflation rates in 1980. The £100,000 possible difference between 1981 (2 × £800,000, if it happens?) and £1,500,000 in 1980 is unspectacular and represents little progress.

Sales are always shown *after* deduction of VAT.

Purchases

Only available within internal sets of accounts, i.e., do not have to be made available in published sets sent to the Registrar of Companies.

As the company is a manufacturer they must represent raw material purchases, which by applying opening and closing raw material stock levels, would give us raw materials consumed. Unfortunately we cannot apply this to sales as we attempt to reach gross profit, as all other factory overheads, direct wages and finished goods in stock (if any) are unknown to us.

Our sole chance is to attempt to apply this to sales, adjusting for stocks, so testing for material content. An anomoly is obvious in the material content in the draft accounts, where purchases look far too high, and yet closing stocks are down! We must ask directors to explain.

Bad debts

Will need the directors' comments on the position shown by the draft accounts — what is happening? Is there a likelihood of further bad debts; could we see the company's age of debt analysis?

Tax

Missing in draft accounts, indicative of losses. 1979 and 1980 figures exceed the liabilities shown in the balance sheets, thus part must have been paid — probably ACT.

Depreciation

Missing from the draft accounts, which must be incorrect; a half-yearly charge should have been made, so worsening the net loss to, say, £160,000 (£5,000 for a half-year).

The £10,000 write-off in 1979 and 1980 seems to indicate that there has been little or no movement in fixed assets.

Net profit

The final summation as between sales less variable overheads which give a contribution to profit subject to deduction of fixed overheads.

Thus when sales rise, variable overheads move with them, but because fixed overheads, and a mid-group called semi-variables have less impact, net profit should accelerate faster than the rise of sales in percentage terms.

The mix of fixed and variable is all important. Obviously if fixed are much higher, and sales expand extremely quickly, then once the break-even point has been passed, profit will be generated very quickly.

So without a full breakdown of fixed and variable expenses we are unable to ascertain whether the 25% rise in turnover in 1980 should or should not have resulted in more than a 20% rise in net profit (£90,000 less £75,000 = £15,000, as to £75,000). Our initial reaction is that the net profit increase of £15,000 *is too low* but extra costs associated with the balance sheet could account for it, e.g., extra loan/bank interest to finance capital expenditure, also excess advertising in the profit and loss account in the year in question, etc.

The draft accounts send a shudder through us — a full explanation is needed.

Tutorial note

The above should be among your thoughts as you quickly read through the accounts. In reality you would work the following ratios:

(a) debtor recovery rate;
(b) stock turnover rate;
(c) creditor repayment rate;
(d) current ratio (sometimes called the working capital ratio);
(e) liquid ratio;
(f) net profit margin;
(g) gross profit margin;
(h) gearing.

Having said the above, however, you should be able to obtain a good idea of what is happening before resorting to the calculator.

Always attempt to substantiate asset values.

2   A LTD

Land and buildings leases

Most probably short leased factory or even shops — we don't know whether A Ltd is a manufacturer, wholesaler or retailer. Shop leases would be probably no more than 21 years in length, whereas factories and warehouses could be longer.

We need to know whether the £74,400 shown was actually paid out in cash for the leased premises and should it not be being depreciated as the leases shorten?

Such leases have very low security value, and our eyes immediately travel to capital reserves of £65,000. Have the leases been revalued, possibly to 'window-dress' the balance sheet? Bankers beware.

Shop improvements

This now guides us as to the line of business; thus the leases are probably of low value, depending on situation. Where are the shops, and how many — a visit needed?

Fixtures and fittings

This will differ from the above, usually relating to internal fittings rather than the shop frontage improvements and structural work included under the previous heading.

When the manager's visit takes place the expenditure on this item and on shop improvements must be carefully considered as to the accuracy of each asset value in the balance sheet. Is depreciation being applied on both and over what period of time?

Motor vehicles

Increase indicates a purchase (and probable disposal). The nominal amount extra spent would appear to be a good sign indicating control, but as we move on to working capital/net current assets the reason soon becomes evident.

Net current assets

A deficit each year of £22,800 and £26,000 respectively. This is the accountant's definition of insolvency – being unable to pay debts (current liabilities) as they fall due. Although the £26,000 shortfall seems little worse than last year's £22,800, because of the rising of all working capital constituents it most certainly is worse. A stranglehold could be forming.

Companies do come back from these positions. It is good to consider the gearing position at this point. If the shareholders are the directors also (which is most probable in a small company), *and* they have much to lose, i.e., their cash *and* future jobs, then they will usually work at the problem.

Debtors

Debtors recovery looks tremendous against sales, but this further indicates a cash business, i.e., shops. So if we could find out how much of sales per annum is on credit (as opposed to cash) we could get somewhere. If, say, ¼ was on credit, then ¼ of £640,000 = £160,000 and with debtors now at £40,000 a 3 month recovery emerges and does not look so good. An incredible thought now arises – that a bad debt element could exist even within the £40,000.

Stock

Levels are expected to rise with the sales push but usually in some near proportion. Questions to ask relating to this vast increase centre around buying policies/slow moving stocks/unsaleable items. Can a reduction be made to free funds for creditors? Also each type of retail outlet has its own rate of stock turnover 'norm', so we now need to know what they sell (we assume they are not fishmongers!).

Creditors

List must be supplied: who are they and how much is owed to each? Is there a good spread or one main supplier? Will one of the creditors be likely to bring an action for his cash in the near future?

Bank account

Pressure will most probably exist. Is the bank secured or not? The bank appears to be 'in the business' for around the cash book figure of £63,000 and with the owners' stake at £1,000 + £65,000 + £38,000 + £2,000 = £106,800 looks comfortable gearing. But if the capital reserve is suspect, even forced, *and* the asset values crumble, the bank could be in a mess, especially if it relies on the company for repayment (rather than the owners' private estates).

Directors' loans

Withdrawable at any time. While they could be capitalised into shares, so preventing this, we as bankers should not readily suggest this. Also a stamp duty is paid on the number of shares issued.

Capital structure

Shows a reasonably nominal share issue of £1,000. Questions to be asked relating to the £65,000 capital reserves. Retained profits of £38,800, although commendable, will prove only a small buffer if problems arise, due to the size of the current liabilities.

Sales

Show a rise of between 14 to 18% (without using a calculator) i.e., £640,000 less £556,000 = £84,000, expressed as to £556,000, which is above inflationary price rises and thus positive growth.

Purchases

In 1980, about 3/5 of sales but worsen in 1981 to 45/64 of sales, i.e., in excess of 2/3.

Thus, subject to adjustments for opening and closing stocks, it is possible that either purchase unit prices are rising, or selling unit prices are falling, or both.

Gross profit margins

These confirm the above, as the 1980 margin, 243 gross profit to 556 sales, must be better than 261 gross profit to 640 sales in 1981.

Tutorial note

In the full question we were being offered the account from one of our competitor banks. The examiner made the comment that cash flows and budgeted accounts into the near future will highlight whether survival is possible. These techniques will be dealt with in Chapter 3, but are outside our present 'scanning' procedures.

3   SENTINEL LTD

Draft accounts

How reliable are they?

Goodwill

An intangible asset — we would like details of how it arose, and is it to be written off against revenue reserves, via the profit and loss account?

Freeholds

Appear to be unchanged. As in Question 1, Manufactures, we would inquire as to possible purchase and sale, but most doubtful as they would have to be in similar figures, as totals are shown at *cost* price. Because they are at cost, we would be interested in purchase dates and a valuation figure at 31.12.80. Could be a hidden reserve. Be careful though, in 1985 great problems exist in selling factories at reasonable prices (the depression).

Plant and machinery

Net values show very low investment, and this could be a very dangerous sign. Questions to ask revolve around the age and continuing effectiveness of the machinery, and the company's future policy thereto.

Motor vehicles

An incredible situation: £120,000 spent thereon. Nil value was shown for this item (lorries, vans, company cars) last year, and while this does not mean necessarily that they did not have any (they could have been fully depreciated but still functional), a complete breakdown of the figure is necessary.

Two very worrying points could arise:

(a)   With no hire-purchase debt showing we must assume the purchases came out of working capital — we will check the net current asset position shortly.

(b)   If £120,000 has been spent on fixed assets, which could possibly be 'non-essential' (i.e., could have been rented), has this been at the expense of correcting the plant and machinery position as discussed above?

Stock levels

Levels of raw materials and work in progress have been reduced — we wonder how much is being produced now, and in the future? Finished goods in hand are abnormal, unless last year's were sub-normal — what is happening? Have items been made to order and a deal fallen through? Have they missed the market in a particular line? These could present real problems.

Debtors

More than doubled, on sales which have nowhere near doubled. Again, warning lights are showing.

We would ask for a debtor breakdown and here we have it. Norton Ltd immediately stands out, and from turnover statistics it appears that they were new customers in the half year commencing 1.7.79. During 1980 sales to them amounted to £3,720,000, almost half of the 1980 turnover, and certainly the reason for the sales explosion. But what is happening to them now? Is the company still selling to them; how long has their £620,000 been outstanding – even though this is only about 1/6 of the Norton turnover above, we must not assume that it is only 2 months of debt, as it depends on when their turnover peaked, and whether they are still buying from the company.

Bank balances

Moved from credit to overdraft, obviously by agreement with bankers. We would wish to know the limit and if excesses were occurring.

Creditors

Have increased threefold, again out of line with the sales increase. Suppliers are almost certainly waiting much longer.

Working capital

In 1979 was quite excessive, it would seem, for a manufacturing company (£260 + £60 +-£400 + £300 + £120, i.e., £1,140 to £280) and cash should have been applied to improve fixed assets (*or* to repay loans if applicable). The situation in 1980 is tolerable (£2,180 to £1,020), but should the Norton debt prove uncollectable and the finished goods stocks prove unsaleable, then liquidation could occur.

Profits

Appear to have been retained, but last year's item £380,000 (made at the *moment* of sale to the debtor) could be swept away if Norton fails to pay.

Ordinary shares

Little to note.

Depreciation

Depreciation in the revenue accounts indicates that the 'expected life' of the assets is about to end.

Raw materials

Amount of these consumed could *possibly* have increased, though much of it will be within stocks of finished goods (£1,140,000), and, as we do not know their mark-up, we cannot comment further.

Debtor analysis

Indicates fairly level trade with other companies (except Norton), but the £20,000 20% deposit on freehold property is a source for concern, i.e., another £80,000 is due on this most fixed of all fixed assets which usually needs more plant and machinery *and* working capital funds to make it functional.

Tutorial note

Again the future is all important and considerable work will need to be done in this area, which will be the subject of Chapter 3, Budgeting Techniques.

2 Ratio analysis applied to historical accounts

INTRODUCTION

The aim of this chapter is to apply selectively ratios used by the banker to past balance sheets and their accompanying revenue accounts, so as to formulate a picture of the enterprise to date, which in itself is a stepping-stone as to what may happen in the future.

Understanding the information supplied by the ratios is of prime importance. Good comments, together with questions you would need to ask management, will bring considerable marks in the examination, whereas mere calculations with few remarks will create no impression.

Ratios primarily relate to performance, activity, stability and growth, and well over 100 ratios exist. As bankers we can probably manage with the following:

(a) Gearing (or leverage) $= \dfrac{\text{Loan capital}}{\text{Equity capital}}$

$= \dfrac{\text{Loans} + \text{Preference shares} + \text{Deferred tax} + \text{Overdrafts}}{\text{Shares} + \text{Reserves} + \text{Directors' loans}}$

(b) Gross profit margin $= \dfrac{\text{Gross profit}}{\text{Sales}} \times 100\%$

(c) Net profit margin $= \dfrac{\text{Net profit}}{\text{Sales}} \times 100\%$

(d) Working capital ratio (or Current ratio) $= \dfrac{\text{Current assets}}{\text{Current liabilities}}$

(e) Liquid ratio (or quick ratio) $= \dfrac{\text{Current assets less stocks}}{\text{Current liabilities}}$

(f) Debtor recovery rate $= 365 \times \dfrac{\text{Debtors}}{\text{Sales}}$

(g)   Creditor repayment rate $=$ $365 \times \dfrac{\text{Creditors}}{\text{Purchases}}$

(h)   Stock turnover rate $=$ $365 \times \dfrac{\text{Average stock}}{\text{Cost of sales}}$

(b) and (c) are performance ratios; (f), (g) and (h) measure activity; and (a), (d) and (e) relate to stability.

1 BETA CARPETS LTD
(Question set in 1980)

The company is a retail outlet.

Balance sheets as at 31 December

	1982		1983	
	£		£	
Fixed assets:				
Vehicles		1,950		2,500
Current assets:				
Cash at bank	2,300		1,700	
Debtors	2,900		3,900	
Stock	3,700		2,900	
	8,900		8,500	
Current liabilities:				
Creditors: trade and hire-purchase	5,200		4,800	
Taxation	250	3,450	290	3,410
		5,400		5,910
Issued capital		500		500
Profit and loss account		90		160
Directors' loans		4,810		5,250
		5,400		5,910
Sales		41,000		62,000
Purchases		27,000		42,000
Gross profit		13,000		18,200

Profit and loss figures for the year ended December 1983

Gross profit		18,200
Rent	2,500	
Other overheads including depreciation	3,630	
Directors' drawings	12,000	18,130
Retained profit		70

Required:

Assess the financial position as disclosed in the trading, profit and loss accounts, and balance sheets above.

15 marks

2   ELSTREE SAWMILLS CO LTD

(Question set in 1977)

The company is a timber wholesaler.

Balance sheets

	£	31.12.83 £	£	Budget 31.12.84 £
Share capital		60,000		60,000
Reserves		62,548		82,548
Deferred taxation		26,184		26,184
		148,732		168,732
Fixed assets		75,973		115,973
Current assets:				
Stocks	35,000		45,000	
Debtors	48,000		56,000	
Group companies	4,538		–	
Cash at bank	4,000		23,759	
	91,538		124,759	
Current liabilities:				
Creditors	18,000		32,000	
Bank loan	–		40,000	
Hire-purchase	779		–	
	18,779		72,000	
Net current assets		72,759		52,759
		148,732		168,732

Trading and profit and loss accounts

	12 months 31.12.83 £	Budget 12 months 31.12.84 £
Sales: Third party	241,000	300,000
Group	28,000	10,000
	269,000	310,000
Materials consumed	72,000	85,000
Direct wages	48,000	54,000
Gross margin	149,000	171,000

	12 months 31.12.83 £	Budget 12 months 31.12.84 £
Indirect wages	52,000	56,000
Rent and rates	5,700	15,000
Insurance	3,600	3,000
Heat, light and power	4,500	5,000
Repairs: Property	800	1,000
Machinery	3,200	3,500
Depreciation	18,000	10,000
Vehicles expenses	10,000	8,500
Administration salaries	12,000	19,000
Pensions payable	1,600	1,600
National insurance	10,800	12,000
Stationery, telephone	3,000	3,000
Professional charges	450	500
Interest: Bank	8,200	10,000
Hire-purchase	950	400
Training board	1,000	1,000
Miscellaneous	1,500	1,500
	137,300	151,000
Profit retained	11,700	20,000

Note: Ignore taxation.

Required:

Work ratios as necessary, commenting on your findings.

15 marks

3   A B EQUIPMENT LTD
(Question set in 1981)

This company is a manufacturer.

Balance sheet as at 31 March

		1979 £	1980 £	1981 £
Fixed assets:				
Goodwill		3,000	3,000	3,000
Vehicles		8,000	7,000	9,000
Fixtures and fittings		2,500	2,250	2,000
Plant and machinery		6,000	4,500	6,500
	c/f	19,500	16,750	20,500

		1979		**1980**		**1981**
		£		£		£
	b/f	19,500		16,750		20,500
Current assets:						
Bank	3,000		4,500		2,000	
Debtors	22,500		24,750		25,000	
Stock	10,000		12,000		20,000	
Work in progress	2,000		2,500		3,000	
	37,500		43,750		50,000	
Current liabilities:						
Hire-purchase creditors	5,000		4,000		7,000	
Trade/sundry creditors	10,000		12,000		14,000	
Current tax	3,000	19,500	2,000	25,750	4,000	25,000
		39,000		42,500		45,500
Issued capital		10,000		10,000		10,000
Profit and loss account		29,000		32,500		35,500
		39,000		42,500		45,500
Sales		90,000		99,000		108,000
Cost of sales:						
Labour		30,000		34,200		39,000
Materials		15,000		17,250		19,700
		45,000		51,450		58,700
Directors' remuneration		25,000		25,000		25,000
Rent		1,500		1,500		1,500
Depreciation		1,500		2,000		2,500

Required:

Work ratios as necessary, commenting on your findings.

15 marks

ANSWERS

1   BETA CARPETS LTD

Gearing

1982	1983
£5,400 to Nil	£5,910 to Nil

Expansion of most businesses is achieved with careful injections of loan capital in controlled situations. It is possibly appropriate that the directors should approach their bankers. The purpose of the loan and its future repayment in both interest and capital terms will be the deciding factors from the bank's viewpoint.

Gross profit margins

1982: $(13/41) \times 100\% = 31.7\%$

1983: $(18.2/62) \times 100\% = 29.4\%$

A very important ratio for retailers, where the bank has great opportunity to test its customer's profit margins against the 'norms' of, in this case, the retail carpet trade:

	1982	1983
Sales	100%	100%
Less: Gross profit	(31.7)%	(29.4)%
Cost of sales	68.3%	70.6%

Therefore: $(31.7/68.3) \times 100\%$ = 46.4% mark-up

$(29.4/70.6) \times 100\%$ = 41.6% mark-up

It appears that the mark-up of purchases, in this semi-luxury market, are rather low, where the 'norm' could be, say, 60%. We enquire of our customer. If, however, their selling prices are very reasonable, we would expect to see a very fast stock turnover rate, which should result in corrected amounts of profit.

Sales have climbed dramatically by £21,000, i.e., 51%, which indicates a year of real growth in the business.

Net profit margin (*before* directors' drawings)

1983: $(12,070/62,000) \times 100\% = 19.5\%$

If a business has a working capital and fixed asset structure sufficient for its needs (often the case with shops) it is ridiculous not to take out the bulk of its profit as drawings. After all, income tax at 30% is a better deal than corporation tax @ 40%, on the £12,000.

We would like comparisons with previous years to make judgments.

Working capital ratio

1982: (8,900/5,450) to 1:1.6 to 1

1983: (8,500/5,090) to 1:1.7 to 1

The above liquidity rates are about right for shops, so as to: (a) avoid creditor pressure; and (b) waste excess funds in working capital.

Current assets could even be reduced as the tax bill will not be due for a minimum of nine months.

Liquidity ratio

1982: (5,200/5,450) to 1:0.95 to 1

1983: (5,600/5,090) to 1:1.1 to 1

Most retailers can manage on, say, 0.5 to 1, so that up to half the debtors and cash could be moved into stocks, which still maintains the correct working capital ratio.

Debtor recovery rate

1982: 365 × (29/410) = 26 days

1983: 365 × (39/620) = 23 days

Recovery looks tremendous, but this is not necessarily so. If retailers mainly sell for cash, we would need a breakdown of their credit sales:

Assume 30% is by way of credit sales:

	1982	1983
Therefore:	365 × (29/123)	365 × (39/186)
	= 86 days	= 77 days

A bad debt possibility could even exist. Enquiries should be made.

Creditor recovery rate

1982: 365 × (52/270) = 70 days

1983: 365 × (48/420) = 42 days

A very satisfactory position exists now, and they may even be taking discount for part of their purchases, for settlement within, say, 30 days.

Stock turnover rate

1982: 365 × (3.3/28) = 43 days

1983: 365 × (3.3/43.8) = 28 days

Perhaps the second most important ratio for retailers, but often difficult to calculate accurately. A monthly turnround of stocks is very good for this trade, and evidenced by increasing sales.

Note: While an average stock level of £3,300 over the two years is not strictly accurate, it is close enough in this case, where opening and closing stock variations are not very great.

Summary

All ratios hold up to scrutiny, particularly in 1983 where excellent results are evident.

2   ELSTREE SAWMILLS CO LTD

Gearing

	1983				1984 Budget	
£		£			£	£
26,184		60,000			26,184	60,000
779		62,548			40,000	82,548
26,963	to	122,548			66,184 to	142,548

i.e.,   0.22 to 1

i.e.,   0.46 to 1

Company very low geared (loans low); shareholders carrying the main risk, especially if reserves are of a revenue nature (out of trading profits made). If capital reserves, we must beware of possible 'window dressing', e.g., assets revalued — enquire.

Note: Deferred tax is a liablity, *not* quasi-capital (SSAP 15), as it could possibly have to be paid over as corporation tax, but this is unlikely if the assets it represents are retained. The liablity originates from the profit and loss appropriation account, and represents tax saved relating to capital allowances. It is capitalised annually to revenue reserves over the life of the asset it represents.

Gross profit margins

1983: (197/269) × 100% = 73.2%

1984 Budget: (225/310) × 100% = 72.5%

Draft accounts indicate that the margin between selling *unit* prices and purchase *unit* prices is being maintained. Thus management are aware of, and able to pass on, prices rising against them (assuming this is happening).

We would also be interested to know whether the profit margin is correct (the 'norm') for the timber industry. Were it below par, we could have questions to ask.

(Note that the operatives' direct wages must be added back to obtain gross profit. Beware of any such anomalies in presentation of accounts.)

Net profit margin

1983: $(11.7/269) \times 100\% = 4.3\%$

1984 Budget: $(20/310) \times 100\% = 6.5\%$

Net profit is the difference between sales and all expenses. Expenses are dividable into variable overheads, fixed overheads and semi-variable overheads (the latter group being somewhere between fully variable and fixed). Here we are fortunate to have a full set of internal (management) accounts, so that categorisation into the above is, with some difficulty, possible.

Thus our conclusion is that when sales rise by 15.2%, i.e., (310,000 less 269,000/ 269,000) $\times$ 100%, net profit should rise faster, and does, at 70.9%, i.e., (20,000 – 11,700/11,700) $\times$ 100%. This reflects management control over variable and semi-variable overheads, assuming fixed overheads stay constant.

The 'mix' of variable and semi-variable overheads to fixed overheads is all important. When the fixed content is large, profit accelerates very quickly once the break-even point has been cleared – possibly the case here.

Working capital ratio

1983: (91,538/18,000) to 1: 5.1 to 1

1984 Budget: (124,759/32,000) to 1: 3.9 to 1

If shortfalls of working capital can be a disaster, the position here is exactly the opposite. Too much working capital is considered wasteful, in that surpluses should be applied to more up-to-date fixed assets. The 'surplus situation' only usually comes about after years of successful trading and certain levelling off as to the annual turnover.

However, this company still seems to be growing and needs £40,000 from us for fixed assets; and at almost 4 to 1, retains probably twice the working capital it needs. This could be its policy, however, where debtors are not pressurised to pay by virtue of the company's liquidity.

Liquidity ratio

Does not merit calculation, in view of above strengths – notably the size of the debtor bank compared with creditor levels.

Debtor recovery rates

1983: 365 × (52.5/269) = 71 days

1984 Budget: 365 × (56/310) = 66 days

The above are probably normal in the present recession of the early 1980s but sight of the company's 'age of debt analysis' may be necessary. However, the point made under 'working capital ratio' above, i.e., deliberate company policy to promote and maintain sales, could apply.

Creditor repayment rates

1983: 365 × (18/72) = 91 days

1984 Budget: 365 × (32/85) = 137 days

Your first reaction could be the seriousness of the situation – who are the creditors, etc. – but all of this pales behind the overall strength of the net current asset structure (see 'working capital ratio' above).

Note: slight imperfections here in that creditors are worked against cost of sales/ materials consumed rather than purchases. We could get to purchases in the draft accounts:

OS (35) + P – CS (45) = C of S (85)

but for better comparison with the previous year we should stay with materials consumed.

Stock turnover rates

1983: 365 × (35/72) = 177 days

1984 Draft: 365 × (45/85) = 193 days

Stocks appear to move very slowly, but this could be correct for the timber business, i.e., seasoning of cut timber. The answer would again be perfectable if we knew the 'norms' of the timber business. We would ask management.

Note: one of the most difficult ratios to construct due to perfecting the 'average stock' position. In this case it is impossible to determine opening stocks for 1983 so for continuity, closing stocks are assumed to be the average for both years – and there the problems lie.

Summary

Looks like a £40,000 loan request to us, from a company in a mature stage of growth.

3 A B EQUIPMENT LTD

Gearing

1979	1980	1981
5 to 39	4 to 42½	7 to 45½
0.13 to 1	0.09 to 1	0.15 to 1

Very low geared, and thus appropriate that management should approach the loan givers if they feel that by taking injections of loan capital their overall business will improve.

At 50:50 level gearing the loan injection would be £38,500, i.e., £45,500 less £7,000.

Gross profit margin

1979
$$\frac{90 - 45}{90} \times 100\%$$
$$= 50.0\%$$

1980
$$\frac{99 - 51.45}{99} \times 100\%$$
$$= 48.0\%$$

1981
$$\frac{108 - 58.7}{108} \times 100\%$$
$$= 45.6\%$$

Falling margin suggests rising manufacturing costs, or falling selling unit prices, or both. Explanations necessary — but occasionally management deliberately reduce selling prices to improve their share of the market. However with a sales rise of 10%, (9/90) × 100, in 1980 and a rise of 9.1% the following year, if such a policy had been adopted, it was largely unsuccessful, rises in turnover being little above inflationary levels, and not representing *real* growth.

Net profit margins

1979: not available

1980: (55*/990) × 100% = 5.6%

1981: (70/1,080) × 100% = 6.5%

*Arrived at thus: retained profit, P/L account 1980 £32,500, less 1980 £29,000, *plus* taxation for the year of £2,000 added back.

Although the trading performance as shown by gross profit margins above was unspectacular, one good point arose in that more was available in gross profit in 1981 — an extra £1,750 over the previous year. This, together with management's control over the administration and selling overheads in the profit and loss account has improved the amount of net profit and retained profit — but only in marginal sums.

Working capital ratio

1979	1980	1981
(37,500/19,500) to 1	(43,750/25,750) to 1	(50,000/25,000) to 1
1.9 to 1	1.7 to 1	2 to 1

Although used as medium-term liabilities under gearing, hire-purchase is added to current liabilities to give the bank the weakest position available.

Improvements have taken place, and at 2 to 1 this *manufacturer* is just on suggested guidelines, although the quality of his product, together with market image could necessitate moves marginally in either direction. But he is probably about right and creditor pressure should not arise, nor are funds being wasted.

Liquid ratio

1979	1980	1981
(25,500/19,500) to 1	(29,250/25,750) to 1	(27,000/25,000) to 1
1.3 to 1	1.1 to 1	1.1 to 1

Again, 1 to 1 is probably sufficient for a manufacturer, which corrects the excess position in 1979.

Note: in the present recession most manufacturers are 'hanging on' in much lower working capital and liquid capital ratios.

Debtor recovery rate

1979	1980	1981
$365 \times (22.5/90)$	$365 \times (24.75/99)$	$365 \times (25/108)$
= 91 days	= 91 days	= 84 days

Slight improvement from three months overall but if there is a spread of debtors, which is assumed, many must be taking well above the average, say four months, and their debt may be uncollectable. Age of debt required.

Unlike Elstree Sawmills (question 2), this company does not have tolerances in its working capital structure, and may have to improve its credit control.

Creditor repayment rate

1979	1980	1981
$365 \times (10/15)$	$365 \times (12/17.25)$	$365 \times (14/19.7)$
= 243 days	= 253 days	= 259 days

We are unable to obtain a breakdown of trade creditors and sundry creditors for any of the three years, which make the above calculations unassessable — directors to supply this information. If, however, say half the total were trade creditors (which is likely), then four month repayments seem ominous.

Note: A further problem is that we really need to make comparisons against purchases, whereas only cost of sales is available, which is subject to opening and closing stock variations. Re-working the latter two years in the above terms and with half total creditors as trade creditors, and one third of work in progress, say, as the material content (see cost of sales):

1979: Opening stocks unavailable

	1980	1981
Closing stocks of raw materials	12	20
Closing stocks of work in progress	0.83	1
Less: Opening stocks of raw materials	(10)	(12)
Opening stocks of work in progress	(0.66)	(0.83)
Add: Cost of sales	17.25	19.7
Therefore, purchases of raw materials	19.42	27.87

Trade creditor repayment rates

$$365 \times (6/19.42) = 113 \text{ days} \qquad 365 \times (7/27.87) = 92 \text{ days}$$

Stock turnover rates

1979	1980	1981
Opening stocks unavailable	$365 \times \dfrac{(11 + 13.25)/2}{15}$ $= 296 \text{ days}$	$365 \times \dfrac{(13.25 + 21.5)/2}{19.7}$ $= 322 \text{ days}$

The above does not necessarily cause alarm, as the material content is very low compared with the ultimate selling price. Thus, the bulk of the costs in the product are not stocks, but wages and overheads, which suggests a specialist manufacturer, e.g., electronics, jewellery, hospital equipment, etc.

Each trade has its stock turnover 'norm', thus we need to know the product.

Summary

The ratios show very little progress, or room for error. Any requests for funds would need careful consideration as to whether repayment of the interest and capital elements were possible.

3 Budgeting techniques

INTRODUCTION

The importance of mastering techniques to project a business into the future is of prime importance to lending bankers, and an area on which the examiner places great importance.

The aim primarily is to construct budgeted revenue accounts (manufacturing/trading, profit and loss, and possibly the appropriation account) from which we will be able to see two main things.

(a)   the resultant cash flow into the balance sheet (net profit plus depreciation, and any other 'book' expenses); and

(b)   whether as bankers we shall receive in full 'interest' on our loan, especially the margin of cover for it.

The secondary aim will be to construct a budgeted balance sheet so as to:

(a)   ascertain budgeted working capital sufficiencies; and

(b)   establish whether the company's structure can readily provide bankers with annual capital repayments on its loan.

The construction of a source and application of funds statement will usually be sufficient to ascertain the above.

THE TECHNIQUES

(a)   *Budgeted revenue accounts*   We must arrive at net profit for the forecast year, and will almost certainly start with budgeted sales, which for most enterprises is the principal (limiting) budget factor (see Question 1).

(b)   *A source and application of funds statement (budgeted)*   This will highlight our secondary aim, by looking at capital movements in the balance sheet (see Question 2).

(c)   *The 'close' (or quick) position*   By obtaining the up-to-date totals for stocks, debtors, creditors and bank (cash book figure) on a monthly basis, we can see, subject to capital movements in the balance sheet, whether a business is making profit — an exercise regularly carried out by accountants (see Question 3).

We work a source and application of funds statement again, but this time from bottom to top, to achieve net profit, or at least funds from trading.

(d) *Budgeted working capital* When turnover rises, so do the constituents of working capital, stocks, debtors and creditors. But the bank account cannot be so manipulated, and this could result in extreme pressure being placed upon it. Timing of the rising turnover is all important, usually highlighted by a cash flow forecast (see Question 4).

(e) *Bank statistics* Taken from the bank's computer we are able to ascertain:

(i)   whether credits into our account represent *all* of our customer's sales cash — if not they could be banking elsewhere;

(ii) possible budgeted sales, when we have been unable to obtain this information as in (a) above. Here we assume continuing debtor recovery rates *and* seasonal or non-seasonal variances in turnover. Slightly a long-shot but an indicator (see Question 5).

Techniques (a), (b), and possibly (c), above are most regularly used.

QUESTIONS

1 CARDBOX LTD
(Question set in 1980)

Balance sheets as at 31 December

	1982		1983	
Uses of capital	£000	£000	£000	£000
Fixed assets at book value		690		726
Trade investments at cost		61		61
		751		787
Current assets:				
Stock valued at the lower of total cost and net realisable value	685		625	
Debtors	421		397	
Cash balances	5		5	
	1,111		1,027	
Current liabilities and provisions:				
Creditors	375		420	
Bank overdraft	126		149	
Dividends	21		–	
Taxation	89		–	
	611		569	
Net current assets		500		458
		1,251		1,245
Sources of capital				
Share capital		700		700
Capital reserves		200		200
Revenue reserves		276		270
		1,176		1,170
Deferred taxation		75		75
		1,251		1,245

Profit and loss account extracts, year to 31 December

	1982 £000	1983 £000
Sales (all on credit): Home	1,906	2,014
Overseas	520	3
	2,426	2,017
Gross profit: Home	630	664
Overseas	172	1
	802	665
Running costs	629	671
Net profit (loss) before tax	173	(6)
Taxation	80	–
	93	(6)

The overseas market has now been lost, but the directors hope that during 1984 the home market will continue to expand at the 1983 rate.

Required:

Budgeted sales and budgeted net profit.

15 marks

2   CARDBOX LTD
(Question set in 1980)

Funds flow statement, year to 31 December 1983

Sources:	£000
Loss on trading	(6)
Depreciation	92
Funds generated from operations	86

Applications:	
Purchase of fixed assets	128
	(42)

Increase (decrease) in working capital analysed as follows:

Stock	(60)	
Debtors	(24)	
Creditors	(45)	
Bank	(23)	
Dividends	21	
Taxation	89	(42)

Required:

From the information given in Question 1 and above, construct a budgeted source and application of funds statement, as far as you are able.

15 marks

3 MONUMENT ENGINEERING LTD
(Question set in 1979)

Balance sheets as at 31 May

	1979 £	1980 £	1981 £
Capital	5,000	5,000	5,000
Profit and loss account	50,000	66,000	73,000
Deferred taxation	21,000	35,000	45,000
Tax	8,000	5,500	13,000
Hire-purchase	–	4,000	7,000
Creditors	70,000	130,000	155,000
Bank	20,000	25,000	22,000
	174,000	270,500	320,000
Plant and machinery	25,000	45,000	46,000
Stock	40,000	80,000	85,000
Work in progress	30,000	34,000	45,000
Debtors	75,000	105,000	140,000
Cash	1,000	4,000	2,000
Patents	3,000	2,500	2,000
	174,000	270,500	320,000
Sales	420,000	630,000	850,000
Net profit	34,000	16,000	7,000
After:			
Tax	15,000	12,000	16,000
Depreciation	2,500	4,500	4,600
Directors' remuneration	30,000	34,000	41,000

Position as at 31 August 1981

	£
Current assets:	
Debtors	200,000
Stock, not subject to lien	70,000
Work in progress	30,000
Current liabilities:	
Preferential creditors	20,000
Trade creditors	175,000
Bank debt (cash book figure)	26,000

Required:

Prepare a report for your manager on the quick figures supplied to the bank over the telephone on 1 September 1981.

20 marks

4 NEW KITCHENS LTD
(Question set in 1979)

Balance sheet as at 31 May

		1979				1980				1981	
	£	£	£	£	£	£	£	£	£	£	£
Capital authorised and issued		100				100				100	
Profit and loss account		3,700				9,100				12,900	
Directors' loans		24,000				26,900				27,200	
		27,800				36,100				40,200	
Fixed assets		7,000				11,800				17,700	
Current assets:											
Stock	42,000			50,300			75,000					
Debtors	31,000			56,900			74,000					
		73,000			107,200			149,000			
Current liabilities:											
Creditors	15,700			44,400			84,500					
Bank	36,500			38,500			42,000					
		52,200			82,900			126,500			
Net current assets		20,800				24,300				22,500	
		27,800				36,100				40,200	

Turnover in 1981 was £380,800 but management expect this to rise to £600,000 for the year to 31 May 1982, and ask for an overdraft of £70,000.

Required:

Consider working capital sufficiency.

15 marks

5 METAL MANUFACTURERS LTD
(Question set in 1979)

Balance sheets as at 31 December

	1979	1980	1981
	£	£	£
Capital authorised and issued	40,000	40,000	40,000
Profit and loss account	45,000	30,000	61,000
Deferred taxation	14,000	36,000	46,000
Directors' loans	18,000	5,000	12,000
Tax	10,000		20,000
Creditors	66,000	150,000	200,000
Bank	30,000	50,000	50,000
	223,000	331,000	429,000

	1979 £	1980 £	1981 £
Freehold premises	25,000	55,000	58,000
Fixed assets	48,000	63,000	73,000
Stock	45,000	55,000	65,000
Debtors	75,000	133,000	231,000
Building society	30,000	5,000	2,000
	223,000	311,000	429,000

	1979 £	1980 £	1981 £
Sales	600,000	485,000	900,000
Net profit (loss)	20,000	(15,000)	31,000
After:			
Tax (refund)	24,000	(11,000)	26,000
Directors' remuneration	35,000	36,000	50,000
Depreciation	5,000	10,000	12,000

Turnover and extreme balances on the company's current account since 1979 have been:

	Turnover £	Highest credit £	Highest debit £
1979	610,000	40,000	18,000
1980	550,000	42,000	41,000
1981	950,000	65,000	19,000
Current year (to March 31)	300,000	45,000	18,000

Required:

From the statistics provided by the bank's computer:

(a) Ascertain, as far as possible, whether customers bank elsewhere.
(b) Calculate the likely budgeted sales for 1982.

20 marks

35

ANSWERS

1 CARDBOX LTD

Budgeted sales, to net profit

	1982 £000		1983 £000		Budget 1984 £000
Sales (W1): Home	1,906		2,014		2,129
Overseas	520		3		Nil
	2,426	100%	2,017	100%	2,129
Gross profit (W2)	802	33.1%	665	33.0%	703
Less: Overheads (W3)	(629)	25.9%	(671)	33.3%	(709)
Profit before tax	173		(6)		(6)
Less: Taxation	80		Nil		Nil
Net profit	93		(6)		(6)

Workings

1 Between 1982 and 1983 home sales rose by 5.7%, i.e., $\dfrac{(2,014 \text{ less } 1,906)}{1,906} \times 100$

Thus £2,014,000 × 5.7% = £115,000 giving £2,129,000 for 1984; overseas sales are assumed to be nil.

2 Budgeted gross profit at an assumed rate of 33%, which looks fairly constant, should be £703,000 for 1984.

3 Budgeted running expenses, if at 33.3% (as 1983), will be £709,000 (1/3 of £2,129,000).

Note: as sales, gross profit and overheads all move upwards by the same percentages, the improvement in net profit will be minimal. In reality a slight improvement should occur as part of the overheads must be fixed, and the greater their proportion to variable overheads, the greater the profit improvement, once the break-even point has been passed. If however, the overheads could be restored to the 1982 levels of 25.9%, a £152,000 profit would probably occur (£703,000 less £551,000), subject to tax. As bankers we would be most interested to enquire into this aspect, suspecting that in 1983 management may have allowed variable overheads to run out of control.

2 CARDBOX LTD

Budgeted source and application of funds statement for year ended 31 December 1984

Sources	£000	£000
Net profit for the year		(6)
Add: Depreciation		92
		—
Funds from operations		86
Add: Other sources:		
Fixed assets sold		?
Loans injected		?
Share issues (rights)		?
		—
		86
Less: Applications:		
Fixed assets bought	?	
Loans repaid	?	
Shares redeemed	?	
Dividends paid	Nil	
Taxation paid	Nil	
	—	(Nil)
		—
Net inflow of funds to working capital (see Note (c))		86 !!
		—

Notes

(a) Depreciation is assumed (you are allowed to make assumptions) £92,000 as in previous years, so that a positive flow of funds into the balance sheet from trading will occur.

(b) The directors will have to be questioned about funds movements of a capital nature within the balance sheet, although tax will be nil (from 1983) and dividends also.

(c) The net inflow or outflow thus obtained will reflect in working capital changes. We need to know the composition of the four constituents. If stocks, debtors and creditors were to remain at their 1983 levels (which is almost possible given that the rise in turnover is only 5.7%), then if the capital movements in (b) above are nil, the bank overdraft could reduce by anything up to the £86,000 (see above).

If, however, stocks, debtors and creditors increase in line with sales (by 5.7%, which is more likely), then the bank balance would be:

	£
Net inflow of funds from trading and capital movements, say	86,000
Less: Stock increase £60,000 × 5.7% =	(3,420)
Less: Debtor increase £24,000 × 5.7% =	(1,368)
Add: Creditor increase £45,000 × 5.7% =	2,565
Improvement in bank	83,777

Clearly businesses continually need to improve their fixed assets, and anything spent in excess of £83,777 would reduce liquidity.

(**Note**: a slight imperfection in the question layout exists. Dividends of £21,000 and taxation of £89,000 are best shown as applications in the capital movement section. Thus the true outflow of working capital in 1983 would have been £152,000 (42 + 21 + 89).

3 MONUMENT ENGINEERING LTD

The 'close' position		at 31.5.81		at 31.8.81
	£000	£000	£000	£000
Stocks		85		70
Work in progress		45		30
Debtors		140		200
Cash		2		Nil
		272		300
Less:				
Creditors	155		195	
Bank	22		26	
	—	(177)	—	(221)
Working capital		95		79

Profit is made when finished goods are sold, and is first felt by the 'cost plus' impact on the debtor bank at the moment of sale (unless of course sold directly for cash) — the balance sheet's corresponding entry being an improvement in the company's reserves.

Thus all trading profit initially finds its way into working capital, and increases the business's lifeblood. So the pool of working capital should grow, though this is not so over the three months above, where the sum of £16,000 has left net current assets (working capital). This could suggest losses have been made during the last three months.

Questions would need to be asked of management, and such questions are most easily seen by constructing a source and application of funds statement:

	£	Example* £
Source		
Net profit for year	Calculate	
Depreciation for year		
	———	———
Funds from operations	Calculate	19,000
Add: Fixed assets sold	?	
Loans injected	?	15,000 total
Capital injected	?	
	———	———
		34,000

Less: Application			
Fixed assets bought	?		
Loans repaid	?		
Share capital repaid	?		
Taxation paid	?		
Dividends paid	?		
	——	( )	(50,000)
		———	———
Net outflow of working capital		(16,000)	(16,000)

Represented by changes in stocks/debtors/creditors and the bank.

The purpose of the close position or quick position is, then, that by calculating the present working capital and adjusting for capital movements (above), net profit, or at least funds from trading which is the cash funds flow, may be fairly accurately ascertained at any moment of time. Accountants have always carried out this exercise for their clients prior to the year end (say after 11 months). Thus they are able to calculate the probable 12 months profit and tax position *before* the year end closes, often recommending purchase of allowable assets to reduce the tax bill.

*Example: If, in the above case, we learnt from management that applications during the three months were £50,000, and funds from other sources were £15,000, then the banker's initial thoughts change. Funds from operations would now become £19,000, and, subject to three months depreciation, profits look to have been made.

4   NEW KITCHENS LTD

Budgeted working capital

When sales rise, a 57½% increase in this case, it can be assumed that debtors, stocks and creditors will also rise. While the rise in each will not necessarily be proportionate to sales, if it were, the following could be the position:

Budgeted working capital:

	£
Stock level, 57½% increase	118,125
Debtor level, 57½% increase	116,550
	234,675
Less: Creditors, 57½% increase	(133,087)
Funds needed	101,588

To finance the above the company has:

		£
(a)	an overdraft requested of	70,000
(b)	an existing fund of working capital	22,500
		92,500
Thus there could well be a cash shortfall of		9,088
		101,588

Notes

Balance sheets to illustrate:

	1981	Budget 1982
	£	£
Fixed assets	17,700	17,700
Stock	Nil	118,125
Debtors	Nil	116,550
Bank	22,500	–
Less: Creditors	Nil	(133,087)
Less: Overdraft needed	–	(79,088)
	40,200	40,200
Capital	40,200	40,200

The 1981 balance sheet assumes all working capital constituents are liquidated at the year end (an unreal situation) so as to indicate that these 'banked' funds are available to finance the 1982 budget. In the 1982 budget it looks as if an overdraft of £79,088 is really needed, but the *timing* of the working capital requirement is all-important, the figures shown being a 1 June 1981 situation (Day 1), where, with capital remaining at £40,200, there has been no profit build-up to ease the situation. The bank would need a cash flow forecast to ascertain the month of the maximum overdraft, which could well prove that the company can manage with £70,000.

Further, with a 57½% rise in turnover, savings may well be made in stock levels. It would be rare not to have the stock turnover faster in 1982, with an increase in activity of this level.

Debtors, on the other hand, may lengthen, so worsening the situation. This is the penalty often paid for pushing for new customers. The £9,088 shortfall could possibly be made up in lengthening creditors, if we knew their repayment position currently.

5 METAL MANUFACTURERS LTD

(a)

	1979 £000	1980 £000	1981 £000	Budget 1982 £000
Bank turnover	610	550	950	300
				X 4
				1,200
Deduct:				
VAT: 3/23	(80)	(72)	(124)	(157)
Sales cash through bank	530	478	826	1,043
Sales in accounts	600	485	900	?
Less: Debtors this year	(75)	(133)	(231)	
	525	352	669	
Add: Debtors last year	Not available	75	133	231
Sales cash through cash book		427	802	

Note: While we are unable to complete 1979, the next two years show that in each case we have received via the account at our branch in excess of the sales cash through the company's books — in 1980 £51,000 (i.e., 478 less 427) and £24,000 in 1981. These could, however, be receipts into the bank of a capital nature — assets sold, loans injected, share rights issues — which we could possibly confirm. But it does look as if we receive all our customer's bankings, negating our thoughts that they bank elsewhere.

We should also check that the bank turnover is the *credit* turnover, and as it probably is not when extracted from the computer, we would have to adjust for opening and closing balances.

(b)

	1981 £000	Budget 1982 £000
Sales	900	D
Less: Debtors this year	(231)	(C)
	669	B
Add: Debtors last year	133	231
	802	A

By assuming A is £1,043,000 from the bank statistics (which indicates that the first quarter of £300,000 applies to a non-seasonal business which would near enough give £1.2 million — information which as bankers we would know) we are able to calculate B at £812,000.

C and D are two unknowns, which may be deduced if we assume the debtor recovery rate will be the same for 1982 as 1981 — a fair assumption. Thus:

		£000		
Sales	=	900	=	100%
Debtor	=	(231)	=	25.67%
		669	=	74.33% Cash recovery

So if £812,000 is a 74.33% cash recovery also, then D (the sales figure we want) could, all things being equal, be £1,092,426, which is 100%.

Note: The above budgeting technique is not the most satisfactory, requiring considerable questions to be asked, but does give us a guide as to the essential item, budgeted sales.

PART TWO   PAST EXAMINATION QUESTIONS AND SUGGESTED ANSWERS

We now look at examination questions in full, which have been structured into lending situations for differing 'groups' of customers:

(a)   private customers;
(b)   private customers buying businesses;
(c)   bridging loans;
(d)   existing retailers;
(e)   wholesalers;
(f)   manufacturers;
(g)   farmers;
(h)   builders; and
(i)   others.

Each group has different 'needs' as to the finance required, and we are usually able to apply to each group certain of the ratios and budgeting techniques already covered.

Questions are reproduced in full and you are encouraged to have a plan of attack, based on the examiner's request for numbered points and short phrases. In other words, essays are not required.

A PLAN OF ATTACK

(a)   The first time you read the question, it should be done slowly. First thoughts are essential and create much more impact than the second read-through.

Stop at the end of each sentence to *underline the main points*. At this point you should *amplify the thoughts in your mind* from what you have just underlined, by *making notes* on the exam paper margins. (**Note**: from April 1985, you not only have 15 minutes' reading time but can mark the exam question paper in the above terms. We firmly believe that success is within your grasp on this first read-through as to the points you underline, and thoughts you note down on the question paper.)

(b)   The script should be sectionalised and based on numbers and short phrases. Consider the following sections:

(i)   the proposition and cost;
(ii)   customer background;
(iii) analysis of historical accounts;
(iv) budgeted accounts (whenever possible);
(v)   a decision whether or not to lend *and* security available if you go ahead.

The decision (v) follows naturally out of the work carried out in the previous sections.

4 Lending to private customers

SECTION 1   OVERDRAFTS AND LOANS (PRIVATE ACCOUNTS)

Introduction

The 'needs' of private customers are ones of immediate shortages of cash to be corrected by future expectations of income or reduced expenditure. The proposition determines the placement of the facility, as to overdraft, loan or flat-rate (personal) loan and in each case the cost should be established. If no time repayment period is given, then make one up — 'say, five years', and test repayment to see whether customer can manage; or is the time period too short?

Customer background is an essential thought area, as dependable customers, even if temporarily embarrassed, will pull through.

There will be little historical data given, but we must attempt to budget income forward as only from this source will our repayment come. Banks never wish to force a sale of its security.

QUESTIONS

1 MR AND MRS LEDGER

(Question set in 1981)

Messrs Balance and Sheet are chartered accountants who have banked with you for many years. The partnership has always been conducted in credit and you have a good opinion of the partners. Recently you received the following letter from Mr Balance:

> Our articled clerk, A. Ledger, is 24 and he banks with one of your competitors. His salary is £4,500 p.a. He is taking his final examinations this year and if he is successful his salary will increase to £5,500. Mr Ledger's wife is my secretary and her salary is £3,500 p.a.
>
> Mr and Mrs Ledger purchased a freehold property last year for £18,000 with the help of a building society mortgage of £15,000. Twelve months ago their bankers granted them a loan of £1,000 (repayable over three years) to enable them to buy essential furniture, and they now wish to borrow £500 to purchase a refrigerator and a washing machine. This request has been declined by their bank and I am writing to ask if you would kindly consider helping them. Mr Ledger tells me that the joint current account is never overdrawn and the present loan account balance is £850.

You reply to Mr Balance that you will be pleased to talk to Mr and Mrs Ledger. At the subsequent interview you learn that:

(i)   mortgage repayments are £90 per month;
(ii)   repayments to existing loan are £37 per month; and
(iii)   the Ledgers wish to repay the new loan over a period of three years.

Assess this request and state on what basis, if at all, you would be prepared to assist.

20 marks

2 THE ANSELLS

(Question set in 1979)

You have held the joint account of Mr and Mrs Ansell for 10 years. The mandate empowers either customer to sign for withdrawals. Mrs Ansell is not known to you, but Mr Ansell is highly regarded as a director of a local private company – A. B. Refrigeration Ltd – the account of which is not held at your bank. He is aged approximately 40, and the joint account is fed by his monthly salary of between £650 and £700 and small dividends totalling £50 p.a. from three public companies. The relative share certificates are held for safe keeping (current value £1,000), together with a certificate for 15,000 A. B. Refrigeration Ltd 25p shares, the dividends on which for the year 1978 amounted to £800, credited to the account in June and December. Your records show that all the certificates are in Mr Ansell's name.

For the past eight years you have been making monthly payments (currently £96.45) by standing order to a leading building society. Also for the past eight years there has been a direct debit (originally standing order) arrangement for £38.20 to be paid each month to a reputable life assurance society. These amounts have been paid regularly.

Both parties to the account have held cheque cards for several years and since 1975 you have allowed them an unsecured overdraft facility of £1,500. Until the end of 1978 this was used satisfactorily, as the following information shows:

Balances

Year	Maximum £	Minimum £	Average £	Dr turnover £
1976	800 Dr	436 Cr	280 Dr	6,600
1977	1,243 Dr	129 Cr	720 Dr	8,300
1978	698 Dr	872 Cr	248 Cr	8,700

During 1979, however, the working of the account has changed radically. The debit balances have rapidly increased and the overdraft now stands at £3,960. Whilst the excesses did not concern you when they first appeared – being of modest amounts, short-lived, and corrected by receipt of Mr Ansell's salary – the position has deteriorated since March. On a close examination it transpires that Mrs Ansell has begun to draw large amounts of cash, and is issuing many cheques to local shops, apparently for clothes and items of jewellery. You ask Mr Ansell to call and see you. He does so promptly and explains that he has just discovered that his wife has started to indulge in extravagant expenditure. He fully realises his financial responsibilities and is anxious to come to an acceptable arrangement with the bank, but without drastic measures being taken if they can be avoided.

What do you see as the most practical solution to the problem? Give full reasons, and outline the implications of the action you propose to take.

20 marks

3 TIMOTHY MARKS

(Question set in 1981)

Mr Timothy Marks has been a customer of yours for many years and you know he is the chairman of two public companies, neither of which is a customer at any of your bank's branches.

Apart from the deeds of his house, which is situated in Surrey and worth around £100,000, and a building society passbook with an up-to-date balance of £3,500, both held for safe-keeping, you have no detailed knowledge of his resources. His account is fed by a substantial income, including dividends amounting to £1,200 p.a., and a summary of his account for the past three years appears below:

Year	Range of balances		Average balance	Debit turnover
	£	£	£	£
1978	462 Dr	1,602 Cr	842 Cr	9,250
1979	192 Dr	1,710 Cr	691 Cr	10,070
1980	60 Cr	1,320 Cr	777 Cr	11,060
1981 (4 months)	982 Dr	1,092 Cr	110 Cr	4,190

Mr Marks has never seen fit to approach you before overdrafts appeared in the past, but you have always believed this was because his business commitments precluded much time being given to his own financial affairs.

In response to a letter which you sent to Mr Marks concerning the overdraft which reached almost £1,000 in March of this year, you receive a four-line reply stating that it was caused by payment of a tax bill for £1,800. Your records show that a cheque in favour of the Inland Revenue was presented at that time and, furthermore, that the position was quickly corrected as the customer had predicted.

You have now received a letter from Mr Marks which says that, after consulting his professional advisers, he considers the stock market is due for a substantial rise over the next few months and asks for a facility of £50,000 to enable him to make investments as and when he feels it appropriate to do so. He asks for your agreement and a note of any requirements or conditions that you may have.

What, in your view are the relevant considerations, how would you deal with the request, and what requirements would you stipulate?

Note: Assume that no credit restrictions apply.

25 marks

ANSWERS

1   MR AND MRS LEDGER

Main points to underline	Amplified
(a) Chartered accountants contact us	Good reference, think highly of Mr Ledger
(b) Mr Ledger 24, articled clerk; and with competitor bank	Could be a good future; does he have prospects with them? Chance to take account!
(c) Finals this year, then £5,500	What are his chances to qualify? Cash incentive (annually).
(d) Mrs Ledger their secretary; her salary £3,500	Is she a valued member of staff with a secure job? Will she continue to work?
(e) House value £18,000 (recently); first mortgage, £15,000; equity £3,000	Lending value, say, 70%: £18,000 × 70% = £12,600
(f) £1,000 loan, 12 months ago	Over how long? If at £850 now, very little has been paid off! How can £37 a month fit in? We must enquire
(g) £500 request	Why declined? We ask him
(h) Joint account; never overdrawn	Can we see his statements without disputing his statement
(i) Mortgage £90 a month	Possibly about right for £15,000 (in 1981)
(j) New loan over 3 years	Personal loan

Suggested answer

(a) **The proposition and cost:**

£500 —   To buy refrigerator and washing machine, over three years

Cost: Flat rate loan (personal loan) say 10½% (1984) thus APR about 20.4%
£500 Principal + £157.36 Interest = £657.36

Therefore 36 monthly repayments: £18.26

(b) **Customer background:**

(i)   New account, but good introduction from employers.

(ii)   Mr Ledger has expectations of a well paid, secure profession with a high future salary. Is he expected to qualify?

(iii)   Joint income good at £8,000 (1981 levels) with £9,000 pending. Will Mrs Ledger continue in her work?

(iv)   Probably both are valued staff.

(v) No lending/security value in their house:

Lending value on houses, say 70% X £18,000, i.e.	£12,600
Deduct 1st mortgage	£15,000
Security value for 2nd mortgage	Negative

(vi) £1,000 flat over 3 years is £1,314.72 (double that asked of us). Therefore with 2 years left the sum of £850 is accounted for, i.e., £36.52 monthly X 24 payments.

(c) **Budgets:**

Income per month is all important:

	Mr Ledger £	Mrs Ledger £
Salary	4,500	3,500
Less: Personal allowances		
Married man (1984/85)	(3,155)	
Wife's earned income relief (1984/85)		(2,005)
Taxable @ 30%	1,345	1,495

Thus tax on £2,840 @ 30% is £852 p.a., and this could be less if there is mortgage relief and other allowances, e.g., professional subscriptions.

So with a net income of £7,148 minimum (8,000 less 852) or £600 a month they must prove to us they can manage.

(d) **Decision:**

We may well lend, unsecured and on personal loan, whether or not the current account is obtained at present.

We would like to know why they have been declined, and hope that they would offer their bank statements, before being asked.

There existing mortgage of £90 a month seems a shade low for £15,000 (possibly £20 short, i.e., have they reduced the capital sum?). But this together with the existing loan of £36.50 monthly and our loan of half as much again seems to make little impact on a net monthly income of £600.

Tutorial note: In this question only the main points to underline in the question and notes to make are given to help you.

2 THE ANSELLS

(a) Proposition and cost

£4,000 plus facility – to clear excesses – over, say, three years probably on loan

Cost: £4,200 say, on loan

- (i) Capital repayments about £120 monthly
- (ii) Interest at, say, 13%, about £45 monthly

(b) Customer background

(i) Mr Ansell is a successful businessman. Had he noticed the overdraft, as we asked him to see us? Possibly not; he could be too absorbed with his work.

(ii) Income good (at 1979 levels) with no previous problems, we assume, over the 10 years he has been with us.

(iii) House bought eight years ago; mortgage about £13,000 from the £96.45 monthly repayments. If he paid, say, £15,000 plus for it in 1971 (£13,000 and £2,000 cash) it could be worth, say, £60,000 now.

(iv) Life policy almost certainly endowment and not linked direct to the mortgage. Thus a good surrender value has been built up – minimum of £38.20 × 12 × 8 plus profits as to two thirds.

(v) What are the private shares worth and does he have a controlling interest? Perhaps not.

(vi) We would know, after 10 years, a great deal about the Ansells – their standing locally; probably his ability and any qualifications; his health; his address to calculate his house value; his dependants; length of time with A.B. Refrigeration, and any connections or relations who may bank with us.

(c) Budgets

The meeting will centre around budgeted income monthly and the Ansells' expenses thereto. Can they afford to repay, say, £4,200 (if more cheques are to come in) over three years, which is £165 per month.

(d) Decisions

We must not become involved in Mr and Mrs Ansells' private financial relationships. We do need an arrangement to clear the overdraft which really Mr Ansell should have noticed.

The £1,000 of public company shares only yield 5% and could possibly be sold, unless a reason exists to retain them.

Security may or may not be taken here. A charge over the life policy would probably be sufficient.

Tutorial note: the word 'say' indicates assumptions, which must be made in most questions. This prevents the data from halting, otherwise the question becomes imponderable.

3   TIMOTHY MARKS

(a)   **Proposition and cost**

£50,000 — stock market occasional investments — time span of facility to be agreed

Interest cost would have to be agreed, possibly about 3% over base rate. Also whether to use a loan account, or an overdraft facility if short-term.

(b)   **Customer background**

(i)   Wealthy — house unencumbered as deeds with us — dividends of £1,200 suggest a £20,000 portfolio if dividend rates are about 6% p.a.

(ii)   Debit turnover for year, say, £12,570 (three times £4,190). Deduct the dividend of £1,200, which gives a net salary of about £900 monthly. Does he have a private account elsewhere perhaps?

(iii)   We can learn much of him by:

–   obtaining the two public companies' annual reports, and
–   examining his cheques/standing orders.

Both essential, prior to our meeting with him.

(iv)   Although his average credit balances are much lower, we assume past conduct of account excellent, which usually is a firm indicator for the future.

(c)   **Budgets and questions**

We would probably visit him — keeping marketing aspects very low key till some future time when he knows us better.

How long will he hold his investment? What will be the interest to the bank? How does he pay this? Will he have a capital gains tax also to find? Could losses be made?

Is the pressure on the account temporary? The tax bill of £1,800 is probably not to do with his salary but other income. What is his life style and what dependants does he have?

(d) Decision

The meeting will be mainly to enable us to know more of him and providing questions are satisfactorily answered we would probably lend.

Security would be the shares themselves or as a possible alternative a charge over his house — one or the other.

SECTION 2   CUSTOMERS WISHING TO BUY A BUSINESS

Introduction

In the present climate, where many people are receiving lump-sums from redundancies, an over-riding need exists to secure income for families. The banker has a most important role to play, as errors in the ultimate decision could lead to the financial ruin of very genuine people.

Prime requirements are to determine sufficiencies of income for the purchaser, whilst protecting the bank's funds and assuring capital repayments and interest.

Within questions in this area, shop purchases predominate, and the following should be carefully considered:

(a)   Purchaser's retail trade experience?
      Experience in this particular trade?

(b)   Source of introduction?
      If from business transfer agent, is integrity satisfactory? Agent obviously concerned with negotiation of sale and subsequent commission.

(c)   Why is present owner selling?

(d)   Is shop freehold or leasehold?
      Leasehold requires special care: adequate term or certainty of renewal must exist to allow borrower to repay advance.

(e)   What is rent?

(f)   What is total cost? How much for stock and goodwill?

(g)   Has stock been inspected and valued?
      Is all stock saleable?

(h)   Has goodwill any value?
      Three years' audited accounts to be seen to assess progress of business. Claims that accounts window-dressed for tax purposes must be ignored.

(i)   Has realistic estimate for working capital been established?

(j)   What is purchaser's contribution?

(k)   Is turnover and profit sufficient?

(l)   Does profit margin compare favourably with retail statistics for this type of shop?

(m)   Is manager to be employed?
      What effect will this have on profits?

(n)   Inspection must be made either personally or by local branch manager if business unknown to bank.

(o)   Charge over premises lease/goodwill required.
Valuation to be made.

(p)   Life policy cover?

4 MR AND MRS CARTER
(Question set in 1979)

Mr and Mrs Carter, both aged 45, have banked with you for 20 years. Mr Carter is a supervisor at the local telephone exchange (salary £4,500) and his wife is earning £15 a week as a part-time assistant in a local grocer's shop. They have no family. A few weeks ago Mr Carter telephoned you to say that, as his employment offered no prospects, he was seriously considering the purchase of a post office and store in Cornwall. He has now sent you the accounts of the business, for which the asking price is £40,000; the present owner is selling because of ill health. The Carters intend to sell their property, which they value at £35,000 and on which there is a mortgage of £6,000. Mrs Carter will sell her shares, value £14,000. Your customers will be calling to discuss bridging finance and a residual overdraft of £5,000 for the business for 12 months.

What points will you wish to discuss with them?

State with reasons whether or not you will be prepared to assist.

20 marks

F. J. Parsons
Trading as Cornish Stores
Balance sheet as at 31 October

	1976	1977	1978 (draft)
	£	£	£
Capital	20,800	21,100	23,100
Bank loan	4,000	3,500	3,000
Creditors	1,900	2,000	2,100
	26,700	26,600	28,200
Freehold premises	15,000	15,000	15,000
Fixtures/fittings	3,500	3,250	3,700
Stock	2,000	2,200	3,000
Debtors	700	900	1,100
Bank	500	250	400
Goodwill	5,000	5,000	5,000
	26,700	26,600	28,200
Sales	20,000	25,000	37,000
Purchases	14,500	18,500	23,000
Post office salary	1,000	1,250	2,000
Bad debts	80	–	150
Net profit	2,000	2,500	4,000
Drawings	1,800	2,200	2,000

5 CUTHBERT BROWN

(Question set in 1983)

Cuthbert Brown is in his late forties and known to you as a foreman gardener at a local factory of a chocolate manufacturer. He receives a weekly net wage of about £90. His wife is a part-time worker at the factory and her net wage averages £35 per week. They live in a maisonette, rented from a local housing association for £20 per week.

Mr Brown calls to see you. At the interview, Mr Brown indicates that both he and his wife have been offered redundancy, involving a cash payment of £8,000 to him, £2,500 to his wife and a further £1,500 jointly from accrued holiday pay and funds in a company savings scheme. They have decided to accept the offer.

They have seen a newsagency business which they are interested in purchasing. The unit is owned by a multiple group.

They have been given the following figures:

	Year ended 30.4.81 £	Year ended 30.4.82 £
Lease at cost	3,000	3,000
Goodwill	10,000	10,000
Fixtures and fittings	3,500	2,000
Debtors	700	800
Stock	6,600	7,500
Creditors	5,500	7,000
Sales	75,000	84,000
Purchases	62,800	70,600
Wages including National Insurance	6,100	6,800
Rent/rates	4,400	4,500
Heat/light	600	700
Sundry expenses	1,000	1,400
Depreciation	500	500
Contribution	500	400

For the first 48 weeks of the current year, the figures are as follows:

	£
Sales	84,000
Purchases	71,500
Stock	8,500
Wages	6,700
Rent/rates	4,300
General expenses	2,000
Depreciation	500

The asking price for the lease, fixtures and fittings and goodwill is £17,500 plus stock and debtors, estimated at £10,000.

Mr Brown believes that he and his wife can possibly run the business without other staff and is confident that he can make a good profit. Since there is a very adequate flat above the shop there will be the additional saving on the house rent.

You question Mr Brown regarding the lease. Apparently it is a standard full-repairing lease granted in May 1980 for a term of 15 years, with rent reviews every five years, the first review being May 1985.

Mr and Mrs Brown have £2,500 invested in a building society account, which they will inject into the business, whilst their current estate car — which is two years old and valued at £2,000 — will be used in the business.

Mr Brown asks you for an overdraft limit of £15,000 to enable him to complete the purchase and provide a little capital with which to run the business.

Required:

State, with full reasons, whether or not you would support the request.

Note: Assume a bank rate of 9% p.a.

20 marks

6   MR AND MRS NIGHTINGALE
(Question set in 1983)

Mr and Mrs Nightingale have been introduced to you by a local solicitor who is well known to you. They are both in their mid-forties and have no family.

Mr Nightingale has a secure job and earns a net monthly salary of about £500. Mrs Nightingale was formerly a state registered nurse but six years ago she had to cease work to look after her infirm mother, who died six months ago.

For some while, the Nightingales have been considering establishing an old persons home and have recently found a suitable property. The price of the property is £50,000 but the vendors have agreed an exchange deal involving the Nightingale's existing house so that the net consideration would be £20,000. There is a mortgage outstanding on the Nightingale's house of £5,000.

Some alterations would be needed to the home to satisfy licensing requirements. A detailed estimate has been prepared at a figure of £7,000. Mrs Nightingale has £8,000 invested in a building society account, being mainly her inheritance from her late mother's estate. She is prepared to invest these funds in the property.

You question the Nightingales regarding the proposed home, and elicit the following information.

They could accommodate up to six old people paying a weekly rate of £85 each. Food would cost about £2.50 per day per person; general expenses, including heating, rates, insurance and telephone, would amount to £5,000 p.a. Since Mr Nightingale would continue with his job, some labour would have to be employed. Cleaning at £5 per day, part-time helpers at £40 per week and holiday cover for four weeks per year at £200 per week have been allowed in the forecast which they have prepared.

After discussions with the appropriate authorities, the Nightingales have good reason to believe that at least five of the six places will be fully occupied for the whole year. No provision has been included in the costs for finance charges nor for replacement of equipment other than routine repairs and renewals, which were included in the general expenses of £5,000.

The Nightingales ask if you can assist them with finance.

How would you respond? Set out the basis, if any, on which you would be prepared to help.

20 marks

7 A. & J. CORNISH
(Question set in 1982)

Alice and John Cornish have banked with you for 20 years. They own a farmhouse and 30 acres situated in a popular tourist area. They have concentrated on growing early potatoes. During the last three years profits have fallen, and they have been considering ways of increasing their income. The business does not take all their time as there is little to do between the lifting of the potatoes in June and planting the following February. They call in January to tell you that they have decided to open a fish and chip and meat pie restaurant five miles from the farm and in the centre of a holiday resort. This would, they say, fit in nicely with their existing business, and they would also keep a few beef cattle to provide the meat for the meat pies.

They wish to purchase for £33,000 a disused garage for conversion into a restaurant, and they have obtained planning consent for change of use. An initial overdraft facility of £134,500 is requested, made up as set out below.

An estimate for the building costs has been sought from a reputable quantity surveyor and quotations for the fixtures and fittings and equipment have been obtained. The Cornishes' accountant has prepared a profit projection and your customers envisage that, once trading commences, repayment of the borrowing over a 10-year period will be feasible.

Summaries of the last three years' accounts, the building estimate and profit projection are given below.

The amounts for fixtures and fittings and equipment may be accepted as accurate. The present balance of the account is £1,000 credit. You already have a legal mortgage over the present farm (which you value at £60,000) and you are offered a legal mortgage over the freehold which your customers wish to purchase.

Required:

Appraise this request and state, with reasons, whether or not you consider the bank should assist.

30 marks

Overdraft request

	£
Purchase of freehold	33,000
Fees	1,500
Building costs	65,000
Fixtures and fittings	10,000
Equipment	20,000
Working capital	5,000
	134,500

Building estimate

	£
Preliminaries	4,000
Drainage	3,000
External works	18,000
Foundations	3,000
Walls	6,000
Roof	6,000
First floor	4,000
Windows and doors	5,000
Floor finishings	3,000
Plastering and decorating	6,000
Plumbing	3,000
Electrical	3,000
Mains services	1,000
	65,000

A. & J. Cornish: Balance sheets as at 30 September

	£	£	1979 £	£	£	1980 £	£	£	1981 £
Fixed assets:									
Freehold property			30,000			40,000			28,000
Plant and machinery			20,000			21,500			18,000
			50,000			61,500			46,000
Current assets:									
Stock	1,000				1,000		1,000		
Debtors	500				500		–		
Cash	–				–		1,000		
		1,500				1,500		2,000	
Current liabilities:									
Creditors	10,000				9,000		3,000		
Bank	6,000				13,000		–		
		16,000				22,000		3,000	
Net current assets			(14,500)			(20,500)			(1,000)
Net assets			35,500			41,000			45,000
Represented by:									
Joint capital account			35,500			41,000			45,000
Sales			34,000			36,000			28,000
Net profit			10,000			5,500			4,000

A. & J. Cornish: Projected trading and profit and loss accounts for the three years commencing 1 July 1982

		Year ended 30.6.83			Year ended 30.6.84			Year ended 30.6.85
	£	£	£	£	£	£	£	£
Gross receipts (note 1)		150,000			180,000			216,000
Purchases (note 2)		53,500			63,000			76,000
Gross profit		96,500			117,000			140,000
Add: Furnished lettings								
(Flat on first floor)		1,500			2,000			2,500
		98,000			119,000			142,500
Deduct:								
Wages and National								
Insurance	36,000			41,400			48,000	
Lighting and heating	5,000			6,000			7,200	
Wrapping and materials	4,000			4,800			6,000	
Laundry and cleaning	2,500			3,000			3,600	
Repairs and renewals	1,200			2,500			3,500	
Motor expenses	2,600			3,250			4,000	
Rates and water	1,000			1,250			1,500	
Telephone, postages, etc.	800			1,000			1,250	
Advertising	1,500			1,500			1,500	
Insurance	850			1,000			1,500	
Accountancy	400			480			550	
Bank charges (note 3)	16,500			13,500			12,000	
Hire of equipment	750			750			750	
Sundry expenses	750			1,000			1,250	
Depreciation	4,500			3,750			3,100	
		78,350			85,180			95,700
Net profit for the year		19,650			33,820			46,800
Farming net income		8,000			4,000			2,000

Notes on projected figures

		£
1	Gross receipts:	
	Fish sales on mark-up 100%	100,000
	Chips sold at 12p per bag	
	½lb potatoes to each bag of chips	
	1 ton of potatoes sold as chips will produce a revenue of £500	
	100 tons of potatoes gives	50,000
	Gross receipts	150,000

2   Cost of purchases: £

	£
Potatoes	
50 tons supplied by Mr & Mrs Cornish at £20 per ton	1,000
50 tons supplied by wholesalers at £50 per ton	2,500
	3,500
Fish: as above	50,000
Purchases	53,500

3   Assumptions:

(a)   Effective interest rate in first year 16%.
(b)   Reduction of bank borrowing £10,000 p.a.
(c)   Bank lending rate second and third years: 15%.

ANSWERS

4   MR AND MRS CARTER

(a)   **Proposition and cost**

£5,000 overdraft; buy post office and sell house; 12 months, say.

		£
Buy: Post office and stores		40,000
Add: Legal fees, say		1,500
Working capital, say		6,000
		———
To find		47,500

	£	
Available: Equity on present house	29,000	
Less: Legal fees, say	(500)	
Add: Sale of shares	14,000	
	———	(42,500)
Overdraft requested		5,000

Cost: over 1 year may be interest only say £600, with the overdraft retained if they are trading profitably.

(b)   **Customer background**

(i)   With us for 20 years — we know quite a lot about them:

   — Do they save or overspend?
   — Have they repaid previous loan, if any etc.?
     Assumed first class.

(ii)   No family and both prepared to work.

(c)   **Historical accounts**

	1977		1978 (draft)	
	£	£	£	£
Sales		25,000		37,000
Less: Opening stock	2,000		2,200	
Purchases	18,500		23,000	
Closing stock	(2,200)		(3,000)	
	———		———	
Cost of sales		(18,300)		(22,200)
		———		———
Gross profit		6,700		14,800
		———		———
Gross profit margin		26.8%		40%
Net profit margin		10%		10.8%

The gross profit margin looks to be excessive for 1978 as, at this figure, the mark-up on purchases would have to be 65%, which is applicable only to the mid-luxury retail trade.

Net profit margins appear to have stabilised, but in 1978 this could only be as the result of applying more overheads. Are the 1978 accounts badly astray — could we see the bank statements — to substantiate the turnover?

(d) **Budgets**

Very little chance exists to push the accounts forward a year or so with possible anomalies in the sales and/or overheads of the draft accounts.

(e) **Decision**

When buying a shop many questions exist:

(i) Purchasers' retail trade experience — the Post Office will have to accept and train the Carters.

(ii) Source of introduction — is the selling agent's integrity satisfactory?

(iii) Why is the owner selling — ill health a 'genuine' reason?

(iv) Can we check the shop's bank account for turnover?

(v) Freehold here (accommodation assumed) — (beware short leases as renewal must be certain; rent 'steps' are high; security value is low for banks).

(vi) How has the purchase price been calculated?

	£
Purchase price	40,000
Less: Fittings at	(3,700)
Goodwill, say twice the profits	(8,000)
Thus value of freehold	28,300

This should be checked. Can a local manager visit for us?

The key factor here is whether the turnover and post office salary can provide a living. Also, will the present house sell quickly? The bank may insist on exchange of sale contracts before the purchase proceeds.

Security to be a first mortgage over the shop, and very ample.

5 CUTHBERT BROWN

(a) Proposition and cost

*£15,000; to buy newsagents shop on short lease; repayment term not stated.

	£
*Purchase price, plus stock and debtors	27,500
Less: Redundancy monies, etc.	(12,000)
Less: Savings	(2,500)
Required to purchase the shop	13,000
Therefore, working capital	2,000

Cost: Year one, assume £13,000 on loan over 10 years

	£
Capital repayment	1,300
Interest at, say, 12½%	1,875
To find	3,175

(Interest is a maximum figure due to the reducing loan account and the swing on current account, although a commission fee would be charged.)

(b) Customer background

(i)   Redundancy — they must find something and will work hard to make a go of it.

(ii) Untrained in newsagency (but achievable).

(iii) A gardener — can he attain business acumen?

(iv) Known to bank — reference satisfactory.

(v)   They have savings and both work, assume no family.

(vi) No equity in their property — rented.

(c) **Historical accounts**

	1982		1983 in full	
	£	£	£	£
Sales		84,000		91,000
Less: Opening stocks	6,600		7,500	
Purchases	70,600		77,500	
Closing stocks	(7,500)		(8,600) say	
Cost of sales		(69,700)		(76,400)
Gross profit	17%	14,300	16%	14,600
Less: Wages and NI	6,800		7,258	
Rent and rates	4,500		4,658	
Heat and light	700		} 2,167	
Sundry expenses	1,400			
Depreciation	500		500	
		(13,900)		(14,583)
Net profit		400		17

Gross profit margins of 17.0% and 16.0% show a worsening position, as there is only a marginal increase in sales (£7,000 being only 8.3% of £84,000). The position is also worse than 1981 when the gross profit margin was 17.5% (overheads: 6,100 + 4,400 + 600 + 1,000 + 500 plus the contribution/net profit of 500 = 13,100, which must be gross profit). Looks to be the reason the multiple is selling.

Furthermore, net profit has now vanished as overheads are rising faster than gross profit.

(d) **Budgets**

If under the Browns' tenancy sales rise another £7,000 during 1984:

	£	£
Sales		98,000
Gross profit at 16%		15,680
Less: Rent and rates, say	4,800	
General expenses, say	2,250	
Bank interest	1,875	
Motor expenses, say	1,000	
Depreciation, say	2,358	
(Lease £17,500/12 years = £1,458;		
motor vehicle, say £900)		(12,283)
Budgeted net profit		3,397

This is before income tax, the bank's capital repayment of £1,300 and drawings.

(e) Decision

It is rare that a multiple pulls out of a newspaper shop unit, but the reason now looks obvious.

There is insufficient living for Mr and Mrs Brown and rent reviews and motor car changes in the future could break them.

Neither is there security for the bank, and it looks as if we would not be able to entertain this proposition. In declining it, we must fully acquaint the Browns with the reason, understanding the position in which they now find themselves.

6 MR AND MRS NIGHTINGALE

(a) Proposition and cost

*£26,000 loan; to buy property for an old peoples home; repayment term not stated.

	£
*Purchase price, plus alteration	57,000
Less: Present house equity	(25,000)
Less: Savings	(8,000)
Add: Legal fees and estate agents	1,000
Add: Stamp duty at 1%	570
	25,570
	say 26,000

Cost: (assume loan is for 10 years)

Year I

	£
Capital repayment	2,600
Interest at say 13%	3,380
	5,980

Year II

	£
Capital repayment	2,600
Interest at say 13% on £23,400	3,042
	5,642

Both items of interest are maximum figures due to the reducing aspect of the loan.

(b) Customer background

(i) Good introduction – local solicitor.

(ii) Mid-forties – sufficient 'time' to make a success (assume health good).

(iii) No family – double income available if Mr Nightingale stays where he is in his 'secure' job.

(iv) Mrs Nightingale is a qualified SRN.

(v) Genuine reason to start the enterprise – six months since Mrs Nightingale's mother died.

(vi) Considered 'for some while' – not a spur of the moment decision.

(vii) All figures available – a good sign showing they are well prepared.

(c) Budgets

Gearing satisfactory : £33,000 of their money against £26,000 of bank's.

Budgeted revenue accounts:

	4 persons £	5 persons £	6 persons £
Receipts:			
Year's rent at £85 per week	17,680	22,100	26,520
Payments:			
Food, £2.50/day/person	3,650	4,563	5,475
Annual expenses	5,000	5,000	5,000
Cleaning, £5 daily	1,825	1,825	1,825
Wages £40 weekly (assume no tax/stamp)	2,080	2,080	2,080
Holiday cover	800	800	800
Bank interest	3,380	3,380	3,380
	16,735	17,648	18,560
Net profit	945	4,452	7,960

As most of the expenses are fixed overheads, profits may be seen to accelerate very quickly, once the break-even point has been passed. In each of the cases above, the bank's interest charge may be met and a positive cash flow into the balance sheet obtained.

Budgeted source and application of funds statement:

	Year I		
	£	£	£
Net profit per year	945	4,452	7,960
Add: Depreciation (assumed)	Nil	Nil	Nil
Funds from operation	945	4,452	7,960
Bank loan	26,000	26,000	26,000
Cash injected	33,000	33,000	33,000
	59,945	63,452	66,960
Less:			
Purchase of property	59,000	59,000	59,000
Capital repayment	2,600	2,600	2,600
Taxation: (carried to next year)	–	–	–
Drawings, minimum, say	1,000	1,000	1,000
To working capital	(2,655)	852	4,360

(d) **Decision**

Will they have five persons all the year round, otherwise drawings would have to be forgone and cover for the bank's annual payment could also be difficult?

Many points exist as to set-up — building alterations regulations, fire precautions, planning permission.

The return for Mr and Mrs Nightingale looks rather slender, although by living in, they will save on housing costs of their own.

Provided we are assured as to income, we may well lend, taking a legal mortgage over the property.

7   A. & J. CORNISH

(a) **Proposition and cost**

£134,500; to buy and convert premises to a restaurant; repayment time not stated.

Facility split as to:

(i)   loan £100,000 over 10 years;
(ii) overdraft £34,500.

Cost:	Year 1	Year 2	Year 3
	£	£	£
	134,500	134,500	124,500
		less 10,000	less 10,000
		124,500	114,500
Interest	@ 16%	@ 15%	@ 15%
Maximum	21,520	18,675	17,175
Capital repayment	10,000	10,000	10,000
To find	31,520	28,675	27,175

(b) **Customer background**

(i) Established customers − living worsening (we should put considerable time into this one, as they need help).

(ii) July to January a free period, therefore they need to diversify.

(iii) Revalued farm property at £60,000 makes the balance sheet value of the enterprise £77,000.

(c) **Historical accounts**

Largely irrelevant − possible questions:

(i) Was there a part sale in 1981 to survive?

(ii) Did the reduction in turnover in 1981 ensue as a direct result of the above?

(d) **Budgeted accounts presented**

(i) Gearing will be very high with the bank putting up most of the capital. How much if any, are they to put in?

(ii) Gross profit margins are 64.33%, 65% and 64.8% respectively − are these the 'norms' for the restaurant (fish and chips) trade?

(iii) Net profit margins are rising, 13.1%, 18.8% and 21.7%, which is expected on a rising turnover with fixed overheads relatively constant and variable overheads controlled, i.e., more pounds of net profit. Are they realistic?

(iv) Can they reach these sales figures? £50,000 taken from chips at 12p per portion is 416,666 portions, divided by 313 days (365 less 52 Sundays) is 1,331 *average* per day, and could be high! When would they start? Before the holiday season or not? If its only a 3-month holiday season how much trade is available in winter? Cash flow is needed to explain sales as it is the principal budget factor.

(v)   Expenses to be queried:

Bank interest is some £5,000 too low in each of the three budgeted years.

What is hire of equipment for?

No oils/fats in purchases or overheads.

VAT is payable on the restaurant side (and now in 1984 on the take-away side). Has this been accounted for?

Is depreciation too low:

Fixtures: £10,000 at 10% say	=	£1,000
Equipment: £20,000 at 25% say	=	£5,000
Total		£6,000 p.a.

Are frying costs in lighting and heating? Is this figure accurate?

Why will farming income rise to £8,000 in 1983?

Is £5,000 working capital sufficient to maintain the cost of purchases? At a little under one tenth of total purchases, or 34 days, it seems adequate for this fresh food trade.

Is the capital expenditure on the buildings accurate; have other tenders been sought? Who gave the quote? How quickly would alterations be completed?

Is the purchase price fair? Has a professional valued the property for them?

(e) **Decision**

The bank is being asked to provide all the risk capital for an enterprise in which the Cornishes have no experience. Also if the budgeted net profit is set too high (as previously mentioned) then after the bank's capital repayment of £10,000 little will be left as cover for drawings. Who produced their budgets?

No mention has been made of finance for beef cattle on their farm, or sales of their home-made pies in the restaurant.

While decisions will all hinge around budgeted sales, the venture looks optimistic and speculative, even if the Cornishes sold up their farm and moved into the flat above the new premises. Perhaps we should casually mention this and their injection of say £77,000 from the farm's net worth, to gauge their reaction. The gearing would then be acceptable and the requirement of

71

£57,500 covered by a charge on the premises and within the 50% lending value for commercial property. Another alternative would be a leased restaurant premises.

The bank would wish to aid these longstanding customers in every way, but would not jump into this project. If it falls through could tourist opportunities, etc., open up, based on their farm?

SECTION 3   BRIDGING LOANS

Introduction

Besides being the staple diet of many solicitors' practices, lending in this area is very common in banking, as the new house often needs to be paid for before the proceeds for the present one are obtained. The two professions work closely together.

The main points to be borne in mind are:

(a)   The undertaking of the solicitor acting to clear the bank will be its security. A legal mortgage is rarely taken.

(b)   Beware of the open-ended bridge where contracts have not been exchanged for the existing house, so that the purchaser can still back out.

(c)   Details of property to be sold.
Price, present mortgage, are contracts exchanged and, if so, completion date? If not, how far has sale progressed? If bridge open-ended, opinion obtained on prospects of early sale and whether price is reasonable.
Will customer reduce if necessary for quick sale?

(d)   Details of property to be purchased.
Price and what mortgage has been arranged?

(e)   What is the completion date? Is property in joint names?

(f)   Firm evidence to be seen of mortgage figures quoted at (c) and (d).

(g)   Has due allowance been made for legal/agents' fees and removal expenses?

(h)   Is fire insurance cover adequate?

(i)   Are solicitors known? If not, status report to be obtained.

(j)   If open-ended and price has to be reduced, could customer repay any residual borrowing? In any event is he able to cover accruing interest, which may be considerable?

(k)   Has form of charge been signed or will bank rely purely upon solicitor's undertaking?

(l)   Could proposition be re-arranged to reduce requirement from bank?

(m)   Have both properties been seen by the manager or someone acting for the bank, and valued?

(n)   Full details of tenancies (if applicable).

(o)   Purchase monies direct to solicitor.

QUESTIONS

8 JAMES BROWN
(Question set in 1980)

James Brown has maintained a satisfactory account with you for 20 years. He has been promoted and will have to move house; he values his present property at £30,000 and there is a building society mortgage of £4,000 outstanding.

He has seen a property for which the asking price is £36,000. The vendor has said that, if contracts are exchanged within three weeks and completion takes place within seven weeks, he will accept £35,000. Brown tells you that the building society has agreed a new mortgage of £14,000 but he cannot be certain that he can sell his present property before he has to complete for the purchase. All expenses (including bank interest) will be met by his employers and he asks you for a bridging loan of £35,000.

Consider this request and state whether or not you would be prepared to assist. Assume that the proposition does not conflict with current government and/or bank policy.

20 marks

9 JACK AND MARY MOORE
(Question set in 1980)

Your customers, Jack and Mary Moore, have been the proprietors of a successful hotel (which you valued at £120,000 last year) for the last six years, and they are currently borrowing £20,000 (limit £25,000) secured by a legal mortgage over the hotel. They have accepted an offer of £145,000 for the business, subject to contract, although £20,000 is to be left on mortgage and repaid over four years.

They wish to purchase a caravan site for £100,000. The site has planning permission for 1,000 caravans to be parked and 200 tents. No accounts are available but the vendors have told your customers that total rents last year were £52,000 and gross profit was £28,000.

The Moores ask you for an overdraft of £125,000 pending the sale of the hotel and a residual facility of £10,000 in case of need. You know that they own a house worth £30,000 with a mortgage outstanding of £10,000.

What points will you wish to discuss with them?

State, with reasons, whether or not you would be prepared to assist.

20 marks

8 JAMES BROWN

(a) Proposition

£35,000; house move, open-ended bridging loan; self-liquidating on sale of present house.

	Existing house £	New house £
Value	30,000	35,000
Less: Mortgage	(4,000)	(14,000)
Equity	26,000	To find 21,000

(All expenses paid by company, including bank charges.)

(b) Customer background

With us 20 years, and very satisfactory.

(c) Questions and enquiries

(i) Both properties to be valued by the branch manager (or his colleague if new house is elsewhere).

(ii) Good margin of £5,000, but open-ended, i.e., will existing house sell at £30,000? There is room for a £1,000 or so reduction within the margin, if necessary.

(iii) Building society to confirm the new £14,000 mortgage.

(iv) A good solicitor's undertaking for net sale proceeds needed. If they are not known we must obtain a status enquiry.

(v) Employers' written confirmation that they will pay *all* expenses, after we confirm our charges to them.

(vi) Is fire insurance arranged on the new property from the date of exchange of contracts?

(d) Decision

Subject to satisfactory replies to all enquiries the bank would assist on this open-ended bridge, where a good margin exists between the two properties, for this long-standing customer.

A legal mortgage may occasionally be needed for a bridge, but here reliance is placed purely upon the solicitors' undertaking, in view of customer's status and the figure involved.

9   JACK AND MARY MOORE

(a)   Proposition

£125,000 overdraft initially (then residual £10,000); (a) original facility of
£25,000; (b) £100,000 to buy caravan site, open-ended bridge; self-liquidating
on sale of hotel.

	Sell £		Buy £
Hotel	145,000	Caravan site	100,000
Less: Overdraft	(20,000)	Stamp duty, 1%	1,000
	———	Solicitors, say	500
	125,000		———
Less: Buyers' mortgage	(20,000)	To find	101,500
	———		———
	105,000		
Less: Expenses say (solicitors and agents)	(2,000)		
	———		
To come	103,000		
	———		

(b)   Customer background

Assumed first class – successful hotel. Why do they wish to leave?

(c)   Questions and enquiries

(i)   Can this open-ended bridge be closed? Are they under pressure to
complete the purchase? If contracts for the caravan site are completed
before the sale of the hotel, which subsequently fell through, they
would be left in very difficult position – £100,000 plus overdrawn,
with interest at, say 14%, i.e., well over £1,000 per month.

(ii)   Who are the purchasers? Are they good for £125,000 and serious
buyers?

(iii)   What budgets are the Moores able to produce for the new venture, and
is the working capital requirement of £10,000 sufficient? Will the rents
rise in the future? Will net profit after all overheads give them a good
living?

(iv)   Is the caravan site valuation considered accurate at £100,000? This
must be checked as it is to be mortgaged to the bank. Also can the out-
going owners justify this figure on past accounting data?

(v)   Is the situation a good one which will lead to good summer bookings?

(d) Decision

The bank would only wish to lend here on a closed-bridge arrangement, where a good undertaking from solicitors acting, to send the bank the new deeds and the sale proceeds, would be required.

Security would then be taken by the bank, most probably a first mortgage over the new caravan site.

5   Lending to established businesses

SECTION 1   LENDING TO RETAILERS

Introduction

Existing retailers greatly need to build the support of the public, their customers, by providing a good service and charging prices that are more or less in keeping with the norms of their trade. The service aspect revolves around the personality of the owners and staff which in itself is a lending criterion, but the gross profit aspect is of prime importance for bankers. Both the accountancy bodies and the Inland Revenue have nationwide statistics to ascertain standard gross profit margins (see below).

Gross profit margins are perhaps the most important ratio for retailer lending – if our customers are below the guideline, they must explain why. Also be prepared to face a possible Inland Revenue investigation, as cash sales undeclared may be suspected.

Working capital is also very important and often a ratio of 1.5 to 1 will be quite adequate. However, be aware that an antique shop, by virtue of its stock pile-up, needs much more; also a food shop may manage with a considerably lower ratio.

Debtor recovery can often be a red herring. If debtors do exist (and often do in the mid-luxury retail trade – furniture, electrical goods, etc.), then this must be calculated against only the total credit sales of the business. Be selective with your ratios.

Always attempt to budget forward using past history of gross profit margins, and paying attention to the likely movement in overheads. Many of these latter items will have to be estimated (see question 3). Insert the word 'say' when you do make an assumption or estimation.

You should always look firstly to try to produce a budgeted trading and profit and loss account – to test for repayment of bank interest, and the surplus profit left over. Of second greatest importance is a source and application of funds statement to show ease of loan repayments and inflows or outflows of working capital.

Independent retail businesses: gross profit ratios at June 1983

	%
Booksellers and stationers	30
Butchers	22
Chemists	27
Dairies	25
Fishmongers	28
Shoe shops	33
Fruiterers/greengrocers	26
Furnishers	31
Grocers	17
Ironmongers	30
Jewellers	34
Men's outfitters	35
Newsagents	20
Women's fashions	32
Electricians/Radio, etc.	32
Publicans	35

QUESTIONS

1 J.D. OFFICE SUPPLIES LTD
(Question set in 1978)

J.D. Office Supplies Ltd have been customers for 10 years.

The account has been trouble-free, and progress has been steady but unspectacular. Until March last year, the business was run by J. Doe, who is now 64. He was then joined by his son, who became a director of the company. The son previously worked for a large chain of retail stationers. Since he joined the business, you have seen a rapid rise in turnover, and agreed to increase the company's limit from £15,000 to £17,500 when the 1977 accounts were produced in December. The deeds of the freehold property are charged to the bank, and you consider them to be worth £25,000.

You have just received a visit from the son, who has requested a loan facility of £40,000 to purchase the adjoining property which has come on to the market at that figure. He says that he is most anxious to complete the purchase as this is a corner site with a yard at the rear which could be used to garage the two new vehicles purchased in the past 12 months. These vehicles and the additional storage space which the property would provide are required because turnover has been built up by making speedy deliveries from stock, and the company has obtained contracts to supply the local authority and an insurance company head office.

The son produces draft figures as at 31 March 1978 to show how he has been building up the business, and says that he expects turnover to reach £240,000 by the end of the present financial year.

Balance sheets for the previous two years are already in your possession and are set out below, together with the draft figures produced at the meeting.

How would you deal with this request in the light of the latest figures and the information given to you at the meeting about the company's plans?

25 marks

J.D. Office Supplies Ltd

	30 September 1976 £	£	£	30 September 1977 £	£	£	31 March 1978 £	£	£
Fixed assets:									
Land and buildings			25,800			25,800			25,800
Fixtures and									
fittings			2,300			1,900			2,700
Vehicles			2,100			6,100			9,400
Current assets:									
Stock	27,100			38,200			59,700		
Debtors	15,400			20,500			29,900		
		42,500			58,700			89,600	
Current liabilities:									
Creditors	19,100			26,200			42,400		
Hire-purchase	–			3,400			6,100		
Tax	2,400			1,900			1,000		
Bank overdraft	8,300			9,700			21,200		
		29,800			41,200			70,700	
Net current assets			12,700			17,500			18,900
			42,900			51,300			56,800
Provision for									
deferred tax			5,400			8,100			11,100
			37,500			43,200			45,700
Represented by:									
Capital			20,000			20,000			20,000
Profit and loss									
account			17,500			23,200			25,700
			37,500			43,200			45,700
									(6 mths)
Turnover			120,000			142,000			90,000
Gross profit			24,000			25,500			14,400
Net profit			3,200			5,700			2,500
After:									
Directors' fees			7,500			10,500			6,700
Depreciation			1,100			1,900			1,500
Tax			2,200			800			700

2 SOFT CUSHIONS LTD
(Question set in 1983)

Simon and Benjamin Jacobs are the sole directors and shareholders of Soft Cushions Ltd. The company has been trading as furniture retailers for over 15 years, making modest profits and providing the directors with a good income. The company has banked with you during its whole history.

By 1981 the company operated eight outlets — three freehold, five leasehold — all situated in suburban areas of a major industrial city. In 1981 the directors decided to acquire two additional units — one in the centre of the city, which started to trade in January 1982, and the other in a new shopping centre in a large neighbouring town, which opened in July 1982. The cost of establishing the two units was nearly £80,000 but each outlet was expected to achieve minimum sales of £½ million.

At the end of September 1982 you received the audited accounts to 30 June 1982. You renewed the overdraft facility at £125,000 secured by legal charges over the three freehold units, professionally valued at a total of £140,000, and the directors' unlimited joint and several guarantee. You were of the opinion that they were good for £25,000 each. The directors attributed the fall in profits in 1982 to the exceptional expenses of opening the new units but were confident of an improved performance in 1982/83.

Over the past 12 months the statistics on the bank account have been as follows:

Quarter to	Debit turnover £	Average balance £	Range £
Dec. 82	775,000	75,000 debit	113,000 debit–50,000 debit
Mar. 83	650,000	85,000 debit	118,000 debit–50,000 debit
June 83	725,000	93,000 debit	122,000 debit–68,000 debit
Sept. 83	700,000	105,000 debit	135,000 debit–60,000 debit

In August 1983 you had to speak to the directors on three occasions regarding excess borrowing above the limit. The position was corrected on each occasion by credits in the bank's credit clearing system and the directors were somewhat resentful of your questioning them. However, they indicated that draft accounts would be available before the end of September and agreed to meet you at that time.

25 marks

Soft Cushions Ltd: Balance sheets as at 30 June

	1981 (Audited) £000	1982 (Audited) £000	1983 (Draft) £000
Freehold property	45	45	45
Leasehold property improvements	12	45	39
Fixtures and fittings	12	30	27
Motor vehicles	9	9	8
	78	129	119
Cash	17	6	5
Debtors/prepayments	57	70	85
Stock	260	340	440
	334	416	530
Bank	–	90	148
Creditors	225	270	366
Tax	17	–	–
	242	360	514
Net current assets	92	56	16
Net assets	170	185	135

	1981 (Audited) £000	1982 (Audited) £000	1983 (Draft) £000
Financed by:			
Capital	20	20	20
Reserves	120	135	85
Directors' loans	30	30	30
	170	185	135

		1981 (Audited) £000		1982 (Audited) £000		1983 (Draft) £000
Sales		1,400		1,800		2,450
Gross profit		330		410		520
Trading profit	92		84		28	
Less: Directors'						
remuneration	28		31		32	
Depreciation	10		22		21	
Bank charges	4		16		25	
Net profit (loss)		50		15		(50)
Less: tax		17		–		–
Profit (loss) after tax		33		15		(50)

3   BURGER BUNN LTD
(Question set in 1982)

Malcolm Bunn and Donald Burger formed Burger Bunn Ltd in 1968 to operate franchised fast-food restaurants. The company banks with the branch of which you are manager. By the end of 1979 the company owned a chain of 13 units, but at that time the directors decided that they needed to rationalise their operation. They concluded that three of the units were satisfactory, six needed refurbishing and four were too small for development and should therefore be sold. The programme for implementing these decisions was agreed as follows:

Refurbished

Sold

Undertaken:
1980   1 unit – cost £50,000   None.
1981   3 units – cost £150,000   1 freehold and 1 leasehold unit realising
                                       £80,000

Proposed:
1982   2 units – cost £120,000   2 freehold units to realise £55,000 each
       (contracts issued for completion   (in hands of agents).
       by October 1982)

The directors call to see you by appointment. They have been offered by the franchisor a new take-away outlet (a restaurant in which meals are prepared for consumption off the premises) in the centre of a major town. The unit has just been shop-fitted and newly equipped by the franchisor, ready for opening in June. The consideration for a new 21-year lease is £250,000, with a rental of £50,000 p.a. renewable in seven years.

The directors explain that, although they appreciate that the timing of this transaction is difficult, they are keen to acquire this site, and they ask for assistance to the extent of a loan of £200,000 and an overdraft of £50,000. As security, they offer a charge over the company's freehold stores and office, which you have recently seen and which you value at £60,000, and a charge over the new lease. Additionally, Bunn and Burger are prepared to guarantee the company's account.

You question Bunn and Burger regarding the potential of the units. They explain that the three unconverted units should each average £2,500 per week, the four refurbished units £4,000 per week each and the two units to be converted £4,000 per week each after conversion. The proposed take-away should average £10,000 per week.

Further, although the purchase margin is likely to remain at the 1981 level, wages as a percentage of sales should reduce significantly to 30%. Overhead expenses (excluding depreciation, finance costs and the remuneration of Bunn and Burger) should not exceed £300,000. The forecasts for 1983 are expected to be in line with 1982 with the exception that the new and refurbished units should be operational for the whole period.

The company's balance sheets for the last three years are set out below.

Required:

A detailed report for your lending controller on Burger Bunn Ltd under the following headings:

(a) the position revealed in the accounts as at 31 December 1981;

(b) the prospects for 1982 and 1983, including budgets and sources and applications of funds;

(c) a recommendation regarding the requested facility with comments on the proposed security.

30 marks

Burger Bunn Ltd: Balance sheet as at 31 December

	1979 £	1979 £	1980 £	1980 £	1981 £	1981 £
Freehold		98,000		98,000		71,000
Fixtures and fittings		187,300		206,900		278,500
Motor vehicles		16,900		23,000		25,600
Computer						18,900
		302,200		327,900		394,000
Cash	50,400		24,600		2,300	
Debtors/prepayments	8,200		6,600		10,900	
Stock	50,200		60,700		70,200	
	108,800		91,900		83,400	
Bank	5,100		–		17,800	
Creditors	120,200		135,200		137,600	
Tax	9,700		7,600		–	
	135,000		142,800		155,400	
Net current liabilities		26,200		50,900		72,000
		276,000		277,000		322,000
Hire purchase	14,100		11,000		25,100	
Loans (5 years)					29,100	
Deferred taxation	6,000		8,400		8,400	
Directors loans	61,900		39,600		34,400	
		82,000		59,000		97,000
		194,000		218,000		225,000
Financed by:						
Capital		20,000		20,000		20,000
Capital reserve		–		–		13,000
Profit and loss		174,000		198,000		192,000
		194,000		218,000		225,000

	1979	1980	1981
Sales	900,000	1,080,000	1,200,000
Purchases	360,000	450,000	505,000
Wages	295,000	360,000	410,000
Gross profit	245,000	270,000	285,000
Net profit (loss)	19,800	24,000	(6,000)
Directors' remuneration	30,000	33,000	28,000
Depreciation	35,000	40,000	50,000
Tax	9,700	10,000	–

ANSWERS

1 J.D. OFFICE SUPPLIES LTD

(a) Proposition and cost

£40,000 loan; to buy property; repayment term not stated.

Cost of loan over, say, 10 years:

	£
Interest at, say, 12½%	5,000
Capital repayment	4,000
Add: Interest on overdraft, say £17,500 at 12½%	2,188
To find, first year	11,188

(The above interest figures could be maximum, due to reducing loan account and the swing on current account.)

(b) Customer background

(i)   Good, steady customer — son now pushing hard to expand business.

(ii)   Existing premises worth £25,000; lending value 50%.

(iii)   Mr Doe now 64 — we assume he will retire soon — are we happy with his son's ability? How old is he, and how many years in the trade?

(c) Historical accounts

Gearing	1976	1977	1978, ½ year
	$\dfrac{5,400 + 8,300}{37,500}$	$\dfrac{8,100 + 9,700}{43,200}$	$\dfrac{11,100 + 21,200}{45,700}$
	0.4 to 1	0.4 to 1	0.7 to 1

Low gearing prevails on a strong capital base, but if the loan is granted a high geared situation of about 1.6 to 1 will develop, i.e. (32,300 + 40,000)/45,700. Profits made will add to the capital base resulting in some improvement of the situation.

Gross profit margins	1976	1977	1978, ½ year
	20%	18%	16%

The fall is disturbing, although this could be deliberate marketing policy to attract turnover and hence more pounds of gross profit, as sales are rising very quickly — we would ask.

Working capital ratio	1976	1977	1978, ½ year
	1.4 to 1	1.4 to 1	1.3 to 1

Rather a weak situation exists, although they are not far under the normal level for their type of trade at, say, 1.5 to 1.

Stocks, however, predominate so that the present liquid ratio is under some pressure, i.e., £29,900 debtors holding back £42,400 creditors, and £3,700 excess in their cash book, i.e., £21,200 less £17,500 agreed. However, provided that a good part of their sales are in cash and with good debtor flows they should manage.

Creditor repayment	1977	1978, ½ year
	75 days	80 days

Workings:

Sales less Gross profit = Cost of sales
Add: Closing stocks – Opening stocks = Purchases

i.e., $\qquad 365 \times \dfrac{26,200}{127,600} \qquad 183 \times \dfrac{42,400}{97,100}$

The above position would have been somewhat excessive in 1978 (when the question was set – though not in 1984), i.e., are creditors likely to press for cash or withhold supplies. Are all creditors trade creditors?

Debtor recovery:

This is incalculable as no split of sales on credit and for cash is given.

(d) **Budgeted accounts**

Given sales, and by making assumptions about overheads, we can just about bring out budgeted net profit:

	1976			1977			1978, ½ year
	£	£	£	£	£	£	£
Sales		120,000			142,000		90,000
Gross profit	20%	24,000	18%		25,500	16%	14,400
Less:							
Directors' fees	7,500		10,500			6,700	
Depreciation	1,100		1,900			1,500	
Overheads	10,000		6,600			3,000	
		(18,600)		(19,000)			(11,200)
Net profit before tax	4.5%	5,400	4.5%	6,500	3.6%		3,200
Less: Tax		(2,200)		(800)			(700)
Net profit after tax		3,200		5,700			2,500

By constructing the trading and profit and loss accounts we notice a falling net profit margin in the half-year to date, which on a rising turnover with fixed overheads constant, indicates lack of management control over variable overheads. Calculating the 'other' overheads for each of the three years is important, £10,000 being 8.33% of sales, £6,600 being 4.65% and £3,000 being 3.33%. If this latter item can be explained and maintained, with depreciation and directors' fees doubled up to make a full year, a good profit 'could' emerge:

Budget full year

	£	£	
Sales		240,000	100%
Gross profit		38,400	16%
Less: Directors' fees	13,400		
Depreciation	3,000		
Overheads	7,992		3.33%
		(24,392)	
Net profit before tax, and bank interest of £7,188		14,008	5.84%

We would ask for professionally drawn budgets to substantiate the above, as an overhead level of 3.33% seems unobtainable in terms of the 1976 figures.

(e) **Decision**

The budgets will have to stand up to close scrutiny before the bank commits itself to financing this most fixed of fixed assets. Present liquidity gives some concern, where stocks have doubled in 18 months, and even though trade is expected to double, most businesses manage on a much smaller increase in stocks, pro rata to sales increases. Also if the two new customers take some time to pay, and being large organisations it is quite possible, a cash flow problem could occur.

Extra accommodation rented would seem the answer, to protect the company's working capital, unless long-term finance can be obtained. The directors are putting nothing in themselves.

2 SOFT CUSHIONS LTD

(a) **Proposition and cost**

£150,000 (£50,000, *say*, on loan); for working capital; term for repayment not stated.

Cost, year 1:

	£
Interest at, say, 13%, £50,000 on loan	6,500
Interest at, say, 13%, £100,000 on overdraft	13,000
	19,500
Add: Capital repayment over, *say*, 10 years	5,000
To find	24,500

(Interest of £19,500 will be a maximum figure due to reducing loan account and the swing on current account.)

(b) **Customer background**

(i) Known to us for 15 years, i.e., we know their track record and assume honesty and ability.

(ii) Past profits made and retained (£135,000 at 30.6.82). Hidden reserve in property increases reserves by £95,000.

(iii) We need to know their health; age; who leads; their private worth; any connections.

(c) **Historical accounts**

	1981	1982	1983
Gearing	$\dfrac{\text{Nil}}{170}$ to 1	$\dfrac{90}{185}$ to 1	$\dfrac{148}{(135+95)}$ to 1
	–	0.5 to 1	0.6 to 1

Company is low geared and the capital base is very strong, especially when the capital reserve on property revaluation is added. It is thus appropriate to contact the 'loan givers' if a good proposition exists.

	1981	1982	1983
Gross profit margin	$\dfrac{330}{1,400} \times 100\%$	$\dfrac{410}{1,800} \times 100\%$	$\dfrac{520}{2,450} \times 100\%$
	23.6%	22.8%	21.2%

Falling margin does not always mean future problems – could be a deliberate marketing policy to encourage sales to increase, so improving the company's market share. Turnover is up, but in this case entirely due to the new shops (£1 million).

Also the gross profit norm for this trade is probably about 30% due to the mark-up they apply, say 43% – are there problems here?

	1981	1982	1983
Net profit margin	$\dfrac{50}{1,400} \times 100\%$	$\dfrac{15}{1,800} \times 100\%$	$\dfrac{(50)}{2,450} \times 100\%$
	3.6%	0.8%	Negative 2.0%

When turnover rises we expect variable overheads to rise proportionately. But as fixed overheads remain constant or virtually so, then net profit should rise even faster than sales. Here a negative position exists on a rising turnover of almost £2.5 million. Given that the new shops have created increased overheads, some exceptional, we still feel that management have lost control of the variable overheads of the business.

	1981	1982	1983
Working capital/ capital ratio	$\dfrac{334}{225}$ to 1	$\dfrac{416}{360}$ to 1	$\dfrac{530}{514}$ to 1
	1.48 to 1	1.16 to 1	1.03 to 1

The 'norm' for retailers in this type of trade, where stock turns over about every two months, is about 1.5 to 1. A potentially dangerous situation now exists as regards keeping creditors 'at bay', and it is essential to check the liquid ratio.

	1981	1982	1983
Liquid ratio	$\dfrac{74}{225}$ to 1	$\dfrac{76}{360}$ to 1	$\dfrac{90}{514}$ to 1
	0.33 to 1	0.21 to 1	0.18 to 1

A very dangerous situation exists, as with stocks being the predominant feature of current assets, the small debtor bank may not be able to fend off creditors, especially if any debtor fails in a substantial amount. 'Norm' should be about 0.6 to 1.

Debtor recovery rate:

This is incalculable as we do not have a breakdown as to sales on credit, against which to set balance sheet debtors.

	1981	1982	1983
Creditor repayment rates	Not available	$365 \times \dfrac{270}{1,470}$	$365 \times \dfrac{366}{2,030}$
		67 days	66 days

The fears within the liquid ratio are slightly negated as creditors (especially in terms of 1984) will accept two months readily. But how many creditors are non-trading (e.g., VAT, PAYE and NI)? What period of time have these been waiting?

	1981	1982	1983
Stock turnover rate	Not available	$365 \times \dfrac{300}{1,390}$	$365 \times \dfrac{390}{1,930}$
		79 days	74 days

Again for this type of retail outlet anything up to two months would be acceptable so it is possible that they may be above the 'norm', which could indicate slow-selling lines.

(d) Budgeted accounts

We can only obtain an estimated budgeted sales figure from the bank statistics, i.e., £700,000 × 4 quarters = £2.8 million, say.

This is likely, as the trading quarters look to be almost level, though there are some improvements in spring and autumn.

	£
Thus: Debit turnover	2,800,000
Adjust for opening and closing bank balances	Assume same
Credit turnover	2,800,000
Less: VAT, 3/23	(365,000)
Budgeted sales (subject to debtors at 30.6.83 and 30.6.84)	2,435,000, say

If the above is so, then the group of 10 shops is making little progress.

(e) Decision

The problem is mainly about control of overheads:

	1981	1982	1983
Gross profit	330	410	520
Less: Net profit	(50)	(15)	50 loss
Total overheads	280	395	570
Less: Items stated			
Directors' remuneration	(28)	(31)	(32)
Depreciation	(10)	(22)	(21)
Bank charges	(4)	(16)	(25)
Other overheads – % of sales	238 17%	326 18%	492 20%

Given that two larger shops have been taken on, how is it that overheads have more than doubled when sales have not? Are certain shops not performing as to their return on capital? Are the Jacobs' shop managers all efficient and to be trusted? Are the Jacobs efficient themselves?! The directors must satisfy the bank in this area, and that they can return to profit on a £2.5 million turnover, providing also for the bank's repayment.

Also their mark-up — we would believe that others in their trade mark up by at least 40%. If this is so then they should be on a minimum gross profit margin of 28% (40 × 100/140).

The company's accountant would be asked to provide budgets for each of the shop units with sales targets and applicable overheads clearly shown, so as to satisfy the bank that this retail company with 10 outlets can return to profit, rather than gradually slide backwards.

3 BURGER BUNN LTD

(a) Proposition

	£		
Loan	200,000	New restaurant	. . . Over 10 years, say
Overdraft	50,000		. . . Recurring
	250,000		

Cost:

		£
Year 1:	Interest at, say, 12%	30,000 max.
	Plus capital repayment 1/10	20,000
		50,000
Year 2:	. . . reducing to say	48,000

(b) Customer background

Established some 14 years ago, now under rationalisation:

Analysis of units	No.	Weekly income £000	Cash received/ (paid) £000	
Original units	13			
Sold	(4)		80	received
			110	to be received (we hope)
Group A				
In good order	3	7.5		
Group B				
Already refurbished	4	16	(200)	paid
Group C				
To be refurbished	2	8	(120)	to be paid
Group D				
New unit	1	10	(250)	to be paid

Points:

(i) In business 14 years, now good profit and loss balance; should know their trade.

(ii) Are units freehold or leasehold (long or short) — assume short leases; enquire (possible security).

(iii) Track record; age and health; ambitions and who follows them in business; connections; house value and equities; will all help our decision.

(c) **Historical accounts**

	1979	1980	1981
Gearing (here capital base stated first)	194 + 61.9 to 14.1 + 6 + 5.1 = 255.9 to 25.2	218 + 39.6 to 11 + 8.4 + Nil (Cr. bal.) = 257.6 to 19.4	225 + 34.4 to 25.1 + 29.1 + 8.4 + 17.8 = 259.4 to 80.4

Working capital ratio
$$\frac{108.8}{135.0} \text{ to } 1 \qquad \frac{91.9}{142.8} \text{ to } 1 \qquad \frac{83.4}{155.4} \text{ to } 1$$
$$= 0.8 \text{ to } 1 \qquad = 0.6 \text{ to } 1 \qquad = 0.5 \text{ to } 1$$

Liquid ratio
$$\frac{58.6}{135.0} \text{ to } 1 \qquad \frac{31.2}{142.8} \text{ to } 1 \qquad \frac{13.2}{155.4} \text{ to } 1$$
$$= 0.4 \text{ to } 1 \qquad = 0.2 \text{ to } 1 \qquad = 0.08 \text{ to } 1$$

Gross profit margin
$$\frac{245}{900} \times 100\% \qquad \frac{270}{1,080} \times 100\% \qquad \frac{285}{1,200} \times 100\%$$
$$= 27.2\% \qquad = 25\% \qquad 23.75\%$$

Net profit margin before directors' remuneration
$$\frac{49.8}{900} \times 100\% \qquad \frac{57}{1,080} \times 100\% \qquad \frac{22}{1,200} \times 100\%$$
$$= 5.5\% \qquad = 5.3\% \qquad = 2\% \text{ (approx)}$$

Creditor repayment rate
$$\frac{365 \times 120.2}{360} \qquad \frac{365 \times 135.2}{450} \qquad \frac{365 \times 137.6}{505}$$
$$= 121 \text{ days} \qquad = 109 \text{ days} \qquad = 99 \text{ days}$$

The above shows:

(i) Very low gearing, therefore appropriate to contact loan givers.

(ii) Disturbing trends, however, exist which will need the directors' clarification. Working capital 'norm' for cash retailers is usually 1.2 to 1, say. Liquid ratio shows tremendous pressure. Can stocks converted to cash hold back creditors? Who are they, i.e., spread, or one large supplier (franchisor) who may put on *extreme* pressure (99 days may show an improvement, but is still very unsatisfactory)? Gross profit margin is falling, but perhaps the rationalisation will correct this. Net profit fall to 2% reflects the need to get out of the 'shop unit' tangle, where some have obviously failed to perform. This fall is in fact most concerning — when turnover rises (up to £1,200,000),we can expect variable overheads to increase in proportion, but as fixed overheads hardly move, a dramatic rise in net profit should occur. This of course depends on the 'mix' between variable and fixed overheads, i.e., the contribution. Here on a rising turnover a net loss of £6,000 has been made, and suggests that management have lost control over variable overheads. Enquiries must be made.

(d) **Accounts budgeted**

	1982	1983
Budgeted sales:	£000	£000
Group A shops: 3 × £2,500	£ 7,500 = 390	£ 7,500 = 390
	× 52	× 52
Group B shops: 4 × £4,000	£16,000 = 832	£16,000 = 832
	× 52	× 52
Group C shops: 2 × £4,000	£ 8,000 = 104	£ 8,000 = 416
Oct., Nov. and Dec	× 13	× 52
First 8 months at, say, £1,000	£ 2,000 = 70	
(closed for 1 month, say)	× 35	
Group D shops × £10,000	£10,000 = 300	£10,000 = 520
	× 30 ―――	× 52 ―――
Sales inc. VAT	1,696	2,158

Restaurant takings are subject to VAT, as now are take-aways (1984 Budget).

Deduct VAT, i.e., 3/23	(221)	(281)
	―――	―――
Sales	1,475	1,877

Therefore budgeted trading and profit and loss accounts:

	1982	1983
	£000	£000
Sales excluding VAT	1,475	1,877
Less: Purchases, 42% (1981 level)	(620)	(788)
Wages, 30%	(442)	(563)
	―――	―――
Therefore gross profit, 28%	413	526
And deducting overheads:		
Less: Overheads	(300)	(300)
Finance costs, interest only	(30)	(28)
Depreciation, say	(60)*	(87)*
Directors' remuneration, say	(30)	(35)
	―――	―――
Budgeted net profit	(7)	76

95

*An extra £370,000 into fixed assets (£120,000 refurbishing and £250,000 on the new restaurant) written off over, say, 10 years = £37,000 p.a. depreciation. Only £10,000 applied in 1982 due to 'part-year' timing aspect. (*The examiner is more interested in the principle*, than an accurate calculation of depreciation.)

Source and application of funds statement for two years

		1982 £000		1983 £000
Sources:				
Net profit for year		(7)		76
Add: Depreciation		60		87
Funds from trading		53		163
Other sources:				
Bank loan		200		Nil
Sales of 2 units		110		Nil
		363		163
Applications:				
New restaurant	250		Nil	
Refurbishments	120		Nil	
Capital repayment to banks	20		20	
	—	(390)	—	(20)
Change in working capital		(27)		143

Represented by changes in stocks, debtors, creditors and bank, although a £50,000 overdraft facility will correct the 1982 outflow.

Note: taxation will not be paid until 1984 at least (on 1983's profits), as the losses of 1982 and allowances will carry forward.

Points:
How accurate are the above sales forecasts? Will the new unit take £10,000 weekly? Can they restore gross profit margin to 28% and control overheads? Can we have an explanation of the lower wages (possibly to do with the take-away)? Ask directors.

Bank will need cash flows and budgeted trading, profit and loss and balance sheets for two years at least to compare with our quick figures above, e.g., to see how the new rental of £50,000 compares with rentals of units sold; to show the certainty of £110,000 to come in from unit sales, etc.

(e) **Decision**

Marginal (this will be the answer occasionally). The whole proposition hinges around budgeted sales and timing of refurbishment (October 1982)/receipt of sale proceeds (which must be certain); also the creditor position. New gearing will be adequate at about 50 to 50, i.e., about 225 + 34.4 + new net profit to 8.4 + 29.1 + 25.1 + 250 bank. Cash flows and budgeted final accounts produced by accountants must highlight the above.

Security:

(i)   Freehold value £60,000 at 50% lending value = £30,000; short leases = little value;

(ii)   guarantees and support;

(iii)   postpone loans possible.

Note: debenture the last thing.

Tutorial notes

1   Students must be aware that a proposition may take two or even three years before enough profit and/or cash is generated to correct inbalances which may exist in the first year of the proposition. Here the question specifically gives you information for not only 1982 but 1983 as well when, with a full year's sales from the new structure, profit emerges, i.e., the chief examiner tries to help you look forward two years.

2   The question is worked in terms of 1984 legislation, i.e., VAT on take-aways.

3   To move from budgeted sales to budgeted net profit is essential to test whether the bank's interest is easily recoverable; while the flow of funds statement is a test for capital repayments and sufficiencies of working capital.

Burger Bunn Ltd is an excellent question to perfect the two main budgeting techniques.

SECTION 2   LENDING TO WHOLESALERS

Introduction

Wholesalers have quick turnovers with associated low gross profit margins. These, then, are two of the main ratios to consider. Beware of improving stock turnovers, as this should not be achieved at the expense of cutting down the range of goods available to retailers, or else they may be lost to competitor wholesalers.

Gross profit margins must be carefully considered, as any fall, however small, can, when multiplied by the volume of sales, have a very serious effect on the year's performance.

Overheads need careful monitoring (rather more than retailers) and the net profit margin should be considered, for management control over expenses.

Working capital and possibly liquidity should also be tested. Gearing will always be your first ratio.

Budgeting assumes even more importance for a wholesaler who, unlike a retailer, cannot assume that customers will, by and large, walk in. Always attempt a budgeted profit statement and flow of funds first. The close position is next in importance and assuming increasing dimensions in the lending banker's armoury.

QUESTIONS

4   GREENE LTD
(Question set in 1980)

Greene Ltd is an unquoted public company whose principal business activity is the wholesale distribution of electrical equipment. The company was formed in 1967 and, following a period of rapid expansion, has spent the last two years consolidating its position. The accounts for the twelve months ended 30 June 1980, prepared under the historical cost convention, are as follows:

Profit and loss account for the year ended 30 June 1980

	£000
Turnover at invoiced selling prices	8,130
Trading profit for the year	520
Proceeds from fire insurance claim	173
	693
Bank interest paid	60
Profit before taxation	633
Taxation	278
	355
Dividends	120
	235
Profit brought forward	895
	1,130

Balance sheet at 30 June 1980

	£000	£000	£000
Plant, machinery and motor vehicles at book value			415
Current assets:			
Stocks		1,781	
Debtors		1,514	
Cash in hand		2	
		3,297	
Current liabilities:			
Creditors	953		
Taxation due 31 March 1981	278		
Bank overdraft	231		
Dividends payable	120	1,582	
Net current assets			1,715
Net assets			2,130

	£000	£000	£000
Financed by:			
Ordinary share capital (shares of £0.50 each)			1,000
Reserves			1,130
			2,130

Source and application of funds statement for the year ended 30 June 1980

Sources:	£000	£000
Trading profit for the year (less bank interest paid)		460
Add: Depreciation		80
Funds generated from trading (at an even rate during the year)		540
Proceeds from fire insurance claim		173
		713
Applications:		
Plant, machinery and motor vehicles	120	
Dividends paid October 1979	110	
Taxation paid 31 March 1980	306	536
		177
Changes in working capital items:		
Increase in stocks	2	
Increase in debtors	4	
(Increase) in creditors	(3)	
Net increase in liquid funds	174	177

The managing director of Greene Ltd recently met the company's bank manager to discuss these accounts and to outline future policy. The explanation and information provided in respect of the accounts included the following:

(a) Proceeds from fire insurance claim, £173,000
   This relates to a fire at one of the company's depots early in 1979. The insurance company had not accepted Greene Ltd's claim for compensation when the accounts for the year ended 30 June 1979 were finalised, but did so soon afterwards.

(b) Dividends payable, £120,000
   The company plans to pay the dividend to shareholders on 5 October 1980.

(c) Plant, machinery and motor vehicles, £120,000
   This represents the cost of replacing assets scrapped during the year.

The managing director expresses the view that the company is now in a good position to resume expansion of trading activities. Greene Ltd plans to open an additional depot for the distribution of electrical equipment in January 1981. Suitable premises have been located which can be leased at an annual rental of £50,000, payable in advance, commencing 1 January 1981. Forecasts prepared by the company's accountant indicate that:

(a) The cost of installing equipment in the rented premises and buying new vehicles will amount to £82,000. Payment will be made in January 1981.

(b) An additional net investment in working capital (stocks, debtors, less creditors) of £60,000 will have to be made in February 1981.

(c) A net monthly cash inflow of £25,000 is expected to be generated by the new depot from March 1981 onwards.

The funds generated from existing activities are expected to be the same in the year ended 30 June 1981 as in the previous year and working capital requirements will remain unchanged. It will, however, be necessary to replace certain fixed assets, and this will result in a further outlay of £60,000 in October 1980 and £70,000 in May 1981.

The managing director points out that Greene Ltd has succeeded in complying with the bank's earlier demand to reduce the overdraft to £250,000 by 30 June 1980, and now requests an increase in the overdraft facility to £400,000.

Required:

A full discussion of the past progress, present financial position and future prospects of Greene Ltd from the viewpoint of the company's bank. You should support your answer with relevant accounting ratios and an appropriate cash forecast.

25 marks

Notes:

1   There are no seasonal fluctuations in the level of business activity.

2   Ignore advance corporation tax.

3   The shares in unquoted companies in the same industry as Greene Ltd have an average dividend yield of 5% p.a.

5   GREEN LIGHT ELECTRICAL CO LTD
(Question set in 1983)

Green Light Electrical Co Ltd has banked with you for 20 years. The company operates an electrical wholesaling business which has enabled John Green and Brian Light to lead a very comfortable life style. They are the only directors and hold 50% of the shares each.

Three years ago, they were approached by a major electrical wholesaler to take over the company for £350,000. Although both of them were in their early 50s and neither of them has any family willing to succeed them in the business, they rejected the offer.

101

In the past two years, trading has been difficult. Last year, they agreed to reduce their remuneration slightly but, notwithstanding this gesture, a small loss was incurred – the first in the company's history. The accounts are reproduced below.

In September 1982, the overdraft facility was reviewed, with the benefit of draft accounts showing the £10,000 loss (the audited accounts received subsequently confirmed the draft figures). The advances controller at head office agreed the facility on the following conditions.

Limit: £175,000
Security: Fixed first charge over the freehold land and buildings, valued at £75,000.
           Floating charge over all other assets.

Quarterly figures were to be produced to the bank to monitor the progress of the company.

Required:

(a) An assessment of the company's position as revealed by the 1982 accounts.
10 marks

(b) A report to the advances controller on the progress of the company during the current nine months with, if appropriate, any recommendation for action for the future.
15 marks
Total 25 marks

Green Light Electrical Co Ltd: Balance sheets as at 30 June

	£	1981 £	£	1982 £
Freehold land and buildings		60,000		60,000
Plant and equipment		30,000		28,000
Motor vehicles		40,000		42,000
		130,000		130,000
Stocks	420,000		460,000	
Debtors	240,000		270,000	
	660,000		730,000	
Directors' loan account	50,000		30,000	
Creditors	400,000		450,000	
Bank	110,000		160,000	
	560,000		640,000	
Net current assets		100,000		90,000
Net assets		230,000		220,000

		1981 £		1982 £
	£		£	
Financed by:				
Capital		50,000		50,000
Profit and loss		180,000		170,000
		230,000		220,000

	1981	1982
Sales	2,350,000	2,450,000
Gross profit	162,000	145,000
Net profit (loss)	5,000	(10,000)
After depreciation	16,000	16,000
Directors' remuneration	36,000	35,000

Quarterly figures

	Sept. 1982 £	Dec. 1982 £	Mar. 1983 £
Directors' loan account	30,000	30,000	20,000
Debtors	265,000	240,000	235,000
Stock	460,000	465,000	460,000
Creditors	450,000	445,000	460,000
Bank	165,000	165,000	175,000
Bank, per statement	148,000	151,000	159,000
Total	1,518,000	1,496,000	1,509,000

John Green told you that he changed his car on 1 January 1983 at a net cost of £10,000. He paid for the car out of his loan account. There have been no other capital purchases.

4   GREENE LTD

(a)   Propositon and cost

£400,000; to finance working capital and fixed asset purchase; repayment or reduction not stated.

Cost:
Depends on the swing on the overdraft, and best seen from the cash flow forecast.

(b)   Customer background

Thirteen years in existence — assume management track record first class.

(c)   Historical accounts

Gearing	1979	1980
	£000	£000
	$\dfrac{403}{1,895}$ to 1 (W)	$\dfrac{231}{2,130}$ to 1
	0.2 to 1	0.1 to 1

The company has a very strong capital base, consisting of shares and retained trading profits. As the gearing is so very low, it is appropriate that management contact the finance givers should a worthwhile project arise. If the facility of £400,000 is agreed to, the budgeted gearing will still be acceptable at 400 to 2,130 plus profits being made.

Working capital	1979	1980
	£000	£000
	$\dfrac{3,462}{1,353}$ to 1 (W)	$\dfrac{3,297}{1,184}$ to 1
	2.6 to 1	2.8 to 1

The company's tax bill is, as usual, to be paid nine months from its year-end. Discounting this item and also the three-month delay on dividends, a very strong position exists for this retailer, who probably needs no more than, say, 1.7 to 1. Tax and dividends are able to be discounted only if the company is making good profits, which looks the case here. Thus their future payment will have *less effect* on working capital.

Even including taxation and dividends, in excess of 2 to 1 exists in 1980.

Liquid capital: this is strong, as the stocks to debtors ratio in 1980 is almost 50:50, so that there is no preponderance of stocks to cause difficulties.

Debtor recovery: this is just adequate at 68 days, but if some customers pay after the normal one month then, because of the average nature of the ratio, others could be taking well over three months; we may need to make enquiries. We also wonder if part of the sales are for cash (cash and carry) — if half were, then the recovery rate would double.

Share valuation,
dividend yield method

$$\frac{120{,}000}{2{,}000{,}000} \times 100\% = 6\% \qquad 1980$$

A 6% return, compared with others in *like* industries who pay only 5%, values our shares at 20% more than nominal value, i.e., 60 pence instead of 50 pence. This is indicative of good performances being made, even though it is only one of several ways of attempting the difficult process of private company share valuation.

Net profit margin

$$\frac{460}{8{,}130} \times 100\% = 5.7\% \qquad 1980$$

This is strong for the wholesale trade, where low margins normally leave only nominal amounts of retained profit to be re-invested in assets each year.

Full management accounts would be needed to compare with previous years, before the new facility was offered.

Working

Calculation of gearing and working capital for 1979 comes from the construction of the 1979 balance sheet, by working the flow of funds statement backwards:

	£000	1979 £000	£000
Plant, machinery, motor vehicles (415 – 120 + 80)			375
Stocks		1,779	
Debtors		1,510	
		3,289	
Less: Creditors	950		
Tax	306		
Overdraft	403		
Dividends	110		
	—	(1,769)	
			1,520
			1,895
Shares			1,000
Reserves			895*
			1,895

	£000		£000
Dividend	120	Net profit	460
Tax	278	Fire claim	173
Reserves 30.6.80	1,130	Reserves 30.6.79	895

(d) Budgeted accounts

The cash flow does not include bank interest, which could be a sizeable amount, say £35,000 (£250,000 average debit balance approximately at, say, 14%). Although the account, including interest at quarterly steps, would exceed the limit in March, after some four months more of £75,000 net inflow (say by October 1981) it should hit credit, which is indicative of profits being made. A strong position is starting to emerge where a full year's net cash flow from the new depot of £300,000 will easily cover the investment of £82,000 made in fixed assets, £60,000 in working capital together with the annual £50,000 rent.

Cash flow forecast (£000)

	1980 July	Aug	Sept	Oct	Nov	Dec	Jan	Feb	Mar	Apr	May	1981 June
Receipts:												
Existing activities	50	50	50	50	50	50	50	50	50	50	50	50
New depot									25	25	25	25
Payments:												
Rent of new depot							(50)					
Equipment and vehicles							(82)					
Additional working capital								(60)				
Other fixed assets				(60)								
Tax									(278)		(70)	
Dividends				(120)								
Net receipts	50	50	50	(130)	50	50	(82)	(10)	(203)	75	5	75
Closing bank (231)	(181)	(131)	(81)	(211)	(161)	(111)	(193)	(203)	(406)	(331)	(326)	(251)

107

(e) Decision

Provided the budgets the company's accountant would be asked to produce from the cash flows stand up to close scrutiny, the proposition looks to be sound, and the bank would lend.

The bank would have been impressed by the two-year consolidation after rapid growth, which shows sound management, last year's overdraft being some £403,000. Working capital is now very strong, and will enable another move forward at this juncture.

The only problem appears to be the security position. Many wholesalers are low on freehold property, working from rented warehouses. If a debenture were taken sufficient cover should be obtained from: (i) other fixed assets; (ii) stocks; and (iii) debtors, even if the lowest of security values (say, 10%, 20% and 30% for (i), (ii) and (iii) respectively) were placed on the assets.

5 GREEN LIGHT ELECTRICAL CO LTD

(In our answer we must move away from our standard format of Proposition, Background of Customer, Historical Accounts, Budgets and Decision, to follow the examiner's requirements which in themselves are a plan of attack.)

(a) Historical accounts

Gearing	1981	1982
	$\dfrac{110}{50 + 180 + 50}$	$\dfrac{160}{50 + 170 + 30}$
	0.4 to 1	0.6 to 1

The company is very low geared, though to a lesser extent in 1982. Here the capital base has fallen for two reasons — a loss of £10,000 and £20,000 directors' loans being withdrawn — which is quite concerning.

Gross profit margins	1981	1982
	6.9%	5.9%

Wholesalers have very tight gross profit margins, which depend entirely on speed of turnover. A fall of 1% on 6.9% is very severe and needs careful explanation by the directors. It certainly was not intentional (marketing policy) as sales have hardly increased. This in itself is very concerning, where a £100,000 rise in sales is far less than inflationary rises on £2.35 million.

Net profit margins:
These have fallen so that a loss now exists — it must be in variable overhead control:

	1981		1982	
	£		£	
Gross profit	162,000		145,000	
Less: Net profit	(5,000)		10,000	
	157,000		155,000	
Less: Depreciation	(16,000)		(16,000)	
Directors' remuneration	(36,000)		(35,000)	
Profit and loss account overheads	105,000	4.5%	104,000	4.2%

The overheads in the profit and loss account are 4.5% and 4.2% of sales respectively, so that the problem is not in control of the variables in this section. Thus all remedies lie in restoring the variables in the trading account, i.e., purchase to sales margins themselves.

	1981	1982
Working capital ratio	1.18 to 1	1.14 to 1

The above looks very low for a wholesaler who probably needs a minimum of, say, 1.5 to 1. But, if directors' loans are left in the business, and the overdraft considered a non-pressing 'loan', then with consideration of creditors only against current assets, 1.6 to 1 is reached. Thus, they should get through, as long as debtors do not fail.

	1981	1982
Debtor recovery	37 days	40 days

The above looks excellent, but if part of the sales were for cash, say a half of turnover, then the recovery rate would double. Do they have cash sales (cash and carry)?

Stock recovery in 1982

	£000
Sales	2,450
Less: Gross profit	(145)
Cost of sales	2,305

Thus recovery $= 365 \times \dfrac{440}{2,305} = 70$ days

At about five times throughout a year, this is about right for an electrical wholesaler. (Data: average business ratios for quoted companies.)

Creditor repayment in 1982

	£000
Cost of sales	2,305
Add: Closing stock	460
Deduct: Opening stock	(420)
Purchases	2,345

All in all the above shows a soundly based company with considerable reserves built up over many years. However, concern is now very obvious over falling trading margins and whether this trend can be arrested.

(b) **Nine-month progress (and the 'close' position)**

In obtaining up-to-date figures for the four working capital constituents on a monthly or quarterly basis, we are able to test for profit:

	£000			
	June 82	Sept. 82	Dec. 82	Mar. 83
Stocks	460	460	465	460
Debtors	270	265	240	235
Less: Creditors	(450)	(450)	(445)	(460)
Bank	(160)	(165)	(165)	(175)
Working capital	120	110	95	60

Profit is first felt in an improvement in working capital (i.e., in the debtor bank at the moment of sale, unless a cash sale). Thus, we would expect to see working capital rising initially, before its funds are applied to other 'sections' of the balance sheet, e.g., better fixed assets, repaying loans.

The above is most concerning — has £60,000 been lost (120 less 60) in the three trading quarters? Questions to ask management lie within the construction of either:

(i) a balance sheet at March 1983; or
(ii) a source and application of funds statement at that point:

Source and application of funds statement at 31.3.83

		£000
Sources:		
Net profit for 9 months: negative (final figure)		(62)
Add: Depreciation for 9 months		12
Funds from trading: negative		(50)
Add: Other sources:		
Assumed		None
		(50)
Applications:		
Directors' loan repaid	10	
Assumed	No more	
		(10)
Net outflow of working capital		(60)
Represented by changes in working capital:		
Stocks: No change: 460 – 460		Nil
Debtors decrease: 270 – 235		(35)
Creditors: 450 – 460		(10)
Overdraft (cash book) 160 – 175		(15)
Net decrease		(60)

110

Thus over nine months £50,000 cash has been lost in trading activities, and if we assume depreciation as £12,000 (three quarters of £16,000), then the nine-month net loss is £62,000.

A very severe erosion of the capital base is now taking place. Can it be halted?

Security cover for the bank

		Lending value £
(i)	The freeholds: Lending value on commercial property about 50%	37,500
(ii)	Other fixed assets: Lending value very low, say 10% or 20%, but the percentage chosen all depends on the quality and movability of the items, say 15% on £72,000:	10,800
(iii)	Stocks: Again 20% to 30% depending on saleability and the impact of *Romalpa* (which must exist here as a wholesaler deals in finished goods — a manufacturer may be able to defeat *Romalpa*, see *Re Peachdart Ltd*, 1983), say 20% on £460,000:	92,000
(iv)	Debtors: Between 50% and 70% depending on quality, say 50% on £235,000:	117,500
	Sufficient margin	257,800

Tutorial note

The balance sheet presentation at 31.3.83, the alternative to a fund flow statement, would be:

	£000	£000
Fixed assets: assume unchanged		130
Less: Depreciation		(12)
		118
Working capital:		
Stocks	460	
Debtors	235	
Creditors	(460)	
Overdraft*	(175)	
		60
		178

Financed by:	£000
Capital and retained profit: assume unchanged	220
Less: 9-month loss	(62)
	158
Add: Directors' loans	20
	178

*This figure will invariably be the company's cash book balance, which is more up-to-date than the bank balance.

SECTION 3   LENDING TO MANUFACTURERS

Introduction

Questions on lending to manufacturing industry are basically to do with two types of proposition:

(a)   working capital – this is usually to cope with increased turnover;

(b)   fixed asset purchases – here much greater care is necessary, especially if a factory purchase or extension, as all other assets may need to be extended in sympathy, i.e., more cash spent on machinery, vehicles, stock and investment in debtors.

Manufacturing industry is complex and the work-force is sectionalised – the shop-floor (operatives and other labour) and many office departments (accounting function, buyers, commercial side i.e., sales, research and development, etc.), which all generate expenses. Thus control of overheads is the main feature of management's ability in the eyes of the lending banker, coupled, of course, with the turnover they are likely to achieve.

Full internal accounts are essential, though examination questions usually give us only published sets (as in each of the four following questions), and we are forced to make assumptions and reconstructions in every question. Look out for window-dressing of the balance sheet, always being ready to question the value of assets presented.

A good range of ratios will probably be needed, especially net profit margins to test for management control of overheads. Working capital sufficiencies will also predominate due to the extra length of a manufacturing company's cash operating cycle. Be careful with working capital; while 2 to 1 may be the pre-depression (of the 1980s) norm, most British companies are hanging on with much lower figures, e.g., 1.5 to 1 say. Others need much more, e.g., a whisky distiller with '7-year stock maturity'. Always ask yourself what line the company is in.

Budgeting must predominate in your answer, and the examiner will invariably give you the wherewithal to achieve this end. Some questions are now being structured 'Required: (a), (b) and (c)' to push you into a plan of attack and towards budgeting.

Again, always look to attempt budgeted profit statements, balance sheets or flow of funds, and possibly cash flows first. If the information is not available, fall back on the close position, budgeted working capital and possibly the bank's turnover statistics.

6 CEDAR LTD
(Question set in 1978)

Cedar Ltd manufacture wooden garden furniture and sheds. They maintain a well-conducted account with overdraft facilities of £40,000, which are used mainly to cover purchases of timber when supplies become available in the summer months.

Ten days ago, they were offered a contract by a well-known chain store, which will entail a 50% increase in sales, commencing May 1978.

To produce the additional goods, it will be necessary to build an extension at the rear of the existing factory, on land which is already owned by the company.

The directors ask for a loan of £60,000, in addition to the £40,000 overdraft facility, to cover the cost of the extension. They produce the 1977 accounts, which are set out below.

What considerations would you have in mind in dealing with this request, and what action would you take?

25 marks

31 December 1977

	£	£
Capital		80,000
Reserves		50,000
Profit and loss account		17,600
		147,600
Current liabilities:		
Creditors	33,400	
Tax (due 30.9.78)	12,600	
Dividend	10,000	
Advance corporation tax	5,000	
		61,000
		208,600
Fixed assets:		
Land and buildings		80,000
Plant and machinery		22,000
Motors		10,000
Fixtures and fittings		2,400
		114,400
Current assets:		
Advance corporation tax recoverable	5,000	
Cash at bank	9,200	
Debtors	51,600	
Stocks	28,400	
		94,200
		208,600

	£
Sales	310,000
Gross profit	93,000
Net profit	33,400
After: Depreciation	10,700
Directors' remuneration	15,000
Tax	12,600

Sales for the first four months of 1978 are £103,000.

7   THE YOUNGERS ENGINEERING LTD
(Question set in 1980)

You have been asked to discuss with Mr Younger, managing director of two companies known as Youngers Industries Ltd and Youngers Engineering Ltd the possible transfer to you of the accounts of his two companies from another branch of your bank. You are told in advance that the engineering company has an overdraft limit of £5,000 and also has a medium-term loan of £20,000, but the other account remains in credit.

To prepare for the interview you have been given the latest balance sheets and funds flow statements of the engineering company (below), and you note that it was formed just over two years ago.

On the basis of your study of the accounts and flow of funds statements you are required to:

(a)   Prepare a brief history of the development of Youngers Engineering Ltd.

(b)   Highlight the trends and/or ratios that appear to you to be significant.

(c)   Formulate questions which can be put to Mr Younger at the forthcoming interview in order to bring out information which will help you to decide whether or not you would accept the transfer of the accounts.

20 marks

Note: Candidates are not required to make a decision whether or not to accept the borrowings.

Funds flow statement for the year ended 31 December

	1978 £	1979 £
Source of funds:		
Profit	12,400	3,600
Adjustment for depreciation	2,000	4,000
	14,400	7,600
Funds from other sources:		
Increase in share capital	100	6,900
Increase in directors' account	17,000	(8,000)
	31,500	6,500
Application of funds:		
Purchase of fixed assets	9,500	65,500
	22,000	(59,000)
Increase (decrease) in working capital:		
Debtors	17,000	5,000
Stocks	31,000	1,000
Creditors	(16,000)	(10,000)
Bank balance – current account	(7,000)	23,000
Inter-company loan	(3,000)	(39,000)
Bank balance term loan	–	(19,000)
Institutional fund mortgage	–	(20,000)
	22,000	(59,000)

Youngers Engineering Ltd: Balance sheet as at 31 December

	1978 £	1978 £	1979 £	1979 £
Fixed assets:				
Land and buildings		–		60,000
Machinery		4,500		6,000
Goodwill		3,000		3,000
		7,500		69,000
Current assets:				
Debtors	17,000		22,000	
Stock	31,000		32,000	
Cash at bank	–		16,000	
	48,000		70,000	
Current liabilities:				
Bank overdraft	7,000		–	
Trade creditors	16,000		26,000	
Inter-company loan	3,000		42,000	
Directors' loan	17,000	5,000	9,000	(7,000)
		12,500		62,000
Insurance company mortgage		–	20,000	
Bank medium-term loan		–	19,000	39,000
		12,500		23,000

	1978		1979	
	£	£	£	£
Share capital	100		7,000	
Profit and loss account	12,400	12,500	16,000	23,000

Sales		130,000	140,000
Gross profit		24,000	20,000
Purchases		90,000	80,000

8 WRIGHT PRESSINGS (NORTHTOWN) LTD
(Question set in 1984)

Wright Pressings (Northtown) Ltd has banked with you for a number of years. The company manufactures pressed components for use mainly in the automotive industry.

Until two days ago, the latest audited accounts you had seen were those for the year ended 30 September 1982 (see at end of question).

In July last year, shortly after these accounts had been submitted to you, your head office agreed to renew the overdraft limit of £175,000, secured by a first charge over the company's factory, valued at £175,000 in 1980, and a debenture, giving a fixed and floating charge. The head office official involved expressed some concern at the increasing solidity of the bank borrowing and questioned the current performance of the company. Further, he requested that monthly figures should be sent to you by the company so that you could monitor progress. The company agreed to this request and figures have been received since September 1983. They have been collated as follows:

Wright Pressings (Northtown) Ltd: Monthly figures (£000)

	1983				1984		
	Sept.	Oct.	Nov.	Dec.	Jan.	Feb.	Mar.
Debtors	268	285	287	266	269	280	286
Stock/Work in progress	156	161	163	166	169	170	173
Trade creditors	200	202	213	210	227	243	258
Bank overdraft	157	167	156	173	172	168	169
Hire purchase	49	46	43	35	42	40	37
VAT	–	21	–	–	20	–	–
PAYE/NI Contributions	13	12	13	11	13	12	13

The March figures were received on Monday, 30 April 1984. On the same day, the borrowing on the account exceeded the overdraft limit as a result of the payment of a cheque for £20,120 dated 19 April, in settlement of value added tax (VAT). You telephoned Mr Wright, the managing director, and during the discussion you questioned him about the monthly figures. In response to your questioning, he commented as follows:

(i)   VAT – this is the amount due from the return for the preceding quarter. The cheque just presented represented the entry in January 1984 covering the quarter period ending 31 December 1983. Normally they pay before the end of the next period; for example, the £21,000 entry in October, covering the quarter to 30 September, was paid in December. Unfortunately, for the next quarter the company was a little later — 19 April — in posting the cheque.

(ii) Pay as you earn (PAYE)/National Insurance contributions — this is the amount due each month. In fact a cheque for £11,498 representing the month of December was also posted on 19 April.

(iii) Hire-purchase — some surplus machines were sold in December for £10,000, clearing £6,000 of hire-purchase debt. A new car was purchased in January for £12,000 of which £9,000 was provided by the hire-purchase company.

Mr Wright also mentioned that he had just received the 1983 audited accounts. He agreed to send a copy of these accounts to you (received 2 May — see below). Additionally, he arranged to meet you today 4 May, to discuss the company's affairs. He commented that he was somewhat reassured that the figures for March 1984 showed that the position of the company had not deteriorated during the current financial year.

Required:

Notes for today's meeting with Mr Wright, including reference to:

(a) the accounts to 30 September 1983;
(b) the monthly figures;
(c) the future of the company.   *30 marks*

Note: Assume that the accounts to 30 September 1982 have already been discussed.

Wright Pressings (Northtown) Ltd: Audited accounts as at 30 September

	1982			1983	
	£	£	£	£	£
Freehold factory	125,000			120,000	
Plant and machinery	110,000			95,000	
Motor vehicles/					
office equipment	66,000		301,000	51,000	266,000
Debtors/Prepayments	276,000			280,000	
Stock/Work in progress	154,000	430,000		156,000	436,000
Creditors	192,000			265,000	
Bank	106,000	298,000		154,000	419,000
Net current assets			132,000		17,000
Net tangible assets			433,000		283,000

118

Financed by:	1982 £	£	1983 £	£
Hire-purchase	80,000		45,000	
Directors' loans	50,000		30,000	
Share capital	50,000		50,000	
Reserves	253,000	433,000	158,000	283,000

	1982	1983
Sales	£1.4 million	£1.2 million
Net loss	12,000	95,000
After: Directors' remuneration	75,000	60,000
Depreciation	36,000	35,000

9 GENERATORS UK LTD
(Question set in 1979 – FSD)

Generators UK Ltd was formed in 1968 by three directors, then in their mid-forties, who had left a major international company, several subsidiaries of which manufactured a wide range of generators. Recognising the growth prospects which could arise from the sale of portable generators of various sizes, they purchased land in West London and built a factory on part of it. Shortly afterwards an increased risk in breakdowns in the supply of electricity through industrial action produced an unprecedented demand for their products, which led to substantial profits being earned. For the past five years a period of consolidation has taken place, and the company is now extremely liquid with no borrowing facilities. The directors have, however, been exploring various avenues for possible expansion.

Following a thorough investigation into the potential in the Middle East countries, the directors have decided to embark on a programme to market their products to many multi-national companies involved in office and residential construction, and irrigation schemes, in several of those countries. Encouraging numbers of enquiries and orders have been received, but they have resulted in difficulty in meeting short delivery dates. An overall increase in sales of more than 50% is expected in the next three years, and existing factory premises and machinery are fully utilised. The need for additional finance is apparent and the directors seek your bank's reaction and advice.

To increase the size of the factory premises by 80% (on land already owned) is likely to cost approximately £280,000 and more plant costing £160,000 will be required soon. In addition the directors believe that a working capital facility may be required despite the large cash resources of the company – though they may not be competent to judge this because none of them has a financial background.

Details of the audited accounts of the company for the past three years appear below and these, coupled with your knowledge of the company and its directors since incorporation, encourage you to wish to assist if possible. Discuss the relevant aspects of the proposition, indicate the possible methods of assistance and what further information you would require now and in the future.

30 marks

Generators UK Ltd:

	September 1976		September 1977		September 1978	
	£	£	£	£	£	£
Fixed assets:						
Freehold property		160,000		152,000		144,000
Plant and machinery		116,000		123,000		128,000
		276,000		275,000		272,000
Current assets:						
Stock and work in progress	362,000		389,000		411,000	
Debtors	489,000		621,000		712,000	
Local authority investments	–		29,000		100,000	
Cash	51,000		38,000		55,000	
	902,000		1,077,000		1,278,000	
Current liabilities:						
Tax payable	102,000		96,000		109,000	
Creditors	341,000		386,000		462,000	
Dividend	46,000		68,000		91,000	
	489,000		550,000		662,000	
Net current assets		413,000		527,000		616,000
Total net assets		689,000		802,000		888,000
Represented by:						
Share capital		180,000		360,000		360,000
Reserves		50,000		50,000		50,000
Profit and loss account		445,000		374,000		462,000
		675,000		784,000		872,000
Deferred taxation		14,000		18,000		16,000
		689,000		802,000		888,000
Sales:		1,800,000		1,950,000		2,060,000
Profit before tax*		211,000		249,000		254,000
Taxation	85,000		72,000		77,000	
Dividend	46,000		68,000		91,000	
		131,000		140,000		168,000
Retained profits		80,000		109,000		86,000

*After charging:	1976	1977	1978
Depreciation	45,000	47,000	51,000
Directors' remuneration	39,000	54,000	42,000
Audit fees	3,800	4,300	6,100

ANSWERS

6   CEDAR LTD

(a)   **Proposition and cost**

£60,000 loan; for factory extension; repayment not stated.
£40,000 overdraft; for existing working capital; repayment not stated.

Cost:

Year 1:		£
	Capital repayment over, say, 5 years, i.e., 8 months	8,000
	Interest at, say, 14%, i.e., 8 months	9,333 max
	Say	17,000

Year 2:		
	Capital repayment	12,000
	Interest on £92,000 at 14%	12,880 max
	Say	24,000

(If a good swing occurs on the current account, interest charges will be much lower.)

(b)   **Customer background**

Assumed first class. We would know:

(i)   number of years in existence (and we would probably hold previous sets of accounts);

(ii)   track record of the directors and their own personal wealth, etc.

(c)   **Historical accounts**

One set is insufficient for analysis but:

(i)   Capital base very sound, with no borrowing/loans at present.

(ii)   Gross profit shows 30% and net profit margin before tax (£46,000) 14.8%, which is very good by any standards.

(iii)   Working capital is very strong, and if one discounts tax due in nine months' time, there seems little need for an overdraft.

(iv)   Debtors exceed stocks so the liquid position, out of the strong working capital position, should give no problems.

(v) Are the reserves of £50,000 of a capital nature, e.g., a revaluation of the land and buildings? We would hope they were of origin out of trading, i.e., revenue reserves. Thus some £67,000 would have been built up in retained reserves, and the land and buildings could still hold a hidden reserve.

(d) Budgeted accounts

The chance to take on further orders is just right for this company, which is in a strong financial position.

	Historical, 1977	
	£	
Sales	310,000	100%
Gross	93,000	30%
Less: Overheads:		
Depreciation	(10,700)	
Directors' remuneration	(15,000)	
Other overheads	(21,300)	6.87%
Net profit before tax	46,000	
Less: Tax	(12,600)	
Net profit after tax	33,400	

We can now estimate the results for 1978 and 1979, assuming:

(i) gross profit margin of 30% prevails;

(ii) the 'other overheads' are all variables, i.e., the worst position and at 6.87% of sales.

	Budgets	
	1978	1979
	£	£
Sales: 4 months to date	103,000	
next 8 months, say	206,000	1977 year +
and 50% more	103,000	full 50%
	412,000	465,000
Gross profit at 30%	123,600	139,500
Less: Overheads:		
Depreciation, say, unchanged	(10,700)	(10,700)
Directors' remuneration, say	(18,000)	(22,000)
Other variable overheads at 6.87%	(28,304)	(31,946)
Net profit before bank interest and tax	66,596	74,854
Less: Bank interest, say	(9,000)	(12,000)
Net profit before tax	57,596	62,854

The above shows that the bank's interest can easily be covered, with a good cash flow into the balance sheet.

Flow of funds statements:	1978		1979	
	£	£	£	£
Sources:				
Net profit	57,596		62,854	
Add: Depreciation	10,700		10,700	
Funds from trading	68,296		73,554	
Other sources:				
Bank loan	60,000		Nil	
		128,296		73,554
Applications:				
Extension to factory	60,000		Nil	
Loan repaid	8,000		12,000	
Tax paid	12,600		?	
Dividends paid	10,000		?	
		(90,600)		( )
Net inflow to working capital		37,696		Positive

The bank's loan repayments can easily be met, and a very strong input into working capital should occur in both years.

(e) **Decision**

This looks an opportunity not to be missed, where good gross profit margins if maintained and little else in running expenses to sour the position, will result in very substantial net profits.

Ten days will probably not have been enough to consider the contract fully — putting one third of all turnover to one customer.

Cash flows and budgeted accounts will be asked of the company's accountant, to compare with our quick efforts. While there may be no need for working capital funds, the need for other fixed assets, notably machinery and motors, must be considered.

Other questions will include:

(i)   estimates and planning permission for the extension;
(ii) the length of the contract term.

Security would be a legal mortgage over the land and buildings, i.e., 50% commercial lending value on £80,000 + £60,000 is sufficient.

7   YOUNGERS ENGINEERING LTD

(a)   **History over the last two years**

(i)   The nominal shareholding has been increased by £6,900 in year 2, showing faith in the enterprise, although directors' loans have been repaid. But good retentions of profit have occurred, and the shareholders' stake is now £23,000.

(ii)   Premises have been purchased with the aid of an inter-company loan and insurance company mortgage.

(iii)   For an engineering company, investment in machinery seems only nominal.

(iv)   Goodwill could possibly be written off to the profit and loss account over a period of time.

(v)   Working capital is very strong if the inter-company loan and directors' loans are considered long-term.

(vi)   The insurance company will almost certainly have a mortgage over the land and buildings, possibly also Youngers Industries Ltd.

(vii)   To have only nominal increase in sales could be disappointing and ratios and questions will centre around the performance to date.

(b)   **Ratios and trends from the historical accounts**

Gearing	1978	1979
	$\dfrac{7 + 3}{12\frac{1}{2} + 17}$	$\dfrac{19 + 20 + 42}{23 + 9}$
	= 0.3 to 1	= 2.5 to 1

A high geared situation now exists, where compulsory interest could bite heavily into profits.

Gross profit margins	1978	1979
	18.5%	14.3%

Showing either selling unit prices falling or manufacturing overheads rising, or both.

Net profit margins	1978	1979
	9.5%	2.6%

As turnover increases, and variable overheads rise proportionately, then with fixed overheads remaining constant, net profit should rise faster than turnover. This is not so here!

Working capital

	1978	1979
	$\dfrac{17 + 31}{7 + 16}$	$\dfrac{22 + 32 + 16}{26}$
i.e.	2.1 to 1	2.7 to 1

Possibly excessive for the needs of the average manufacturing company — best applied to better fixed assets.

Debtor recovery and creditor repayment:
These indicate that while there is little change in the former (£17,000 to £130,000, and £22,000 to £140,000) creditor repayments have been greatly extended (16 to 90, and 26 to 80 which is almost 1/3rd or 17 weeks).

Return on capital employed

	1978	1979
	$\dfrac{12.4 \times 100\%}{3 + 17 + 12.5}$	$\dfrac{3.6 \times 100\%}{42 + 9 + 20 + 19 + 23}$
	= 38%	= 3.2%

This shows a disastrous fall, brought about by the loans taken to cover the property purchase. This level of return in a manufacturing company would be unacceptable.

(c) **Questions as to the transfer of the accounts (the future)**

Questions can only be constructively asked of the managing director with knowledge of the other group company in mind. Its accounts, albeit in published format only, could be obtained from Companies House. What are its strengths — they could be considerable, working in credit and granting £42,000 loans!

(i) What are the future plans for the group — are budgeted accounts and cash flows prepared and may we see them?

(ii) Why has the engineering company made such weak profits this year? What do they make — and what then is their gross profit 'norm'? Interest will have affected their net profit. Are overheads being controlled by management?

(iii) What are the company's intentions as to repayment of the loan structure?

(iv) Are creditors happy to allow 17 weeks, or is this mainly an inter-group debt?

(v) Why buy a factory in the second year of trading?

(vi) Are the loans secured?

The bulk of questions centre around future profitability.

8   WRIGHT PRESSINGS (NORTHTOWN) LTD

(In this answer we must move away from our suggested layout – Proposition/ Customer Background, etc. – and follow the examiner's requirements, which are in themselves a plan.)

(a)   **The accounts to 30.9.83**

Gearing

	1982	1983
	$\dfrac{80 + 106}{50 + 253 + 50}$	$\dfrac{45 + 154}{50 + 158 + 30}$
	= 0.5 to 1	= 0.8 to 1

In 1983, while still low geared, a severe erosion of the capital base has occurred. This is very evident in the fall in the company's reserves (losses made), together with the directors' reducing their loans by £20,000.

Overheads:
Net losses have been made in both years, and on a falling turnover we would expect to find fixed overheads having a larger impact on overheads overall, but a £95,000 loss could well mean lack of management control, predominantly over variable overheads:

	1982		1983	
Sales	1,400,000	100%	1,200,000	100%
Less: Directors' remuneration	75,000		60,000	
Depreciation	36,000		35,000	
	1,289,000		1,105,000	
Thus, other overheads	1,301,000	93%	1,200,000	100%
Loss	12,000		95,000	

A 7% rise in other overheads in 1983 is very disturbing and will need considerable discussion with the directors.

Working capital ratios	1982	1983
	1.4 to 1	1 to 1

While profits are first felt in improvements in a company's working capital, losses have the adverse effect, which, subject to other capital movements in the balance sheets, is predominantly the case here.

The company is a manufacturer, and the 'norms' associated with their longer cash operating cycle (stock turnover rate both finished goods and raw materials, add debtor recovery rate, less creditor repayment rate = net days) are, say about 2 to 1.

At 1 to 1 this looks dangerously low if creditors apply pressure. With this level prevailing we must consider the liquid ratio.

Liquid ratio	1982	1983
	0.9 to 1	0.7 to 1

While no generality exists, 1 to 1 is considered about right for most manufacturers so at 0.7 to 1 a precarious situation could arise, especially if one of their sizeable debtors fails to pay up. Thankfully debtors are much larger than stocks, which eases the position somewhat.

Debtor recovery	1982	1983
	72 days	85 days

A lengthening of credit given indicates either slackness in the company's credit control department and/or the possibility of bad debts. Enquiries would have to be made; also as to the level of prepayments, the exclusion of which would improve the above recovery rates.

Flow of funds statement for 1983:

Sources:	£	£
Net profit/(loss)		(95,000)
Add: Depreciation		35,000
Funds from trading		Negative (60,000)
Other sources		Nil
Applications:		
Hire-purchase repaid	35,000	
Directors' loans repaid	20,000	
		(55,000)
Net outflow		(115,000)
Represented by changes in working capital:		
Stocks increased		2,000
Debtors increased		4,000
Creditors increased		(73,000)
Overdraft increased		(48,000)
		(115,000)

The highlights (or lowlights) are the losses coupled with a rise in overhead content, and the serious net outflow of working capital aggravated by directors' loan repayments which seem to have maintained the directors' life-style, as their remuneration had fallen by £15,000. Note also hire-purchase repayments, the size of which (£35,000) suggest too short a repayment period and possibly too much committed to hire-purchase. Also the flow of funds indicates no investment in fixed assets, an area which every manufacturing company must continually seek to improve.

(b) The monthly figures supplied

The September 1983 monthly figures should be quickly checked with the balance sheet presented at that point of time for anomalies:

(i) Debtors differ by £12,000 (£268,000 to 280,000) but could be pre-payments.

(ii) Stocks appear to be spot on, but this asset can be most difficult to value accurately and is always suspect.

(iii) Balance sheet creditors of £265,000 closely agree with the monthly figures presented, i.e., £200,000 plus VAT accrued at 30.9.83 of £21,000, and the remainder could well be 3 or 4 months' PAYE outstanding.

(iv) Bank and hire-purchase accepted as about right.

The second, and even more important, use of monthly figures for working capital is to test whether profits are being made:

	Sept. £000	Oct. £000	Nov. £000	Dec. £000	Jan. £000	Feb. £000	Mar. £000
Current assets (per a/c's)	436	446	450	432	438	450	459
Trade creditors		202	213	210	227	243	258
VAT unpaid	21	21	21	20	20	20	20
New quarter							+20
PAYE accrued, 4 months, say	48	48	48	48	48	48	48
	265 (per a/c's)	271	282	278	295	311	346
Add: Overdraft	154 (per a/c's)	167	156	173	172	168	169
	419	438	438	451	467	479	515
Working capital	17 (per a/c's)	8	12	(19)	(29)	(29)	(56)

By the insertion of VAT and PAYE as ongoing expenses until they are paid, a negative working capital position exists of some £56,000 at the end of March i.e., a net outflow of £73,000, which subject to capital transactions, suggests substantial losses have been made. A flow of funds statement, constructed from the change in working capital backwards and up to net profit/loss will confirm the position for us:

Flow of funds statement, half-year to 31.3.84:

Sources	£	£	
Net loss, about		(74,000)	(final figure)
Add: Depreciation (6 months) say		17,500	
		———	
Funds from trading		(56,500)	
Other sources:			
Machines sold		10,000	
Hire-purchase obtained		9,000	
		———	
		(37,500)	
Applications:			
New car purchased	12,000		
Hire-purchase repaid	6,000		
Existing hire-purchase repaid,			
6 months, say	17,500		
	———	(35,500)	
Net outflow of working capital		(73,000)	

It would now appear that over the last 6 months some £74,000 of losses have taken place, and the position is serious.

(c)   **The future**

Gearing at 31.3.84

$$\frac{169,000 + (45,000 + 9,000 - 23,500 \text{ say})}{50,000 + 30,000 + (158,000 - 74,000)}$$

i.e.   1.2 to 1, high

Considering the rate at which losses are being incurred, the above, a shift into high gearing, by denuding the capital base rather than extending loans, would be unsatisfactory to the bank.

The bank is, however, 'in for £175,000' and must look to its security:

	£	
Freehold factory, with buildings being depreciated in line with SSAP 12; (any hidden value; possibly not in the 1984 depression) at 50%, say	60,000	
Other fixed assets, at 10%, say	15,000	
Stocks, at 20%, say	31,200	minimum
Debtors, at 30%, say	84,000	
	190,200	

Asset values and lending values thereto are always difficult to assess where the quality of the asset is the main feature. All would now need very careful valuation, although the above guide (minimum perhaps) may well cover the bank, subject to the strength of the fixed aspect of the charge.

Serious difficulties prevail, and urgent action is needed. Concern exists as to management control, predominantly to do with overheads. Unless the future can be corrected, by accountants' investigations, a receiver could have to be appointed.

9   GENERATORS UK LTD

(a)   Proposition and cost

£280,000; for factory extension   Repayment
£160,000; for plant and machinery   terms not
£ Extra; for working capital   stated

Cost: Minimum of £440,000 over, say, 15 years

		£	
Year 1:	Capital repayment	29,333	
	Interest at, say, 14% (in 1979)	61,600	max.
Say		90,000	

(b)   Customer background

Assumed first class

(c)   Historical accounts

Gearing	1976	1977	1978
	14,000	18,000	16,000
	675,000	784,000	872,000

Exceptionally low geared, with a tremendous capital base, where retained profits predominate.

Net profit margins	11.7%	12.8%	12.3%

To have 12% of sales left over after paying all overheads is incredibly strong, notwithstanding that it will attract more taxation and possibly dividends. Retentions are being made out of this figure annually. The only cause for concern is that there is no *real* rise in turnover. Thus the company needs to expand/diversify providing that the three directors (now mid/late fifties) are keen to do so.

Working capital:

This looks to be about 2 to 1 each year (without calculation) – probably about right, and as stocks are not less than debtors, the liquid ratio will be adequate (or even excessive – in 1978 it is 1.3 to 1).

Debtor recovery	1976	1977	1978
	99 days	116 days	126 days

Our first thought is a worsening position which needs correcting. This is also suggested by the high liquid capital ratio above. But this company has tremendous strength in its capital base and is in a mature stage of its life-span. So why insist on debtors paying up more quickly; the present situation probably maintains their sales turnover from customers established over many years.

(d) **Budgets – the future**

The directors, although mid to late fifties are still keen enough to expand. They may have other members of their family about to join them. The working capital requirement gives us the main problem:

If sales rose by 20% in the first year, then:

	£
Stock level 20% increase	493,000
Debtor level 20% increase	854,000
	1,347,000
Less: Creditors 20% increase	(554,000)
Funds needed	793,000
Obtained from:	
Existing working capital	616,000
Overdraft necessary	177,000

This overdraft would only be needed if the above levels of stocks, debtors and creditors were reached immediately, i.e., 1 October 1978, which of course never happens. Indeed as the above figures, which are probably year-end (not start of year) totals, materialise an overdraft of £177,000 will never be needed. This is due to the fact that as profits are made *during* the year, they reduce the overdraft need as each month passes. We would need a cash flow forecast to see the points where the overdraft is likely to peak.

To expand the company will be best advised to shake off its preponderances of slow debtor recovery and slow net asset to sales turnover, i.e., sharpen up its management financial control. If its three main working capital constituents could be cut immediately by, say, one quarter more cash would be available into its bank:

	£
Stocks down 1/4	308,000
Debtors down 1/4	534,000
Investments	100,000
Thus: Bank balance	224,500
	1,166,500

Less: Tax	109,000	
Creditors down 1/4	346,500	
Dividends	91,000	
		546,500
Working capital		620,000

So with more working capital in the form of cash, a 20% rise in sales in the first year is achievable without an overdraft, subject of course to cash flow time points:

		£
Stock level £308,000 + 20%	=	369,600
Debtor level £534,000 + 20%	=	640,800
		1,010,400
Less: Creditors £346,500 + 20%		(415,800)
Funds needed		594,600

Obtained from existing working capital of £620,000

(e) **Decision**

This is a very strong business, and a delight for the lending banker.

It needs to up-gear its financial control, probably needing a good accounting 'ear' on the board, and its strength should easily carry it towards a planned 50% rise in turnover, which is needed (as the interest is still there) after its 'rather protracted' period of consolidation.

Cash flows and budgeted accounts will be needed together with indications of the long-term future of the company. This will satisfy the bank as to repayments of its loan (where the 15-year repayment suggested may be reduced, or even extended).

As the time point of the exam question is May 1979 (FSD) the *actual* performance since September 1978 can be monitored for some eight months.

Monthly or quarterly figures for the constituents of working capital will probably be called for in the future. The 'close' position will then indicate whether the expected profits are materialising, and show us if pressure develops on working capital.

Security would probably be a legal mortgage over the factory:

$$
\begin{array}{rl}
 & \text{£} \\
 & 144{,}000 \\
+ & 280{,}000 \\
+ & \text{any hidden reserve} \\
\hline
 & \text{as to 50\% lending value}
\end{array}
$$

The bank may, technically, be under-secured but would probably accept this, in this case.

SECTION 4   LENDING TO FARMERS

Introduction

Farming questions centre predominantly around land purchases. The approach to be followed is similar to all business propositions. Check for efficiency from accounts seen to date, and attempt to budget forward to prove that the customer can cope with interest and capital repayments.

Points

(a) Farm purchases are often put out to the Agricultural Mortgage Corporation (the farmer's 'building society') if any doubt exists as to servicing. Here the bank provides a bridging loan if needs be. Banks do not always entertain 25-year farm loans.

(b) Check farmer's valuation of livestock and crops (from weekly magazines). Visit the farm.

(c) Attempt to ascertain and check the farmer's gross income per acre, for different types of crop/livestock usage. This is the total income per crop acre less variable overheads applied per acre (machine time, seeds, fertilisers, etc. — labour tends to be considered a fixed overhead).

(d) Security can be:

   (i)   legal mortgages over property;

   (ii)   assignments of the monthly Milk Marketing Board cheque to the bank;

   (iii) an agricultural charge — a farmer's debenture but without a legal charge over property.

QUESTIONS

10   J. APPLEYARD
(Question set in 1981)

You are manager of a branch which serves a predominantly agricultural community. The farming land is considered to be generally good and the majority of the farms are mixed.

You have recently visted Mr J. Appleyard, a long-standing farming customer, and during your visit you were able to confirm the annual request for an overdraft facility of £10,000 pending receipt of harvest proceeds. However, Mr Appleyard also enquired whether your bank would be able to assist with a 20-year loan in connection with the purchase of the farm. It appears that Mr Appleyard's landlord died recently and that the executors of the estate are prepared to sell the farm at £500 per acre, recognising his (Mr Appleyard's) right as a tenant and bearing in mind the improvements that he has carried out during his tenancy, as reflected in the 'Tenant's Rights' item given in the farmer's balance sheet, which is given below.

Mr Appleyard is 45 years old, married, and has one son. At present he rents the 250-acre farm at the full commercial rent of £30 per acre. The farm is equally divided between corn growing and milk production from his 100-strong pedigree herd. You know that it is Mr Appleyard's policy to find the cow replacements from his own young animals (that is to say, 'followers') but that the bull calves are sold early and that beef production forms no part of the farm enterprise. You also know that your customer enjoys a good reputation in the local farming community and that the farm's record for the production of both cereals and milk is better than the national average. The plant and machinery are very modern and need not be replaced for many years.

Believing that the bank would not be sympathetic to any request that called for 100% bank finance, Mr Appleyard has raised a family loan of £30,000 which will be treated as non-interest bearing and non-reducing provided that the lenders are offered security in some shape or form to protect their investment.

To support his request Mr Appleyard has prepared a farmer's balance sheet as at 31 March 1981, together with a projected budget for the next twelve months. You know from your records that the trading accounts and balance sheets are satisfactory.

Required:

Make a detailed appraisal of your customer's application, highlighting all the factors which would be relevant to the eventual decision.

20 marks

J. Appleyard: Farmer's balance sheet as at 31 March 1981

Current liabilities:	£
Bank	7,000
Trade creditors	3,000
Current taxation	5,000
Capital account	103,500
	118,500

Current assets:	
Stock	40,000
Plant and machinery	45,000
Tenant's rights	25,000
Milk Marketing Board	5,500
Crops for consumption	3,000
	118,500

Budget for the coming year

Income:	
Milk sales	66,000
Calf sales	4,800
Corn sales	10,800
	81,600

Expenditure:	£	
Personal drawings	4,000	
Labour charges	6,000	
Rates	500	
Rent	7,500	
Seed	2,500	
Fertilisers	3,500	
Sprays	2,500	
Animal feeds	20,000	
Repairs/fuel	3,000	
Sundries	5,000	
Interest	1,000	
Depreciation	5,000	
	60,500	
Net profit	21,100	81,600

11 T. AND E. NANT
(Question set in 1980)

T. Nant, aged 61, and his son Edward, aged 31, are tenant farmers who have been in partnership since Edward left agricultural college 10 years ago. They farm 175 acres of rented land, 100 acres being arable and the remainder grass, and they now have the opportunity to purchase the arable land as sitting tenants for £60,000.

T. Nant has £10,000 available and the partners ask you for a loan of £50,000. Balance sheets for the last three years are given below.

Consider the request and state the points which you would wish to discuss with the partners. On what basis, if at all, would you be prepared to assist?

Note: Assume that the present cost of borrowing is 15% p.a., on which basis annual repayments would be £154 per thousand pounds over 25 years.

T. and E. Nant: Balance sheet as at 31 January

	1978		1979		1980	
	£	£	£	£	£	£
Sheds, machinery and vehicles		10,000		10,200		13,400
Current assets:						
Stock	8,000		7,000		10,000	
Debtors	900		800		900	
Bank	1,000	9,900	5,000	12,800	7,000	17,900
		19,900		23,000		31,300
Current liabilities:						
Creditors		2,000		1,600		1,700
Net assets		17,900		21,400		29,600
Capital accounts:						
T. Nant:						
Balance forward	10,000		11,900		14,900	
Share of net profit	4,000		6,000		9,000	
	14,000		17,900		23,900	
Drawings	2,100	11,900	3,000	14,900	3,500	20,400
E. Nant:						
Balance forward	5,500		6,000		6,500	
Share of net profit	2,000		3,000		6,500	
	7,500		9,000		13,000	
Drawings	1,500	6,000	2,500	6,500	3,800	9,200
Net capital		17,900		21,400		29,600
Sales		25,000		39,000		53,000

20 marks

ANSWERS

10   J. APPLEYARD

(a)   Proposition and cost

£95,000 loan (250 acres at £500 = £125,000 less £30,000); farm purchases; over 20 years.

Also £10,000 overdraft for seasonal use only.

Cost, Year 1:

	£
Loan, capital repayments	4,750
Interest at, say, 15% in 1981	14,250
	19,000

(Interest is a maximum figure for the loan account which is gradually reducing. In year two the interest charge will be some £750 lower.)

(b)   Customer background

(i)   First class farming customer — long-established, with excellent farming community reputation.

(ii)   High yields; above national average.

(iii)   Considerable effort put into this tenanted holding (tenant's rights £25,000 could include buildings, concrete yards, etc.), which his family could lose on his death or retirement, i.e., son not an automatic tenant. The landlord would have to make a payment to him/his estate, at the point of cessation.

(c)   Historical accounts

Gearing for farmers is usually very low, currently £7,000 of the bank's money, to £100,500 built up over the years. It would be almost impossible for a farmer to service a high geared situation.

Of the other ratios we assume gross and net profit margins are above the normal levels; working capital will be high, represented predominantly by stocks (growing crops and dairy cows). His debtor for one month's milk is £5,500, as this is paid regularly and directly into his bank. Crops for consumption are drawings.

(d)   Budgeted accounts

(i)   It is most probably a very appropriate time for him to gear up his enterprise, due to the strength of his existing capital base.

138

Budgeted gearing would be very acceptable at £125,000 of loans (bank and family), as to £350,500 of his money (capital £103,500 less £3,000 drawings, plus the £250,000 hidden reserve in the land if valued at a minimum figure for arable land of £1,500 per acre, i.e., 250 × £1,500 less the purchase price).

(ii) Can the loan of £95,000 be serviced?

	£	
Budgeted net profit	21,100	
Less: Interest	(14,250)	
	6,850	
Add: Rent saved, say, £30 per acre × 250	7,500	(given)
	14,350	

Flow of funds:	
Net profit	14,350
Add: Depreciation	5,000
Funds from farming	19,350

This gives ample cover for the annual capital repayments of £4,750.

(e) **Decision**

The bank will undoubtedly lend to this first class farmer, who has a wonderful opportunity to buy his farm and secure the future for his family.

We would like to know how many years he has been a tenant, to see the build up of his capital of £100,500, and thus be able to project his retentions forward, so attempting to prove his £21,100 retained for 1981/82. Out of this figure our annual repayment must come. A cash flow may be called for. Also, can we confirm the net profit margin of about 26%, i.e. (21,100/81,600) × 100, as normal for his enterprise, and achievable in future?

Once the budgets are cleared the bank would lend on first mortgage, and would be most happy for the family to take a second mortgage behind them.

Tutorial note

A landlord often allows a sitting tenant to buy at a considerably reduced rate. This avoids the landlord's having to buy him out on his retirement/death, assuming the son is not granted the tenancy. The payment under a tenant's right can be in excess of the balance sheet figure, but the valuation of a land agent will be necessary to determine the exact figure.

Also the landlord, allowing the lower figure, makes tax savings when capital gains tax is assessed.

Finally, if the landlord did not reduce, he would have to sell the enterprise tenanted, as eviction is not possible, under new legislation.

11 T. AND E. NANT

(a) Proposition and cost

£50,000 on loan; to buy 100 acres of arable land; over 25 years.

Cost: Annual repayments given at £7,700

(b) Customer background

(i) Assumed first class tenanted farmers.

(ii) Considerable value built up in the tenancy over the years (£17,900 to £29,600 in the last three years).

(iii) Edward, the son, should have provided his father with the impetus to make improvements, especially if Edward is committed, and there always existed the chance of his taking over the tenancy.

(c) Historical accounts

Gearing:
Gearing is normally very low in farmers' balance sheets. There is no borrowing to date.

Budgeted gearing would be acceptable at £50,000 the loan, as to £29,600 existing net worth, plus £10,000 inject from external funds, plus say £90,000 hidden reserve in the 100 acres:

Land:	£	Finance:	£
100 acres at £600 per acre	60,000	Capital injected	10,000
		Bank loan	50,000

Revalued at, say, £1,500 per acre = £150,000

Thus: revaluation reserve £90,000.

Net profit margins	1978	1979	1980
Net profit	£6,000	£9,000	£15,500
Margin	24%	23%	29.3%

An improvement is shown, but we would need internal accounts to check the efficiency of this farming enterprise, in terms of intensive or non-intensive farming methods. We would then be able to check their gross income per acre per activity, e.g., dairy, sheep, beef, wheat, barley, potatoes, etc., with the national or even regional 'norms'. This is income per acre less variable overheads associated thereto.

There is little else to comment on in the accounts — retentions of profit take place; net profit sharing has altered to 50% father, 42% son; and farmer's working capital very high and often found at this level.

(d) **Budgeted accounts**

As with any other business, farmers are usually required to produce a cash flow and budgeted accounts (at least to net profit). Can the Nants do this for us, to prove they can furnish the £7,700 repayments? The rental on the 100 acres will at least be saved — 100 acres at, say, £30 per acre rent = £3,000 saved.

(e) **Decision**

A tremendous opportunity exists to obtain 100 acres freehold, predominantly for the benefit of the son; also, at £600 per acre, where arable farmland should be considered between £1,500 and £2,000 per acre. (A landowner usually allows his tenants to buy at a reduced price as a tax saving for him, and to save having to buy out his tenant's right. Otherwise he could be in difficulties as eviction of the tenant is not usually possible.)

There are some doubts, however, that the Nants could manage the loan. Sales of £53,000 divided by 175 acres are about £300 per acre, which seems reasonable (barley sells at £250 to £270 per acre). But how was the rise from £39,000 last year managed? This needs explaining. Also the stock of £10,000 looks low for a 175-acre farm. It could be explained that in January 'work-in-progress' (growing crops and livestock) are low.

Certain doubts do exist here, so it could be that the bank may decline the offer, but bring in the AMC, and bridge the purchase.

SECTION 5 LENDING TO BUILDERS

Introduction

Questions on this topic fall into three distinct categories:

(a)   The modernise/renovate builders, where, to make the question more difficult, the property in question is to be bought by him (question 12).

(b)   The small 'builder' who buys one plot and erects one detached or two semis (question 13).

(c)   The developer who is to build houses or factory units on a site, probably where roads and sewers have to be made.

The 'developer' questions are obviously the most involved, and question 14 (Smith Builders) is a good example as it requires a list of the points a banker should discuss, and the method for controlling and securing the advance.

The most important aspects in each of the propositions are:

(a)   reputation of customers;
(b)   margin of safety, in this very volatile trade;
(c)   control, probably by loan account;
(d)   security – usually a 'top-and-tail' job.

12 P. AND K. SMYTHE
(Question set 1983)

Patrick and Kerry Smythe are brothers who have been in partnership for over 15 years. They are builders, involved mainly in repairs to domestic property, including work for the local authority, modernising and redecorating houses owned by the authority.

In the past you have agreed overdraft facilities of up to £7,500 against the security of a second mortgage over Patrick's house (value £22,000; first mortgage £9,000) and Kerry's house (value £20,000; first mortgage £8,000). Currently, there is an overdraft limit of £2,500, agreed last October, but today the account is in credit £1,300.

The Smythes have arranged an appointment with you for today. They explain that they have been offered the opportunity of buying a block of six terrace houses for £20,000. Three of the houses are empty but the remaining three are tenanted on controlled rents totalling £18 per week exclusive of rates. Their proposal is to develop the three empty houses. They have costed this work at a total of £10,000 for the three houses, and advise you that the houses would sell, after development, at a minimum of £12,500 each.

From their personal resources they can jointly find £5,000 which they are prepared to inject into the venture. They ask you for an overdraft limit of £25,000 for a period of nine months.

The partnership accounts for the past three years are given below.

How would you respond to this request?

20 marks

P. and K. Smythe: Balance sheets as at 31 December

		1981			1982		1983
Fixed assets:	£	£	£		£	£	£
Motor vehicles		4,900			3,700		6,000
Plant equipment		600			700		600
		5,500			4,400		6,600
Cash	400		600			500	
Debtors	2,500		6,000			1,500	
Stock	1,000		1,500			2,000	
Work in progress	2,000		2,500			3,500	
	5,900		10,600			7,500	
Bank	3,500		5,000			2,500	
Creditors	2,500		3,600			4,800	
	6,000		8,600			7,300	
Net current assets		(100)			2,000		200
Net assets		5,400			6,400		6,800

143

Capital accounts:	1981 Patrick	1981 Kerry		1982 Patrick	1982 Kerry		1983 Patrick	1983 Kerry	
Balance forward	2,400	2,400		2,700	2,700		3,200	3,200	
Profit	7,300	7,300		8,500	8,500		9,700	9,700	
Drawings	7,000	7,000		8,000	8,000		9,500	9,500	
	2,700	2,700	5,400	3,200	3,200	6,400	3,400	3,400	6,800
Sales			42,000			53,000			66,000
Net profit			14,600			17,000			19,400
After depreciation			1,200			1,500			2,200

13 JOHN GODDARD
(Question set in 1981)

John Goddard, aged 42, has been with a national building company all his working life and is currently a works foreman. He has maintained a satisfactory current account with your bank for ten years (present balance credit £2,500). He now wishes to branch out on his own and he tells you that he can buy a plot of land for £40,000. Detailed planning permission for building eight flats has been obtained. Goddard also tells you that:

(i)   he can purchase the land from his own resources;
(ii) building costs will be £16,000 per flat; and
(iii) the flats can be sold for £30,000 each.

In support of (ii) and (iii) he produces letters from a local architect and estate agent confirming the figures. You consider that the writers of both letters are competent men.

A loan of £70,000 is requested. Goddard says he can complete the development with this facility as he is certain that at least two flats will be sold before the whole block is completed.

Consider this request and state, with reasons, whether or not you would recommend the advance.

20 marks

14 SMITH BUILDERS
(Question set in 1980)

You have received an exploratory letter from Mr J. Smith of Smith Builders, a firm of general building contractors who have maintained a satisfactory account with your branch for the last 10 years. In the letter Mr Smith requests an appointment to discuss in detail a request for borrowing facilities to help to purchase and then develop an area of land which carries outline planning permission for six detached houses. The proposed purchase price of the land is £32,000. In his letter Mr Smith mentions that he has confirmation from a reputable local firm of solicitors that, under the terms of a will of a deceased relative, he will very shortly receive funds which he could place towards the financing of this project. However, your customer cannot consider the purchase of the building land until he knows how much he is likely to be able to borrow from your bank.

Your file shows that the firm has a good reputation for general building and maintenance contracts, but that this would be the first housing development it had undertaken. Mr Smith, who is a skilled bricklayer, has a small work-force, including his son and three others, who between them have plastering, carpentry and plumbing skills.

Required:

In readiness for the forthcoming interview, prepare notes on:

(a) preliminary questions to be put to Mr Smith about the proposition; and

(b) the basis on which the bank would be prepared to advance moneys in respect of the purchase and development cost, including a note of the method by which the bank would control the lending.

25 marks

12 P. AND K. SMYTHE

(a)   Proposition and cost

£25,000; to buy 6 terraced houses, refit and sell 3 of them; self-liquidating.

	£
Buy 6 terraced houses	20,000
Refit 3 of them	10,000
Less: Capital injected	(5,000)
	25,000

Cost: 9 months interest on £25,000 max at, say, 16% (speculative) – say, £3,000.

Also add good commission fee.

(b)   Customer backbround

(i)   In the trade 15 years; only work in repairs and modernisations (not structural builders).

(ii)   Some reputation as they have worked for the local authority.

(iii) Past facilities have been agreed. Did they honour them? We assume so.

(iv)   As bankers we should know a considerable amount about them, track record, local reputation especially if they have banked with us for some time. This knowledge will be paramount in this case.

(c)   Historical accounts

Capital base:
Capital base of £6,800 may, at first sight, seem small for a 15-year business. But it is quite adequate, as they do not need more net assets to run this two-man business, which will bring in subcontractors if necessary.

Net profit margins	1981	1982	1983
	34.8%	32%	29.4%

Although a fall exists, the profit is sufficient each year to give the brothers a reasonable living. Unlike retailers/wholesalers/manufacturers the net profit margin rarely indicates management control, as the building trade suffers great fluctuations. One job may be profitable, but the next a loss, e.g. the quote was not accurate, or the weather was bad.

Working capital:
Working capital looks ridiculously low but most builders have a pile-up of
work in progress which even carries from one year to the next on long contracts.
Only when the work is complete (unless payments on account for stages
reached exist) will a correction of working capital take place.

Also creditor pressure should not occur as there is some £5,000 leeway in the
bank overdraft.

(d) **The future project**

Many questions need to be asked:

(i)   Will the three houses sell at £12,500 each? We should visit the site and
      see the work to be done, so as to make a judgment.

(ii) When will they be sold? Are they expecting to complete one first to
      help the cash flow?

(iii) What materials will be needed and the costs thereto? Has a complete list
      of development costs been produced?

(iv) Will the properties when complete be up to a good standard, so that
      potential buyers will easily obtain a mortgage on the property?

(v)   How close is the existing work in progress to completion, or does this
      overlap with the new project? What is their definite starting date?

(vi) When will the tenanted properties become vacant (age of occupants)?
      Will these be renovated too? They are tying up £10,000 in these three
      houses, which will devour the bulk of the expected profit.

(e) **Decision**

This could be a most profitable contract for the brothers (and the bank too!)
since they are working within their existing practical experience.

	£	£
Sell 3 at £12,500		37,500
Less: Purchase price	10,000	
Renovation	10,000	
Bank charges, say	3,300	
Sundry items, say	2,000	
		(25,300)
Possible profit		12,200

We would prefer a brief cash flow, prepared with the brothers present, to
highlight cash movements and maximum overdraft points.

Assuming we feel comfortable with these brothers, especially as to their management ability to complete this project we would lend:

$$\text{Budgeted gearing} \qquad \frac{25,000 \text{ (bank)}}{6,800 + 5,000 \text{ (customers)}}$$

But the high gearing aspect is to be self-liquidating in this case.

Security:

		PS	KS	
(i)	2nd mortgages:	£	£	£
	House	22,000	20,000	
	75% lending value	16,500	15,000	
	Less: First mortgage	9,000	8,000	
	Security value	7,500	7,000	= 14,500

(ii) 1st mortgage over properties

3 tenanted	assume nil value	
3 renovated	at 75% × £37,500	= 28,125
		42,625

This is sufficient even if smaller lending percentages (which are fluent at the best of times) are used.

13 JOHN GODDARD

(a) Proposition and cost

£70,000 loan; to build 8 flats; repayment from sales.

Cost: Depends on time span of project:

say, one year at 15%: £10,500, plus commission

(b) Customer background

(i) No experience or track record as a builder. His whole life in the trade (now a foreman) does not mean he can manage a building (structural) enterprise.

(ii) Savings of £2,500 on current account, and over 10 years we will probably know quite a lot about him — items held in our registers, personal memoranda cards, etc.

(c) The future project

To build 8 flats, on land with planning permission:

	£	
Plot	40,000	
Flats	128,000	(8 × £16,000)
	168,000	

i.e., Cost £21,000 each, sale price £30,000 each.

Questions to ask:

(i)   When would the work start?

(ii) How long would completion take?

(iii) What will his cash flow be? Considerable time will now have to be taken on planning his cash.
Are his building costs considered accurate?
Can he really complete and sell flats, *in a block,* so that buyers will move in?
Stage payments will not be possible with flats in a block.
If he has to finish the block before anyone moves in, which seems likely, he could need an overdraft of £128,000.

(iv) Will the flats sell, when completed? If they do not go he could be in severe trouble with such a high overdraft. However, if four were sold at £30,000 he would almost clear the bank.

(d) Decision

On the information supplied the bank would almost certainly decline this proposition.

Given that Mr Goddard is prepared to stake £40,000 (from where, we would enquire) he has no track record, and the project has quite a few worrying aspects.

Why does he want to go in such a big way on his first project? As constructive bankers, with a keen customer with some £40,000 to invest, we should attempt to suggest alternatives, not merely turn him down. Why not buy a plot of land for one house with, say, half of his £40,000? Use the other half, together with a smaller overdraft, to complete a single house. Thus stage payments may be forthcoming and he would prove his business ability.

14 SMITH BUILDERS

(The question asks us to move from our normal suggested layout.)

(a) **Questions to put to Mr Smith**

    (i)   Where is the site, and how certain is planning permission?

    (ii)   What will each house sell at?

    (iii) Could we please see his development drawings and plans?

    (iv) How much is each likely to cost to build? There are national house-building costs based on pounds per square foot of accommodation. If we see the plans and work out the sizes we can roughly check his figure.

    (v)   Are the houses to be stage-built so as to use subcontract labour more efficiently? Thus the first to be finished could be sold and taken before the whole site is finished.

    (vi) What is the expected demand for the houses? Are they the right type and price for the area?

    (vii) Will buyers' stage payments be requested? This is now normal and provides income as stages of the building proceed. Payments are made by the purchaser's building society.

    (viii) Is a road to be put in, or will the six houses be built alongside an existing road (which is considerably cheaper)? If he has to build a road and lay sewers he must pay for this, and the local authority may ask the bank to join in (and be liable on) an indemnity to prove that Smith will do this work satisfactorily.

    (ix) Is there any problem with availability of materials and skilled labour?

    (x)   Is he registered under the National House Builders Association which, with the giving of their certificate, will enhance the chances of a mortgage for potential buyers?

    (xi) Has he drawn up a cash plan to highlight his requirements from his bankers? (**Note:** a customer attending an interview with such a plan may usually be considered prepared for his banker's questions, which in itself is a good management sign.)

(b) **The advance from the bank**

The timing shown on the cash flow forecast will form the basis for discussion.

The bank will normally advance one half of the cost of land, road and sewers.

As building proceeds, the bank will require certificates from the architect or surveyor acting as to work done:

    (i)   costs up to the top of the walls;
    (ii)   costs up to roofing;

(iii) costs up to plastering;
(iv) costs up to completion;

whereupon the bank will advance a (standard sum of a) further two thirds.

For example:		Bank lends £
Land £32,000 (no service road):		16,000
		———
Per house (as certificates received):		
Walls £6,000		4,000
Walls £6,000 + roof £3,000	+	2,000
Walls £6,000 + roof £3,000 + plastering £3,000	+	2,000
Completed, an extra £4,500	+	3,000
		———
		11,000
		———

The easiest way is to transfer each payment from loan account to current account as certificates are received. The bank keeps a schedule of work done on each property.

When the house is sold the bank will need to join in the conveyance of the property to the purchaser – the bank nearly always takes a legal mortgage over the site at the onset. Thus it receives by way of solicitors' undertaking a cheque to reduce its loan account for:

One sixth of £16,000
Plus: £11,000 work done
Plus: interest applicable to one house
Plus: an extra sum to be agreed.

This latter sum aims to clear the bank's loan account when, say, four or five of the houses are sold, so that if one or two remain unsold, the bank is not left with a non-moving debt.

The bank would probably insist on stage-building, one or two at a time, and on this basis pay great attention to the cash flow. It will also need to see a budgeted profit and loss account for the development, knowing that builders should have a good margin for error. This copes with material price increases, delays to do with bad weather, or having to lower selling prices for the last one or two which are perhaps not so well sited. Taking the development under legal mortgage is also essential.

Positive answers to all the above will usually ensure that the bank finances its builder customers.

6 Other lending propositions

INTRODUCTION

Very few questions are set in this area, although *finance for international trade* is most likely to be the type of question to arise, for both importers (see question 1) and exporters. Exporters usually require the discounting of bills of exchange for their sale monies. These can be applied to inland trade also (see question 2). For inland trade the bank will only discount bills after a 'good' acceptance by the drawee. Foreign bills are occasionally discounted before acceptance (a 'negotiation') but a report will usually be obtained on the buyer from agents abroad. If the bills are drawn under a letter of credit or acceptance facility they will be more acceptable still. The Export Credits Guarantee Department are able to provide insurance cover for exporters, which again helps lending bankers.

Wages and salaries advances occur on a separate account usually. This prevents the bank's preferential claim being eroded by the rule in *Clayton's* case, and also assists with administrative convenience. Limits for preference are £800 per employee, up to a maximum of four months. This topic is usually examined in Practice of Banking 1.

Finance for capital transfer tax depends on the integrity and financial standing of the representatives acting. If not known they must be properly identified and introduced, together with a good report on the solicitor. A death certificate must be seen, together with a list of all assets and liabilities. Representatives sign a joint and several mandate, and the solicitor should agree to produce probate in their favour, whereupon they can effectively charge estate assets.

QUESTIONS

1 STOPPERS LTD
(Question set in 1980)

Stoppers Ltd have banked with you for over 50 years. They have always obtained their supplies of cork from Portugal on open account terms; the documents have been sent to your branch and released against a receipt.

The sellers are now asking for payment against the documents and the directors are prepared to agree, although this will necessitate an overdraft facility of up to £20,000 for short periods. You are asked to agree to this facility against the security of the goods.

Consider this request and detail the points you would wish to cover in an interview with the directors.

20 marks

2 CLOTHIERS LTD
(Question set in 1979)

Clothiers Ltd manufacture woollen garments and have been incorporated for 10 years. They have made steady progress and their latest balance sheet is given below. Their trade at present is exclusively with 10 wholesalers, but they now wish to tender for a contract to supply £50,000 of ladies' coats to a mail order firm. The terms of the contract will be to deliver the coats in batches to the value of £12,500 at two-monthly intervals, with the mail order firm accepting three-month bills on delivery of each batch.

The directors consider that, if their tender is successful, they will require assistance from the bank. They prefer not to have an overdraft and ask whether you would discount the bills.

Set out the points you would consider in assessing this request, and state with reasons whether or not you would recommend the proposition.

20 marks

Clothiers Ltd: Balance sheet as at 30 June 1979

	£		£
Capital, authorised and issued	25,000	Freehold premises	30,000
Reserves	30,000	Plant and machinery	8,000
Profit and loss account	30,000	Stock	25,000
Tax	10,000	Debtors	50,000
Creditors	30,000	Bank	12,000
	125,000		125,000

Sales	£200,000
Net profit	£15,000

ANSWERS

1 STOPPERS LTD

(a) **Proposition**

£20,000 overdraft, occasional; to produce advance for imports; self-liquidating.

(b) **Customer background**

Assumed first class — 50 years in business.

(c) **Historical accounts**

Most probably held.

(d) **Points and decision**

(i) Goods themselves are the security — they must be saleable, and their price stable.

(ii) Directors' integrity and stability of company essential — this is a 'trust' facility.

(iii) Here the goods will be used by the company. If to be resold we would check if contracts exist for sale.

(iv) Some goods are not acceptable, e.g., perishables, fashion items, or specialist market. These do not apply here.

(v) Processing could cause delay if the commodity is to be contract sold. Not so here, as used in own business.

(vi) If a normal contract sale, a margin of safety would be taken so as not to lend up to the total produce import price. Not so here.

(vii) Memorandum and articles of association to be checked. Is borrowing within the company's powers?

(viii) Will a cash flow be produced to show the calculation and time usage of this import?

Security could be by:

(i) Mortgage by registration of a bill of sale, but this is rarely done. Not so here.

(ii) Pledge where the importer allows the banker to hold the documents or has the items warehoused in the bank's name pending their sale. Not so here — to be used by the company, we assume.

155

(iii)   Letter of hypothecation from the company to the bank, pledging the goods but without the stipulations in (ii) above. This form could well be taken by the bank to be released to the customer when the goods actually reach them, against the customer's trust receipt.

Tutorial note:

Most produce loans are to importers, who will sell on their goods as soon as they take possession of them. Payment has to be made before either possession (still on board ship), or contracts for their sale are finalised (warehoused), or both. Produce loans are an integral part of UK trade, without which importers could not continue to act.

2   CLOTHIERS LTD

(a)   **Proposition and cost**

£25,000 (see budget); discounting facility; self-liquidating.

Cost:
To be agreed with customer; probably 2% or 3% over base rate. (14% is used here, i.e., 2% over assumed base rate of 12% — see budgets.)

(b)   **Customer background**

No information supplied — assumed first class.

(c)   **Historical accounts**

Very strong, the main features being:

(i)   Capital base £85,000; no loans.

(ii)   Net profit margin 7½% which if retained (subject to tax) is creditable.

(iii)   Working capital very high at 2.9 to 1, i.e., 87 to 30 ignoring tax to be paid in nine months. Thus this build-up either needs applying to better fixed assets *or* using to finance expansion, as in this case.

(iv)   Debtors are one quarter of sales, and thus recovery must be about three months.

(d)   **Budgets**

Gearing to be:

$$\frac{\text{£25,000 bill facility}}{\text{£85,000 + profits for year}}$$

By discounting its customers' bills of exchange the bank holds them until the 3-month maturity point, so taking a possible risk of non-payment. The facility of £25,000 is made up of two bills of £12,500, which at certain time point

156

will be held by the bank, i.e., the second will be received and discounted before the first is paid (see cash flow). The above low gearing of 0.3 to 1 maximum (if profits are not considered), would be most acceptable to the bank.

Cash flow for the contract:

	Start				Months						
	1	2	3	4	5	6	7	8	9	10
Point of sale	12,500		12,500		12,500		12,500			
Bill due				12,500		12,500		12,500	12,500

Cash if discounted:								
(i) Bill	12,500	12,500		12,500		12,500		
(ii) Less: Discount fee 14%, say	(437.5)	(437.5)		(437.5)		(437.5)		
Net	12,062.5	12,062.5		12,062.5		12,062.5		

The above shows a discounting fee to their bankers of £437.50, i.e., £12,500 × 14% for 3 months.

Budgeted working capital:
If the contract is accepted (£50,000) and the existing turnover continues (£200,000), an overall increase of 25% will occur:

	£
Stocks may need to rise 25%	31,250
Debtors as before (extra 25% discounted)	50,000
	81,250
Less: Creditors, a 25% rise	(37,500)
Needed	43,750

Provided by existing working capital of £40,000, plus profits to be made.

The above position may 'come on-stream' immediately the contract commences.

(e) **Decision**

Without discounting, an overdraft for working capital could be necessary, unless existing three months for debtors could be shortened.

We assume there is sufficient profit in the contract to 'lose' £437.50 in charges.

The bank would almost certainly provide the facility subject to:

(i)   status enquiry on the mail order firm;

(ii) bills being properly accepted by the mail order firm, and their bankers confirming the directors' signatures; and accepting bills being in compliance with their memorandum of association;

(iii) Clothiers' memorandum also being checked for the power to discount bills;

(iv) cash flows for possible pressure points, and to see that the existing turnover will continue.

SECTION B — BANK SERVICES

PART THREE

7 The marketing environment

INTRODUCTION

From April 1985, candidates will be required to answer only *two* rather than three questions in Section B of the Practice of Banking 2 syllabus. Section B deals primarily with the range of services offered by the banks to their customers. Chapters 8 and 9 look in detail at the services offered to personal customers and business customers respectively.

However, this short chapter sets the scene by looking at the overall marketing environment within which the banks operate. Question 1 looks at the importance of the principle of market segmentation in the marketing of bank services, while question 2 is a practical application of market segmentation to marketing at branch level. Questions 3 and 4 look at the relationship between the banks and their competitors. Question 3 looks at the problem of the decline in the share of personal sector deposits going to the banks, and how this might be reversed. Question 4 looks at the difficult issue of if and when a bank manager should recommend a competitor's service in preference to one provided by his own bank.

General marketing questions will only very rarely appear on the Practice of Banking 2 paper. Candidates should, however, be prepared to discuss the relationship between the banks and their competitors in the provision of financial services. This is an area which is likely to be subject to rapid change, and it would be advisable to watch for developments through your bank's circulars and marketing intelligence reports, and in the financial press.

QUESTIONS

1 What do you understand by 'market segmentation'? Discuss the reasons for the statement that a bank's marketing activities are more effective with market segmentation than without.

20 marks

2 You have recently been appointed manager of your branch at Oldtown-by-Sea, a minor seaside resort with a population of approximately 40,000 inhabitants. In addition to the seasonal holiday trade, the branch serves a prosperous farming hinterland of some 10 miles in radius. Because of the town's pleasant climate it is a favoured retirement area, and the town has a higher proportion of retired people than the national average. The retail shops are adequate and benefit from the holiday trade; the professions are well represented; but the commercial/light industrial sectors are modest with the firms thinly spread throughout the town.

Before your appointment you were told that your predecessor had suffered from poor health for the last three or four years and that, although no worthwhile accounts had been lost, the branch's business had remained static. Managerial commitment to local affairs had, by force of circumstances, been missing and you are asked by your head office to send them your plans to develop your branch's business in one of the town's personal/business sectors. To assist you, a copy of a recent marketing survey has been provided and an extract is given below.

Extract from recent branch survey

The competition comprises branches of three other major clearing banks. Each of the other banks is of a similar size to your own branch.

	Town's population in socio-economic groupings	Branch's share of town's banked personal sector
A	15%	33%
B	20%	31%
C	45%	28%
D	15%	21%
E	5%	10%

Branch's share of town's other banked business

Commercial and industrial	20%
Farming	17%
Professional	30%
Retail	23%
Hotel and guest houses	25%

Required:

Prepare a plan for your head office showing:

(a) the market segment you have chosen, giving your reason(s);   *10 marks*

160

(b)　your short-term plans (i.e., for the coming year) to develop the branch's
　　　business in that segment.　　　　　　　　　　　　　　*10 marks*
　　　　　　　　　　　　　　　　　　　　　　　　　　　Total 20 marks

3　The clearing banks' share of personal sector deposits has declined consistently
over a number of years to the point where their share is now little over one third
of the total. Their share of *new* deposits has halved since 1980, and is now only
about one fifth of these deposits.

Required:

(a)　Discuss reasons for this decline.　　　　　　　　　　　*12 marks*
(b)　Suggest ways in which you think the clearing banks could respond to arrest
　　　the decline.　　　　　　　　　　　　　　　　　　　*8 marks*
　　　　　　　　　　　　　　　　　　　　　　　　　　　Total 20 marks

4　Are there any circumstances which should cause a branch manager to recommend a competitor's services rather than similar services of his own bank? What
are they?

　　　　　　　　　　　　　　　　　　　　　　　　　　　20 marks

ANSWERS

1 'Market segmentation' is the recognition that the market for a good or service is not homogeneous. Some parts of the market are likely to be highly receptive to a particular good or service, while other parts of the market may show little or no interest in the product. Put into the context of banking, particular bank services are likely to appeal to some customers or potential customers, but not to others.

Market segmentation may arise from a number of causes, though they are not necessarily independent of each other.

(a) *Socio-economic grouping* It is possible to classify households in the UK into a variety of socio-economic groupings. This is usually done on the basis of the occupational status of the head of the household, and an example is shown below.

Social grade	Occupation	Social status
A	Higher managerial and professional	Upper middle class
B	Intermediate managerial administrative and professional	Middle class
C1	Supervisory, clerical and junior managerial/administrative/professional	Lower middle class
C2	Skilled manual worker	Skilled working class
D	Semi and unskilled manual worker	Working class
E	State pensioners, widows, casual workers	Lowest level of subsistence

Whilst such classifications may conceal differences, they are useful in that the banking needs of one socio-economic group may be somewhat different to those of another group. For example, the bulk of the market for will appointments is likely to lie in the higher socio-economic groups, since a bank appointment requires a significant size of estate to be worth while.

(b) *Occupation* Though occupation is the basis of most schemes of socio-economic grouping, individual occupational groups may have particular banking requirements. For example, the self-employed are the obvious market segment for personal pension plans through the bank's insurance broking subsidiary.

(c) *Age* Different age groups may have different banking requirements. For example both students and old age pensioners will need the use of a bank account; but the requirement for other ancillary services is likely to be quite different.

(d) *Family life cycle* The stage the individual has reached in the family life cycle will influence his requirement for banking services. For example, a single person in employment may be thinking in terms of savings facilities or personal loans for car purchase. By contrast a family with children may have need for such services as life assurance and mortgage facilities, while customers approaching retirement may need investment advice and advice on the making of wills.

(e) *Regional dimension*　There can also be a regional dimension to market segmentation.

    (i)   An area like the south coast of England has a high concentration of retired people, often the better-off retireds. Clearly, such a locality is a good target market for those services with particular appeal to the retired.

    (ii) Branches in suburbia are likely to have a higher proportion of socio-economic group A and B customers, and to be a good market for such things as investments and life assurance.

    (iii) At a local scale, branches on a university or polytechnic campus are likely to have a disproportionate demand for services which appeal to the young.

A bank which identifies the market segment for a particular service, and focuses its marketing effort on the service for that segment, is more likely to succeed than one which veers off in the general direction of the total market. There are several reasons why this greater success should be achieved.

(a) *Size of marketing budget*　The bank is enabled to adjust the size of its marketing budget to the size of the market segment it is seeking to reach. Clearly, where this market segment is restricted in size (for example, the administration of estates) a large promotional expenditure could not be justified.

(b) *Choice of marketing medium*　Knowledge of the market segment which it is desired to reach for a particular service, enables the bank to select which of the various media it should use. For example, is the particular market segment best reached by advertising or by a 'mail shot' or by direct selling through agents?

    (i)   Within advertising, knowledge of the market segment allows the bank to decide which is the best advertising medium to use, the local press, the national press, television and radio. Also, within advertising media, whether to go for an 'up-market' newspaper or periodical or the 'popular' press.

    (ii) With mail shots, knowledge of the market segment allows a more selective and cost-effective exercise. Marketing information systems are available which enable the bank to target particular localities which have a high proportion of the type of people who comprise the market segment.

(c) *Staff training*　Marketing to a given sector may require a particular approach to achieve high levels of success. By knowing the market segment for the given service, suitable staff training can be undertaken to ensure the correct approach. For example, the type of approach which staff might take in recruiting new student accounts is likely to be very different from that dealing with services which appeal particularly to the retired.

Thus, we can see that market segmentation makes sense for a bank, since it allows alternatively:

(a) the achievement of a higher level of business for a given level of marketing expenditure; or

(b) the same level of business with a much lower level of marketing expenditure.

163

2 (**Note:** There is no necessarily correct answer to the first part of this question. There are several possible sectors of the branch's business which could be developed. The answer here looks at perhaps the most obvious one.)

Chosen market segment

The market segment chosen for development is the personal sector, and more specifically socio-economic groups A and B. There are several reasons for making this choice.

(a) Socio-economic groups A and B consist of the highest occupational group households: higher and intermediate managerial and professional people. They are thus a high income group with a potential demand for a fairly wide and profitable range of services.

(b) Oldtown-by-sea has a significant concentration of households in socio-economic groups A and B. Nationally, only around 17% of households fall into these two groups, but here the proportion is double this. In particular, there is a very strong concentration of group A people: 15% as against approximately 3½% nationally. Thus, socio-economic groups A and B are attractive, not only because of their high income status, but also because they are very much better represented in the town than nationally.

(c) The branch already has an above average share of customers in this market segment. With three other banks of equal size, our branch might be expected to take around 25% of the market share for each segment of the market; but for groups A and B our branch has around one third of the market share. This makes A and B attractive as a market segment to develop, since the bank can capitalise on:

    (i) its local reputation as 'the bank' for this sort of customer; and

    (ii) the tendency for the large body of customers already in account in groups A and B to recommend the bank to their colleagues, friends and neighbours who are also likely to be in the same socio-economic groups.

At the same time, it can capitalise on its existing customer base in socio-economic groups A and B, by attempting to market a broader range of services to these customers.

Short-term business development plan

Having identified personal customers in socio-economic groups A and B as the market segment for development, it is necessary to formulate a plan to develop this business. This plan is likely to have twin objectives:

(a) increasing the range of services used by existing customers; and

(b) recruiting new customers in socio-economic groups A and B.

Objective 1: Selling more services to existing customers

(a) As the first stage in the development of a suitable plan, the manager will require information.

    (i) A break-down of the existing customers, so that those in socio-economic groups A and B can be identified. (Since the marketing survey is able to quote the proportion of these two groups which bank with the branch, presumably this information is already available.)

(ii) An inventory of the type of services likely to appeal to personal customers in socio-economic groups A and B. These could include the services of the Trust Company (executorship, investment advice and management, and taxation advice), the insurance service, and possibly money market deposits.

(b) A 'mail shot' could be organised for suitable customers offering details of some of these services and/or the opportunity to discuss them further with experienced staff of the Trust Company. The mail shot might also include the opportunity to request quotations for the customer's various insurance needs.

(c) A further possibility is to arrange regular 'clinics' held at the branch by staff from the Trust Company, where customers could obtain information and guidance on general problems concerning taxation, investment, executorship and the making of wills. This could lead on to the selling of a bank service to help the customer solve a particular problem.

Objective 2: Attracting new customers in socio-economic groups A and B

Attracting new customers is obviously a rather different proposition to selling more services to existing customers, particularly as most people in socio-economic groups A and B are likely to have banking facilities already.

(a) Some business may be generated from the goodwill towards the bank from existing group A and B customers. For example, the caring attitude shown by the bank in the suggested 'clinics' at the branch may possibly sway some non-customers to consider opening accounts.

(b) The 'clinics' and the back-up investment and trustee services might be made available to selected non-customers. They could be reached, for example, by a 'mail shot' on those addresses known to be residential areas for the target socio-economic groups.

(c) Some local advertising or local sponsorship may also help, though the effect of this is more diffuse.

3   Reasons for decline in clearing bank's share of personal sector deposits

Personal customers hold money on deposit with banks and other financial institutions for a number of reasons, though they may be summarised as largely falling into one of the following categories:

(a) *Ability to make payments*   Holding money on a bank current account has traditionally had the advantage of allowing the depositor to participate in the banking payments mechanism. Transfer of all or part of a current account balance, by means of a cheque, is a very widely acceptable means of settling indebtedness without the risk and inconvenience of cash.

(b) *Investment*   Balances held on deposit may not, for the moment, be required for spending. The attraction of a deposit here is that interest may be payable: the depositor receives either income on his deposit or else the capital growth of his deposit.

(c) *Access to other services*   A deposit may be held with an institution, not simply for the benefits it directly gives, but also to take advantage of other services. A traditional reason for saving with a building society is that it enhances the chances of obtaining a house mortgage at a later date.

The declining relative share of the clearing banks in personal sector deposits must reflect the loss of competitive edge of the banks in one or more of the above mentioned areas.

(a) *Payments mechanism*   Clearing bank current accounts remain the major means for settling indebtedness. However, the banks have lost their dominance of this reason for holding deposits.

   (i)   There is now increased competition from other deposit-taking institutions, which offer comparable chequeing facilities. These institutions include the National Girobank, the Trustee Savings Banks plus a number of schemes giving cheque book facilities in association with building society deposits.

   (ii)   There is also greater customer awareness of the relative costs of cheque account facilities with different clearing banks and with other banks and financial institutions. There is greater customer awareness of the opportunity cost of leaving idle balances on current account, so that the proportion of current account balances in total clearing bank deposits has continuously fallen. These trends have only partially been counteracted by 'free banking' for personal customers with the clearing banks.

   (iii)   Banking hours are less convenient than those of competing financial institutions such as building societies.

(b) *Investment*   The clearing banks have steadily lost ground as the building societies have gained in terms of their share of personal sector deposits. The major reason for this lies in the placement of investment balances. The building societies have hitherto paid interest net of tax, while banks have paid interest gross. Moreover, building societies have been at a competitive advantage:

   (i)   by offering consistently higher after-tax rates on ordinary share accounts than those offered on bank deposit accounts;

   (ii)   by taking an increasing proportion of their deposits on high-interest share accounts.

Another increasingly important competitor for bank deposits has been National Savings investments, such as National Savings certificates and National Savings Bank investment accounts. These have offered highly competitive rates of interest and, in the case of index-linked National Savings certificates, protection against inflation. The increased attraction of National Savings in the late 1970s and 1980s reflects the Government's desire to fund a larger proportion of the PSBR from the non-bank private sector.

At the same time, savers have become much more conscious of the interest differentials on different types of savings media. This has come about through advertising and the work of consumer organisations. They are far more likely to shop around today before placing their funds.

(c) *Access to other services*   A bank account remains a key to a wide range of ancillary services to meet the needs of personal customers. However, even here, there are countervailing trends:

   (i)   There is an increasing tendency for a number of ancillary financial services to be available to individuals whether they are in account with the bank or not.

(ii) The range of financial services available from other institutions, notably the building societies, non-clearing banks and money shops is expanding dramatically.

Possible clearing bank responses

The solution to halting the decline in personal deposits probably lies in:

(a) making the clearing banks more competitive in the personal sector, both in term of price and quality of service; and

(b) more effectively marketing the bank's product range.

Possible developments which might assist in the achievement of these aims are the following:

(a) Extended opening hours, so that the banks compete on a more level footing with the building societies in terms of convenience. There is already a trend towards Saturday opening amongst the clearing banks which clearly helps to make bank deposits a more convenient way of holding funds.

(b) Technology can also help to increase the convenience of holding bank accounts:
   (i) The ATM networks of the clearing banks allow for a 24-hour cash service; and the linking together of the banks into reciprocal ATM arrangements will enhance this.
   (ii) The development of EFTPoS (Electronic Funds Transfer Point of Sale) will allow bank customers to purchase goods and services without the bother of writing cheques. EFTPoS should make having a bank account more convenient.

(c) The banks might also attempt to improve their price competitiveness, although there are limits on how far this can go, particularly as it is likely to provoke retaliatory action from other institutions.
   (i) The renewed interest in 'free banking' for current account customers is one aspect of this.
   (ii) Offering more competitive interest rates on larger personal sector deposits and promoting them more effectively is another possibility.

(d) The development of new product packages may also stimulate the volume of deposits with the banks.
   (i) The proliferation of student account packages over the last decade has been one obvious area, where the banks have competed hard to attract new personal customers.
   (ii) The more recent attempts to offer packages to attract young savers, offering money boxes, etc., or linked to the purchase of household items with a cash gift deposited on the new account, are an example of re-packaging the product to make it more attractive.

(e) The logical extension of this is the idea of the banks as 'financial supermarkets' or 'one-stop banking'. By offering a range of 'off-the-shelf' financial services such as insurance, travel facilities, estate agency, etc., not only can these services be sold to existing customers at a profit, but also it is hoped that non-customers may begin by buying these ancillary services and then later become customers. In this way, the deposit base would be raised.

(f) The banks must also seek to improve their public image. As recently as 1983, a National Consumer Council report suggested that many people regarded banks as unfriendly and impersonal. This stands in contrast to the building societies which had a much more open and friendly image.

4   In the marketing of banking and financial services, banks may sometimes find themselves with conflicting objectives:

(a)   They are commercial organisations, with the objective of providing financial services at a profit.
(b)   They have a fiduciary duty to their customers to see them properly advised on financial matters.

Clearly, there is a possibility of conflict between what is profitable, and what is best for the customer. Yet this conflict may be less common than might, at first sight, be thought.

The first point which meeds to be made is the distinction between short-run and long-run profit:

(a)   Selling a bank service to a customer, where it is known there is a superior alternative available from another institution, obviously earns the profit which comes from this sale.
(b)   However, such action may be to the long-term detriment of the bank:
      (i)   When the customer discovers he has been poorly advised, there may be a loss of goodwill.
      (ii)   The customer may not come to the bank for other services because of his bad experience. Clearly the bank would lose the profit from not selling these other services.
      (iii) In extreme cases, the customer's loss of faith in the bank might even lead to the loss of the account.

Thus, the branch manager needs to weigh up the short-term advantage that the bank would gain by selling a sub-optimal service to a customer, against the long-term loss to the bank. This calculation will include a consideration of the following variables:

(a)   To what extent is the competitor's product superior? Clearly, there will be more temptation to sell the bank's service, the narrower is the gap between the bank's and the competitor's service.
(b)   How likely is the customer to make use of other bank services at a later date? Clearly, if a customer is likely to use other bank services, the potential long-run loss in going for a quick return is greater.

Secondly, the bank manager needs to fulfil his fiduciary duty to the customer. In part the provision of the best advice on financial matters is a moral obligation. But again there is a marketing and profitability angle. There is always the risk of the image of the bank in the market being damaged by acquiring a reputation for seeking profits at the expense of its customers.

Thus, on many occasions, it will be in the bank's longer-term interest to honour its fiduciary duty, and to recommend the services of a competitor where these clearly serve the customer's interest better than the bank's equivalent service. An example

168

which frequently confronts bank managers is where a customer needs investment advice. For example, a financially unsophisticated customer receives a legacy of £5,000. The easy course for the manager to adopt would be to suggest placing the funds on deposit account. However, the customer's interest may be better served by suggesting investing part of the legacy at least in National Savings or a high-yield building society account.

8 Bank services for personal customers

INTRODUCTION

This chapter examines the principal bank services for personal customers. Questions 1 to 10 look at individual services or groups of services which fulfil a particular need. The thing that each question has in common is that it is fairly direct:

(a) It is clear from the question which service or services you are required to consider.
(b) You are usually required to explain the nature of the service and what advantages it offers to the customer.

By contrast, the remaining questions, 11 to 18, are of the 'problem type'. From the facts provided in the question, it is necessary to develop an answer which does the following things:

(a) identifies the problem(s) or opportunity(ies) faced by the customer in the question;
(b) matches one or more bank services to the needs of the customer identified in (a);
(c) explains to the customer why he should make use of the particular bank service(s) to solve his problems. This latter is the 'marketing element' of the question: the customer is encouraged to use the service since he is led to see how it can be of value to him.

In preparing for the examination, it is essential to have a good working knowledge of the mundane as well as the more specialised services used by personal customers. This will include their main features, and their selling points – what advantages they offer to the customer. However, it is important not to become too 'compartmentalised', and to recognise that a question may call for several relatively divergent services. For example, a question primarily about business customer services may also have an element of personal customer services in it too.

We shall meet some examples of this in the next chapter. But equally, it is vital to avoid the 'pepperpot approach' – including a wide range of services in the hope that some will be relevant. The secret is to analyse the question carefully to ascertain what the customer requires; and to deal with those services directly relevant to his requirements.

QUESTIONS

1 You have been asked to contribute a talk to the local Sixth Form College Business Club on the subject of 'Banks and the Provision of Consumer Credit'.

Outline the main bank services you would wish to mention in your talk, and list their main features.

20 marks

2 Following the success of your talk to the Sixth Form College Business Club, you have now been asked to speak to a Townswomens' Guild meeting. Your subject this time is: 'How can Banks Help the Home Buyer'.

Outline the main bank services you would wish to mention in your talk and detail their main features.

20 marks

3 Outline the services which banks can offer to personal customers who wish to invest in equities (stocks and shares).

20 marks

4 Over the past 20 years there has been a proliferation of authorised unit trusts offering a variety of investment opportunities.

What are the main sorts of unit trusts offered by banks? Write brief explanatory notes about each of the types of scheme you have identified.

20 marks

5 Your customer, Peter Brown, has called by appointment to see you. He has seen a bank advertisement offering customers help with their insurance problems. He feels that, with his family commitments, he needs some form of life assurance. However, he says that he finds the subject confusing and asks if you will briefly explain to him the main types of life assurance, and what their particular advantages are.

20 marks

6 Explain what is meant by 'personal pension plans'. Does the bank have a service which may help a customer find an appropriate plan?

20 marks

7 What are the advantages of appointing the bank as executor under a will? Is there any way that the bank can assist, even though it has not been appointed to act?

15 marks

8 Colonel Holt-Saunders, a very good customer at your branch, calls to see you today. He informs you that his co-trustee in the family trust, John Holt-Saunders, has died. The trust maintains an account with you, and the colonel tells you that they are having difficulty in finding a member of the family to take over as co-trustee, while he himself is finding management of the trust increasingly onerous.

172

What opportunities, if any, does this situation offer to the bank?

20 marks

9 When Michael Stratton, a successful author, calls to see you to discuss his over-draft, he tells you that he needs a temporary facility of £3,500 to meet a demand for back tax from the Inland Revenue. It appears that he has always managed his own tax affairs but on his own admission they have become badly disorganised resulting in the accumulation of arrears of tax due.

You are happy to provide the overdraft, but is there any other bank service you might usefully offer to Mr Stratton, and what benefits would it give him?

10 marks

10 Your local college is mounting a course for trainee travel agents. You have been asked by the bank to provide a talk followed by a discussion on 'Travel Services Offered by the Banks'.

Outline the main services you will wish to mention in your presentation.

20 marks

11 As manager you have been advised by your head office that part of your bank's policy for the coming year is to increase the number of current account customers, particularly in the higher wage-earning sector.

In the light of this policy you have been undertaking a survey of your branch business and have discovered that one of your larger industrial customers still pays its work-force by cash, which is collected by a security firm each week. You know that the work-force is predominantly skilled and would fall into the category identified by your head office. You have therefore requested an initial meeting with the company's financial director and a member of the non-unionised work-force to discuss in outline the benefits that would accrue if payment of wages were made by means of a transfer to a bank account for each employee.

Required:
A consideration of the benefits and services that you would discuss at the forth-coming meeting.

Notes: Candidates may assume that consideration has already been given to the provisions of the Consumer Credit Act and that no further reference is required. In addition, candidates may disregard the provision set out in the Payment of Wages Act 1960 for alternative method of payments.

20 marks

12 You have been appointed to the managerial team of a branch shortly to be opened in one of the country's new towns.

The development of the new branch's industrial business has been assigned to one of your colleagues, but it is your responsibility to develop the strategy for the personal sector.

You understand from the various reports issued by the New Town Commission that the estimated population of the town, when fully developed in about five years' time, will be approximately 75,000. It is expected that the working population will be predominantly skilled and semi-skilled to meet the needs of the light industry which is being established, and would therefore fit into socio-economic group C, although there will inevitably be smaller proportions in the other categories. The housing policy of the local council indicates that only a very small proportion of the housing stock will be earmarked for private ownership, with the balance remaining in the public sector.

Required:
Discuss:

(a) the most likely financial and banking requirements of the expanding work force;
10 marks
(b) the traditional and/or specialist bank services that would seem most likely to satisfy those needs. *10 marks*
Total 20 marks

13 You have received a letter from Mr White, managing director and majority shareholder (he owns 90% of the issued share capital) of White's Engineering Ltd, one of your old-established customers. In his letter he mentions that he will be calling to discuss temporary overdraft facilities to meet corporation tax that is now due. From the balance sheet figures given below you expect no difficulty in acceding to the request, although an exact amount of the overdraft required is not stated in the letter.

You know from Mr White's file that he is 58 years old, a widower with two sons, both of whom are involved in the business which has operated from its original factory for many years. Your branch holds the unencumbered deeds of his house, which you value at approximately £45,000, together with various uncharged stock exchange security certificates with a valuation of approximately £15,000. No other documents or securities are held, either for Mr White or for the company.

Required:
From the general information already in your possession and the balance sheet and profit and loss figures given below, identify the areas in which Mr White might have problems and indicate those bank departments and services which could assist in solving or mitigating those problems, to the mutual benefit of the bank and the customer.

Balance sheet of White's Engineering Ltd as at 30 June

Current liabilities:	£	Fixed assets:	£
Trade creditors	34,000	Land and factory (at cost)	25,000
Hire purchase creditors	6,000	Plant and machinery	10,000
Current tax	10,000	Vehicles	7,000
	50,000		42,000
		Debtors	35,000
		Stock	20,000
Issued share capital	20,000	Work in progress	5,000
Profit and loss account	35,000	Cash at bank	3,000
	105,000		105,000

Profit and loss account for year ended 30 June

	£	£
Gross profit		100,000
Directors' remuneration	15,000	
Salaries/wages	45,000	
Heat and light	3,000	
Insurance	1,500	
Motor expenses	2,000	
Rates	750	
Hire purchase interest	750	
Depreciation	4,000	72,000
Net profit before taxation		28,000

20 marks

14 You have been asked to interview Mr Brown, who is not a customer of your bank. At the meeting Mr Brown produces the following letter from Mr Smith, one of your long-standing customers:

Dear Sir,

I am writing to introduce Mr Brown, as a potential customer of your bank. He has been known to me for the last 15 years or so as a local workman. He tells me that, quite unexpectedly, he has inherited an appreciable sum of money and he needs banking facilities and guidance. As your bank has helped me in the past I have suggested that he seek your assistance.

Your faithfully,
signed A. Smith

During the interview Mr Brown tells you that he is married with two grown-up sons. He has his own modest unencumbered property, but has no plans to buy a larger house. He would like to use the money to care for his family, but he emphasises that he does not understand finance. Mr Brown then produces a cheque for £120,000 from a firm of solicitors who have handled the estate under which he has benefited.

Describe the various specialist services the bank provides which would meet Mr Brown's specific needs and give a brief outline of the benefits to him of each of those services.

20 marks

15 Mr and Mrs Jones are both in their early forties and are proprietors of a small chain of six hairdressing salons, one of which incorporates their living accommodation. They bought the chain of shops, which operate through short-term leases, four years ago through an outside source of finance which handled all matters relating to security for a five-year medium-term loan, the security being mortgages over the leases of the premises.

The interest rates were high and this, coupled with the loan reduction programme, has resulted in their living most carefully since the purchase was completed. As their bankers, you have been supporting the business by way of an unsecured overdraft up to £2,500, and Mr and Mrs Jones have requested an interview to discuss renewal for a further 12 months. You have available the following audited accounts:

Balance sheets as at 30 June

	1983 £	1984 £		1983 £	1984 £
Hire purchase creditors	3,000	1,500	Debtors	300	400
Trade creditors	500	750	Stock	500	400
Bank	2,250	2,300	Motor vehicles	4,000	2,500
Mortgages	8,000	4,000	Shop improvements	2,000	1,500
Capital accounts	18,050	21,250	Goodwill	25,000	25,000
	31,800	29,800		31,800	29,800

Required:

In readiness for the interview, prepare a note of the bank services which might be of interest to Mr and Mrs Jones in view of their changing financial circumstances. In each case show briefly the benefit which the service in question would confer upon your customers.   *20 marks*

16   John Williams is a director of a public company which banks with a competitor bank. Mr Williams and his wife have maintained a satisfactory joint account with you for over 10 years. From your records you notice that a monthly salary of about £1,400 is received and the standing order payments include a monthly transfer of £155 to the local building society. Additionally, your securities clerk tells you that, today, the balance on the current account is £500 credit, with the salary credit due next week, and on the deposit account £1,500 credit. You are also holding in safe custody a building society passbook showing a balance of £2,500.

Mr Williams calls to see you today by appointment. He explains that he has decided to purchase a house outside the town in preparation for his retirement in five years' time. He has submitted an offer of £75,000 which has been accepted.

You question Mr Williams regarding his present house. The house was placed with a local firm of estate agents one month ago and an offer of £65,000 − £5,000 below the asking price − has just been submitted but with a condition that completion is to be delayed until 3 August. You learn that the property was purchased 10 years ago with the help of a mortgage of £12,000, of which about £8,000 is still outstanding.

Mr Williams asks if he can issue a cheque next week for £7,500 and complete the purchase at the end of May.

How would you reply to Mr Williams?

In helping him, what considerations would you have in mind and what security requirements would you need?

(4/82)   *20 marks*

176

17 While preparing for an interview with Albert Smith, you observe that:

(a) the account was opened six months ago in the joint names of Albert and Molly Smith;

(b) two credits, both from Beta Plastics Ltd have been received each month, the monthly average of the two credits being £800;

(c) the balance on the account is £400 credit and this month's credits have not yet been received.

At the interview, Mr Smith explains that he is 29 years old and is Works Manager at Beta Plastics, earning £160 per week, whilst his wife is secretary to the managing director and paid £90 per week. They opened the bank account since the company required all the work force to have their salaries paid monthly into a bank account. He and Molly were married 12 months ago and live in a rented flat costing £30 per week.

Two years ago, Mr Smith purchased a sports car costing £2,900. The garage arranged hire-purchase on which the final monthly payment of £100 was made last month. Mr Smith wishes to buy a new, more economical car costing £5,500 but on special discount at £5,000 to include 12 months' car tax. A friend has agreed to purchase the sports car for £2,000 and Mr Smith has saved £1,000 in a National Savings Bank account. You agree to a loan of £2,000 repayable at £100 per month.

Could you help Mr Smith in other ways? If so, identify the services and give reasons for your suggestions.   (4/83) *20 marks*

18 You agree to hold an 'Open Day' at your branch for the upper sixth form of a local school. The students, all aged 18, are to arrive at 4.00 p.m. They will be escorted round the office by the office manager, after which you have agreed to answer their questions.

Various questions have been submitted to you in advance of the visit, including the following:

I have been offered a temporary job, starting in January, prior to going to university next autumn. The work involves a delivery service throughout UK, France and West Germany and I will be required to travel, using my own motor-bike, with very little advance notice.

One condition of the job is that my monthly pay and reimbursement of travelling expenses are credited directly to a bank account.

Can you indicate to me what help your bank could offer me whilst I am working next year?

(9/83) *15 marks*

ANSWERS

1 The main types of consumer credit services which would be mentioned in the talk are as follows.

Overdrafts

(a) These represent an agreed 'line of credit' with the customer: the customer is permitted to overdraw his current account up to some specified limit.

(b) Overdrafts are repayable on demand, or are subject to regular review. Consequently, they are best suited to help the personal customer finance:
  (i) peaks of expenditure;
  (ii) delays in the receipt of income or other payments.

(c) Overdrafts offer the personal customer a number of advantages as a source of consumer finance:
  (i) Flexibility – the customer can draw as little or as much of his overdraft facility as he needs from time to time, so long as he stays within his agreed limit.
  (ii) Low cost – interest rates are variable, and typically lower than the true cost of credit from other sources, especially if the borrowing is secured. Since interest is charged on a day to day basis, on the overdrawn balance outstanding only, the cost of borrowing is minimised.
  (iii) Minimum formality – an immediate answer as to whether the facility will be available can usually be obtained from the bank; and there is the minimum of documentation and form-filling.

(d) Overdrafts will normally only be available to established customers.

(e) They have the disadvantage that there is no programme of scheduled repayments. Consequently, overdrafts do not impose the same financial discipline that servicing a loan provides.

Personal loans

(a) This represents a loan made to a personal customer:
  (i) for a fixed period of time; and
  (ii) at a fixed rate of interest.

(b) The term of borrowing is usually up to three years.

(c) They are most suitable for financing the purchase of consumer durables.

(d) The particular advantages of personal loan finance are as follows:
  (i) Certainty – unlike an overdraft facility, the customer knows in advance how long the finance will be available to him. So long as he maintains his repayments, the facility cannot be revoked.
  (ii) Discipline – there is a regular programme of repayments to ensure the loan is cleared in the specified time.
  (iii) Budgeting – since the interest rate is fixed, repayments remain the same for the life of the loan; and this assists the customer to plan his expenditure.
  (iv) Discounts – armed with a cash loan, the customer can shop around to obtain the best value for money in his purchase, and take advantage of any cash discounts.
  (v) Insurance – there is usually life assurance cover as part of the loan package, which ensures the loan will be cleared in the event of the customer's death.

Credit cards

(a) Credit cards provide an alternative means of effecting payment to cash or a cheque. But they are also a form of revolving credit:
  - (i) the cardholder is allowed to make purchases up to his credit limit; and
  - (ii) as he makes his monthly payments, the balance of his credit limit becomes usable again.
(b) Credit cards are a convenient and safe way of carrying 'spending power'.
(c) Once a credit limit has been agreed in response to the cardholder's application, he has a revolving credit facility available to him whenever he needs it. There is no need regularly to renew the facility as with an overdraft.
(d) Using a credit card can assist the customer's budgeting:
  - (i) Peaks of expenditure can be absorbed by fuller use of the credit limit.
  - (ii) The monthly payment can be timed to coincide with the receipt of a salary.
  - (iii) The detailed monthly statements give a clear picture of the customer's expenditure.
(e) By using his credit card rather than cheque book, the customer has the added bonus of reducing his bank charges.
(f) Under the terms of the Consumer Credit Act 1974, a cardholder who makes a purchase using a credit card, and who is supplied with defective goods, has a claim against the credit card company for restitution as well as against the supplier. Currently, the limit *above* which this protection arises is purchases of £100 or more.

Hire purchase

(a) This is a source of finance whereby the customer acquires the use of a good, and after the payment of the required number of instalments, the good becomes his. All the major banks have finance house subsidiaries which provide hire purchase credit.
(b) Consumers may make use of the instalment credit facilities of finance houses in two ways:
  - (i) By making a direct application for a hire purchase facility to the finance house (via their branch bank).
  - (ii) More typically, by buying a good on hire purchase from a retailer on hire purchase. Though ostensibly the transaction is with the retailer, the finance agreement is made with a finance house who pay the retailer, and collect the instalments from the customer. This is known as point of sale credit.
(c) Consumer hire purchase normally involves a fixed programme of instalments during the course of the contract:
  - (i) The customer obtains use of the good.
  - (ii) He is able to pay for it out of future income.
(d) It is most suited to the purchase of consumer durables.
(e) It is, however, likely to be a more expensive source of consumer finance than an overdraft or personal loan.

2 In the talk it would be desirable to mention the following services:
(a) house mortgage;
(b) bridging finance;
(c) insurance services.

House mortgages

(a)   The bank's house mortgage service offers finance for the purchase of both freehold and leasehold property, to first-time buyers and to people selling one property and buying another.

(b)   There are two alternative types of mortgage available:

(i)   *Repayment mortgages*   Monthly repayments are made which cover the interest accruing, and clear the borrowing within the specified life of the mortgage.

(ii) *Endowment mortgages*   Monthly repayments cover only the interest accruing on the borrowing. The principal is repaid at the end of the mortgage term by the proceeds of an endowment life assurance policy.

(c)   Interest rates and the terms on which the facility is made available are competitive with house mortgages offered by building societies.

Bridging finance

Where a customer wishes to complete the purchase of his new property before he completes on the sale of his existing property, he will have a financing requirement.

(a)   The bank is prepared to advance funds to allow completion on the purchase, the borrowing to be cleared with the sale proceeds on the existing property.

(b)   Usually, the finance can be provided against the informal security of a solicitor's undertaking to account to the bank with the net sale proceeds. It may, however, sometimes be necessary to take a legal mortgage over the existing property, especially where the bridge is likely to be for an extended period of time.

(c)   Normally, the bank will finance 'closed bridges': situations where contracts have been exchanged on both the purchase of the new property and sale of the existing property, but where the date for completion on the sale is later than that on the purchase. However, in appropriate circumstances an 'open-ended bridge' may be possible, where the existing property has not yer been sold, but the customer wishes to complete the purchase of the new property.

(d)   In all cases, the bank must be satisfied that the transaction will be self-liquidating, and that the customer is able to service the interest payments on the loan.

(e)   Bridging advances are always taken on a separate loan account, rather than by overdrawing a current account, since interest on the latter would not be eligible for tax relief. The borrower can obtain tax relief on a bridging advance of up to £30,000 for a year (in approved cases longer) as well as a separate tax relief on a house mortgage on the new property of up to £30,000.

Insurance services

House purchase raises a number of requirements for new or revised insurance cover. The bank's insurance broking service can arrange suitable cover for customers:

(a)   life assurance cover, particularly in relation to endowment mortgages;
(b)   mortgage protection policies;
(c)   redundancy, accident and sickness insurance;
(d)   house insurance;
(e)   household contents insurance.

180

3   The banks provide a diverse range of services which are of assistance to personal customers wishing to make equity investments.

Purchase and sale of investments

(a)   The bank will buy or sell stocks and shares on behalf of customers through the bank's stockbroker.
(b)   The service offers convenience to the customer, especially the small investor who may not have his own broker.
  (i)   The customer merely has to give his branch an instruction to buy or sell: the bank will do everything else.
  (ii)   When settlement day arrives, the bank can debit or credit the customer's account as appropriate without the need for the customer to take any further action.

Investment advice

As a result of the case *Woods* v *Martins Bank Ltd and another* (1958), banks are understandably wary of giving advice on equity investments at branch level. However, banks are prepared to:

(a)   submit a request for advice to the bank's stockbroker; and
(b)   pass on the broker's report without comment to the customer.

Investment management

Most major banks offer an investment management service to their customers through their executor and trustee departments. This advice may be provided in two ways:

(a)   The bank provides advice on charges in an investment portfolio, but the customer must sanction any buying or selling of investments.
(b)   Discretionary management: the bank has full power to exercise its own initiative in managing the portfolio, and may buy or sell as it sees fit without reference to the customer.

The investment management service offers a number of advantages to personal customers:

(a)   The customer receives professional investment guidance at a reasonable cost (as compared to alternative sources of professional advice).
(b)   Convenience: the customer is relieved of the necessity to monitor his investments, and to initiate action as market conditions change.

However, the investment management service is not really suitable for smaller portfolios (say under £50,000 though some banks will accept portfolios of as little as £10,000).

(a)   The overhead costs are high on a labour-intensive service. Only larger portfolios generate sufficient revenue to justify management costs.
(b)   Risk spreading: with small portfolios it is difficult to achieve an acceptable spread of risks (investment mistakes tend to have a bigger proportionate effect).

Unit trusts

All the major banks offer their own unit trust investments, of which they are the managers. Unit trust investment offers a number of advantages, particularly to the smaller investor who still wishes to invest in equities:

(a) It is possible to achieve a greater spread of risk than in a separately managed portfolio of equivalent value.

(b) The investor is relieved of the need to manage an investment portfolio against a changing stockmarket.

(c) Administrative problems associated with holding equity investments (allotment letters, dividend counterfoils, income tax certificates etc.) are minimised. A number of separate equity holdings are replaced by one unit trust holding.

(d) Dealing costs are proportionately reduced, since a few large buying or selling transactions by the trust managers replace a multitude of separate small transactions.

(e) Authorised unit trusts enjoy exemption from capital gains tax on gains made during investment switches within each trust.

(f) If investors employed an investment manager directly (e.g., the bank's investment management service) as private investors they could not offset the management charges against their tax liability. However, unit trust managers may allow their own management charges against taxation on the profits earned by the unit trust fund. Thus, indirectly, the personal investor effectively enjoys tax relief on his investment management charges.

(g) There are a wide range of unit trusts available calculated to meet the needs of most investors:
  (i) income, or capital growth or balanced funds;
  (ii) a variety of different industry and country specialisations.
  Moreover, there are a number of special schemes designed to appeal to particular classes of investor (see Question 4).

Miscellaneous services to investors

(a) *Safe custody* The bank will hold for safe-keeping the certificates evidencing ownership of stocks and shares. This is a very important service for holders of bearer securities:
  (i) Safety of the bearer share certificates is essential since, as they are negotiable by simple delivery, they are the equivalent of cash.
  (ii) The customer is relieved of the chore of watching for the declaration of payment of a coupon, and sending those coupons to the company concerned to collect payment of the dividend or interest.

(b) *Nomineeship* All the major banks maintain nominee companies; and it is possible for a customer to have his shareholdings transferred into the name of the nominee company. This can be particularly convenient as the following examples make clear:
  (i) Charities, trusts and similar bodies are relieved of the need to have their investments re-registered in the name of new officials or trustees, every time a change of personnel takes place.
  (ii) Customers residing abroad can rely on the bank to handle the administrative chores of holding investments in UK companies.

182

(c)   *Valuation service*   As an extension of their computer services, most banks will provide an up-to-date valuation of a customer's portfolio for a small fee.

4   An *authorised unit trust* is one authorised by the Department of Trade to invite the public to subscribe for units in the fund. To gain authorised status, the unit trust must be managed according to the following principles:

(a)   Investments must be made in stocks and shares quoted on a recognised stock exchange. However, up to 25% of the fund may be held in shares traded on the unlisted securities market.
(b)   No single holding may exceed 5% of the total value of the fund. However, as an alternative, up to six holdings may each form up to 7½% of the fund, provided:
    (i)   the number of separate holdings in the fund exceeds 20; and
    (ii)   no 10 holdings exceed 55% of the fund.

In order to attract as large a volume of investors' funds as possible, the banks have devised a variety of different types of unit trust and a variety of different unit trust schemes, designed to cater for the diverse needs of investors.

Types of unit trust

The banks offer a variety of different unit trusts offering the chance to invest in funds which are managed to maximise growth of income or growth of capital, or to achieve a balance between growth and income; while some funds are directed at particular sectors of economic activity or towards investment in particular countries.

As an example, one major clearing bank recently was offering the following unit trusts for subscription by the general public:

(a)   Growth Investment Unit Trust – designed to achieve a balance between capital and income growth;
(b)   Capital Trust – designed to achieve a high level of capital growth;
(c)   Income Trust – designed to achieve good levels of income;
(d)   Financial Trust – designed to achieve long-term capital growth;
(e)   Extra Income Trust – designed to give high and growing levels of income;
(f)   Portfolio Investment Trust – a balanced capital growth and income fund, but designed for the larger investor;
(g)   North American Growth Trust – invested almost wholly in US and Canadian stocks and shares;
(h)   Smaller Companies Trust – invested primarily in smaller companies with good growth prospects;
(i)   Recovery Trust – designed to achieve long-term capital growth through investment in companies which have been weak performers, but which have recovery potential.
(j)   Japanese and Pacific Growth Trust – invested in equities in Japan and Australia plus other Asian countries;
(k)   Energy Trust – invested in equities in the energy sector in the UK and overseas.

Unit trust special schemes

(a) *Savings plans*   The investor voluntarily invests a regular amount each month in a specified unit trust. There are two main advantages to the investor:

    (i)   Timing of investment − by making regular small investments, the investor is relieved of the anxiety of ensuring he does not buy at the 'top of the market'.

    (ii) 'Pound cost averaging' − with the investment of a fixed sum each month, fewer units are bought when unit prices are high, more when unit prices are lower. The result is that the average cost of units is less than the average price of units over the same time period, for example:

Customer invests £24 per month in a unit trust

	Unit price	Units purchased
Month 1	£2.00	12
Month 2	£2.40	10
Month 3	£3.00	8
Month 4	£2.40	10
		40

Total cost of units = £96
Average cost of units = £96/40 = £2.40
Average price of units over 4 month period

$$= \frac{£2.00 + £2.40 + £3.00 + £2.40}{4} = £2.45$$

(b) *Unit trust linked life assurance*   This is the most important of the special schemes, alone accounting for over a quarter of all new investment in unit trusts.

    (i)   The investor gains the advantage of life cover.

    (ii) Unlike an endowment policy, the premiums are invested in units in a nominated unit trust, so that the investor has a more direct equity stake.

(c) *Withdrawal plans*   This ensures that the investor receives a minimum level of income from his holding every year. Where the income distribution on the unit trust is not sufficiently high to generate this income, the unit trust managers make up the shortfall by redeeming some units.

However, such schemes are not without their dangers:

    (i)   Where unit prices are falling, there can be a substantial erosion of capital to maintain income.

    (ii) Some investors may naively treat the scheme as a form of annuity, and not realise the potential reduction in their capital.

(d) *Share exchange scheme*   Shareholders with an existing investment portfolio may wish to off-load the management of their investments; but the size of their portfolio is too small to be a suitable case for investment management service.

    (i)   Unit trusts may be the logical solution to their problem.

(ii) To encourage them to make the change, the share exchange scheme may allow them:
  – to exchange their present shareholdings for units at a price better than that prevailing on the stock market; or
  – to sell their present shareholding and invest in units, with the unit trust managers paying the broker's commission.

5   In selecting an appropriate life assurance contract, Peter Brown must be advised to consider what his needs are. Though there are many types of life policy, they may be classified into two broad groups:

(a) Those which provide either a lump sum of continuing income (annuity) at the death of the life assured. This makes provisions for the dependents.
(b) Those which provide a lump sum or continuing income at the death of the life assured; but which in addition provide benefits where the life assured survives to a certain age. This group can be regarded as more akin to a form of investment: in return for regular premium payments, benefits will be provided in the future.

Simple life cover

These policies provide only cover against death of the life assured. They do have the advantage of protecting the life assured's dependents against the financial consequences of his death for a very small premium.

(a) *Term assurance*   The sum assured will only be paid if the life assured dies within the term of the policy. With such policies, substantial cover can be obtained very cheaply. But they acquire no value if the life assured survives the term of the policy.
(b) *Convertible term assurance*   This is the same as a term policy. However, it offers the life assured the opportunity to convert the policy into an endowment policy or perhaps another term policy without further medical examination.
(c) *Mortgage protection policies*   This is insurance cover arranged on the life assured for the duration of a mortgage.
  (i) The policy ensures that, should the life assured die, the mortgage will be cleared.
  (ii) The amount payable under the policy reduces in line with the repayment of the mortgage.
(d) *Personal accident and sickness assurance*   Though not 'life cover', these policies protect a family from the effects of loss of income.

Life cover with investment

Premiums on this type of policy are higher, but they are a form of investment in that payment is certain to be made under them.

(a) *Endowment assurance*   The sum assured is payable at the death of the life assured or his survival to a specified date. Policies may be either:

(i)   'with profits' – the life assured receives the sum assured together with accrued bonuses which are a share in the profits made by the life assurance company; or

(ii)   'without profits' – the life assured simply receives the sum assured.

Understandably, 'with profits' policies attract a higher premium.

(b)   *Linked life assurance* A conventional endowment policy has its premiums invested in the general fund of the life assurance company; and its value depends on the bonuses declared by the company. By contrast, a linked life assurance policy has its premiums invested in specific assets, usually units in a unit trust.

    (i)   The value of a linked policy is thus directly geared to the value of the underlying units purchased by the premiums.

    (ii)   This means that the surrender and maturity value can be subject to substantial variation, and can fall as well as increase.

(c)   *Whole life assurance* This is similar to endowment assurance, and policies can be written with or without profits. The main difference is that premiums are lower for equivalent sums assured; but no benefits are realised until the death of the life assured, and premiums must continue to be paid up to death.

(d)   *Personal pension plans* Where a customer is self-employed or has self-employed income, he can place up to 17½% of his pre-tax earnings into a personal pension plan, and gain full tax relief on these premiums. The pension plan, when it matures, enables the purchase of an annuity to be financed which provides a retirement income.

    Annuities These are the reverse of a conventional life assurance contract.

    (i)   The customer pays over a lump sum premium to a life assurance company.

    (ii)   In return, the company makes regular income payments to the customer immediately or commencing at some date in the future (deferred annuity).

Clearly, the branch manager cannot be expected to be an expert on life assurance. However, he should be able to help the customer to sort out what his main requirements are; and to introduce the customer to the bank's insurance broking subsidiary, which will be able to obtain competitive quotations on suitable policies, and provide more detailed advice to Mr Brown.

6

Target market

Personal pension plans are a form of insurance contract. They are most suited to the needs of the following groups:

(a)   persons engaged in any trade or profession on their own account or in partnership (i.e., the self-employed);

(b)   directors and other company employees not included in a company pension scheme;

(c)   employed persons in an occupational pension scheme, but with additional independent earnings.

Types of scheme

There is a great diversity of schemes available from the insurance companies, but they break down into three main types.

(a) Pension-funded contracts:
  (i) Premiums buy a guaranteed minimum annual pension.
  (ii) Bonuses are declared by the life office underwriting the plan, and these may increase the amount of the pension above the guaranteed minimum.
(b) Cash-funded contracts:
  (i) Premiums buy a guaranteed minimum cash lump sum at the end of the plan; and this may be supplemented by bonuses declared by the life office.
  (ii) The lump sum is used to purchase a pension (an annuity) at the end of the plan.
  (iii) Clearly here, unlike in (a), there is no guaranteed pension: it all depends on annuity rates at the time the lump sum matures.
(c) Unit-linked contracts:
  (i) Premiums are invested into units in a specific fund (akin to a unit trust).
  (ii) When the plan matures, the units are re-purchased by the life office at their current valuation.
  (iii) The lump sum generated is then used to purchase an annuity.
  (iv) Clearly this type of scheme entails the greatest degree of uncertainty:
    — uncertainty as to the lump sum the units will generate at maturity; and
    — uncertainty as to how big an annuity the sum will purchase which depends on current annuity rates.
  Nevertheless, it is the most popular of the three types of scheme.

Advantages to a customer

For the appropriate customer, a personal pension plan is highly advantageous:
(a) It provides pension benefits for customers outside the protection of an occupational pension scheme.
(b) It is a highly tax-efficient form of investment. A maximum of 17½% of the customer's pre-tax income from self-employed or independent sources can be paid as premiums under a pension plan; and the amount of the premium is netted off the customer's income before assessment for income tax.
(c) There is a diversity of pension plans available, so that the customer can readily find one suited to his particular needs.

Where a customer wishes to take up a personal pension plan, the bank's insurance broking subsidiary will be able to assist with advice, and by obtaining quotes from life offices.

7   The administration of estates by the banks' executor and trustee departments or subsidiaries is one of the oldest established specialised banking services. Appointing the bank as executor of a will offers the customer a number of advantages:

a) *Continuity* The bank, as a corporate entity, 'never dies'. This avoids the inconvenience and possible dangers of a personal executor dying before the testator (the customer); and thereby at best requiring the customer to remake his will and at worst leaving his estate without an executor.

(b) *Impartiality* Death can often lead to family quarrels about the administration of the deceased's estate. Appointing the bank may prevent this problem arising, since the bank is seen to be above family disagreements.

(c) *Expertise* Most executorships are routine; but if problems should arise in winding up the estate, the bank can offer 'in-house' expertise on the management and realisation of assets, and on the taxation and other implications of winding up an estate.

(d) *Knowledge of customer's affairs* The bank is in the privileged position of already knowing a great deal about the customer's financial affairs. For this reason, it may be able to expedite the winding up of the estate.

Against these advantages, it must be remembered that this is a labour-intensive and hence fairly costly service to operate. Consequently it will not be appropriate to offer the service where customers will only leave a relatively small estate (it is unlikely that an estate under £25,000 could be profitably administered).

Even though the bank has not been appointed as executor under a customer's will, it may still administer the estate. The bank could take out letters of administration on behalf of the deceased customer where either:

(a) he dies intestate; or
(b) the named executor(s) in the will have pre-deceased or do not wish to act.

Clearly, the bank may only adopt the role of administrator of the deceased's estate with the agreement of his next of kin.

8 Colonel Hold-Saunders' problems clearly relate to the continued management of the family trust, which will include management of the assets in which the trust funds are invested, and payments to beneficiaries under the trust. In the case of both investment decisions and payments to beneficiaries, the terms of the trust deed must be strictly followed.

The bank could capitalise on the opportunity these problems have created, by offering an introduction to its trustee service. Colonel Holt-Saunders should be told that, provided the existing trust deed permitted the change, the bank could act as trustee managing the assets and making disbursements in accordance with the trust deed.

The particular advantages of appointing the bank as trustee are as follows:

(a) *Continuity* The bank, as a corporate trustee, 'never dies'. Thus the present problem caused by the death of a trustee, and difficulty in replacing him, will not arise again.

(b) *Confidence* It is essential that the present trustees and beneficiaries repose complete confidence in the integrity and good faith of a new trustee. This is particularly important if the family trust is 'discretionary', giving the trustee wide powers over the management of the trust assets and the payments to beneficiaries. The bank is an organisation whose integrity is beyond question.

(c) *Experience* The banks have a long 'track record' in trusteeship stretching back more than 70 years in the case of some banks.

(d) *Expertise* Banks have considerable 'in-house' expertise when it comes to resolving problems relating to the trust, such as the effective management of the trust assets and taxation.

As with all executor and trustee services, trusteeship is expensive to operate. Consequently the branch should be sure the trust fund is sufficiently large to be remunerative to the bank. However, in the present case, there seems every likelihood that this is so.

9 Mr Stratton's problem has clearly arisen from his inability to manage his own tax affairs as a person with a rising income from self-employment. The obvious service to which Mr Stratton might usefully be introduced is the bank's taxation advice service.

(a) The bank would complete Mr Stratton's tax return, ensuring that he took full benefit from the various allowances available to self-employed persons.

(b) The bank would also negotiate on Mr Stratton's behalf with his inspector of taxes. With the bank's greater expertise in tax matters, these negotiations might well be more beneficial than if he conducted them himself.

(c) The bank could also provide longer-term advice on steps which Mr Stratton could take to mitigate the effect of taxation. One obvious example is to take out a personal pension plan (see Question 6).

(d) The savings which may accrue to Mr Stratton from the more efficient management of his tax affairs may more than cover the commission charged by the bank for the service.

10 Whether people are travelling abroad on business or holiday, there are three basic needs which bank services can fulfil:

(a) the need to be able to buy goods and services while abroad;
(b) the need to make remittances abroad particularly prior to departure;
(c) the need to have adequate insurance against the risks associated with foreign travel.

Spending abroad

The traveller must be able to settle for goods and services abroad in currencies other than sterling.

a) *Bureau de change service* The banks maintain foreign tills in larger branches, while even in smaller branches foreign currency may be obtained on a few days' notice. The advantages of this service are clear cut:

(i) It is essential for a proportion of the traveller's funds to be held in the form of cash, to allow immediate payments to be made on arrival (e.g., for taxis, gratuities, etc.).

(ii) The bank provides currency at a good rate and with minimal commission as compared to some of the alternative 'specialised' bureau de change outlets.

(iii) The bank will accept orders from travel agents to obtain currency on behalf of their clients.

(b) *Travellers cheques* The banks will supply travellers cheques in sterling and in a range of other currencies too. The advantages of using travellers cheques are:

    (i)   Security – if the cheques are lost or stolen, the customer will be reimbursed by the bank.

    (ii)   Wide acceptability – UK banks issue travellers cheques based on the large international organisations such as Thomas Cook, Visa, Mastercard and American Express. Consequently, the cheques are universally acceptable.

(c) *Credit cards* All the major UK credit card companies are linked to an international credit card group (Mastercard and Visa). Thus, UK credit cards are widely ccepted for payment in hotels and retail outlets around the world. Credit cards offer a number of advantages:

    (i)   wide acceptability;

    (ii)   convenience – the customer uses his normal credit card, and does not have to place a special order for his travel requirements;

    (iii) stand-by value – a credit card is available to meet unforeseen payments;

    (iv) credit – holiday spending can be spread over an extended repayment period.

(d) *Eurocheque facilities* This allows a customer to use his ordinary cheque book or a special Eurocheque book abroad to draw cash from a bank. It is necessary for the customer to be issued with a special Eurocheque card since, to prevent the fraudulent use of stolen cheque cards abroad, the UK clearing banks withdrew their ordinary cheque cards from the Eurocheque scheme in May 1983.

(e) *Open credits* This is an arrangement with a specified bank and branch abroad that the customer may cash his own cheques at that branch. It is rarely appropriate for most travellers since it is inflexible, and offers nothing that the other means of payment (travellers cheques, credit cards, Eurocheque) do not. However, it might be suitable for a person making a prolonged stay abroad in the same place (e.g., a UK student studying abroad).

Though exchange control has been suspended in the UK it still applies in many other countries. The bank will be able to advise on restrictions on the import and export of currency in the countries the traveller proposes to visit.

Payments abroad

Where a UK business or holiday traveller needs to make payments abroad, the banks can arrange to remit funds overseas. The service may be useful where:

(i)   accommodation or other facilities need to be paid for in advance; or

(ii)   where additional funds are needed during the trip abroad, perhaps because of an unforeseen emergency such as a car breakdown.

Remittances may be effected in a number of ways:

(a)   Bankers draft

    This is a 'cheque' drawn on the bank itself in either sterling or currency. I can be made payable to whoever the traveller wishes to make payment; an then sent to the payee.

(b)   Mail transfer

    The bank sends instructions (by airmail) to an overseas bank to make pay ment to a specified beneficiary.

(c) Telegraphic transfer
This is similar to a mail transfer but the payment instruction is cabled to the overseas bank. Consequently, funds can be moved to the beneficiary very quickly.

Insurance

Through its insurance broking subsidiary, the bank is able to offer a range of insurance cover for the various risks associated with overseas travel. For example, health and accident insurances; cover for personal effects; 'green cards' for motorists who insure their cars through the bank's broking service.

11 Clearly, it is necessary to 'sell' the idea of payment of wages into a bank account to both employer and employees:

(a) From the company's point of view, the benefits lie in avoiding the cost and inconvenience of making wage payments in cash.
(b) From the employee's point of view, the benefits are those of having a bank account.

Benefits to company

(a) The services of the security firm can be dispensed with, with consequent cost savings.
(b) There will be cost savings on the making up and distribution of cash wage packets.
(c) Less time will be wasted through employees having to collect their cash wage packets each week.
(d) Where the changeover is accompanied by a switch to fortnightly or monthly payments, there will be savings in administrative costs.
(e) Insurance costs will be less, as there will no longer be the security risk of large amounts of cash held on the premises.
(f) Where the company can take advantage of BACS (Bankers Automated Clearing System) wages data can be given to the bank as computer tapes, with worthwhile savings through not 'generating paper'.

Benefits to employees

Here, it would be sensible to stress those aspects of bank services which are likely to appeal to the particular type of potential customer:

(a) The employees will enjoy greater security than if their wages are paid in cash.
(b) Access to a variety of useful bank services will be gained:
  (i) budget accounts;
  (ii) personal loans;
  (iii) house mortgages;
  (iv) insurance services;
  (v) savings facilities;
  (vi) credit card.

(c) The convenience of having a cheque card to make payments, particularly since, in a case like this, the bank may be prepared to grant cheque card facilities as soon as the account is opened.

(d) Through the issue of regular statements a record is provided of income and expenditure.

(e) In the circumstances of the case, the bank would probably be prepared to offer concessionary terms on commission charges.

(f) The employees will benefit from the enhanced status of having a bank account.

12

(a) **Banking requirements of expanding work-force**

It is highly likely that a large proportion of the new work-force will not have bank accounts, and so the question is primarily one concerned with the 'unbanked'. The banking requirements of the new work-force are likely to be relatively straightforward and to include the following:
  (i) a safe way to hold their income prior to the need to spend it;
  (ii) easy access to their money when they need it;
  (iii) a means of making payments, other than by cash, for example where payment needs to be made through the post or where an unforeseen payment needs to be made and cash is not available;
  (iv) a way of saving surplus income on which interest can be earned;
  (v) instalment credit to finance the purchase of consumer durables (cars, videos, freezers, etc.);
  (vi) revolving credit to allow peaks of expenditure to be financed;
  (vii) assistance with the budgeting of income and expenditure.

(b) **Bank services for the expanding work-force**

The following services would satisfy the banking requirements of the work-force as identified in part (a) of the question:
  (i) Having a current and/or deposit account will provide the work-force with safety in respect of their money. This will obviously be particularly true where their wages are paid directly into a bank account rather than as a cash wage packet.
  (ii) Money held in a current or deposit account is normally withdrawable on demand from the account holding branch. Moreover, cash may also be obtained outside banking hours by use of an automated teller machine (ATM).
  (iii) Making payments:
    (1) A current account cheque book is a widely accepted alternative means for effecting payment. Normally, new customers would have to run a satisfactory account for at least six months before a cheque card is issued; but the bank may be prepared to treat this as a special case and to relax the rule to attract customers amongst the new work-force. If this is the case, the cheque book becomes a highly effective means for making payments.
    (2) Regular payments can be made on behalf of the customer by standing order or direct debit.

(3) Provided the customer is considered satisfactory to the credit card subsidiary, a credit card provides a widely acceptable alternative means of payment.

(iv) Savings are provided for through an interest-bearing deposit account, while many banks have higher interest special schemes for regular savers.

(v) Instalment credit needs can be met by either:
(1) a personal loan from the bank itself; or
(2) a hire purchase credit facility from the bank's finance house subsidiary.

(vi) Revolving credit requirements could be provided by the bank's credit card subsidiary. Provided the customer was satisfactory, a revolving credit limit would be available which would allow the customer to use his credit card to make payments, or to draw cash.

(vii) An additional budget account would be helpful in allowing the customer to budget his annual expenditure against income, and in allowing peaks of spending in the year to be funded from a temporary borrowing on the budget account.

13 Mr White's problems lie, primarily, in the area of his own financial position and ensuring the company can be handed on to his sons when he retires or dies.

(a) With his house and investments plus his 90% stake in White's Engineering Ltd, Mr White faces a significant CTT (capital transfer tax) liability.

(b) This CTT liability may make it difficult to hand on the business to his sons, since shares in the company may need to be sold to outsiders to meet the tax liability.

(c) From the company's accounts and other material in the question, it would appear that Mr White has not made any provision for his retirement.

(d) Should Mr White wish to realise a proportion of his shareholding to finance his retirement, he may also face a CGT (capital gains tax) liability.

Taxation problems

Whether Mr White waits for the business to pass to his sons as part of his estate, or whether he hands on the business during his lifetime, the transfer will be subject to CTT.

Mr White would find an introduction to the bank's trust company useful. They would provide advice on how to make best use of the various exemptions available to minimise CTT liability:

(a) how to make use of exemptions on lifetime transfers;

(b) how to make use of 'business property relief' in transferring the business to his sons;

(c) how to make use of life assurance policies, where the premiums are paid by Mr White out of income, but the benefits accrue to his sons rather than forming part of his estate.

The manager cannot be expected to be an expert on CTT. But he should be able to point out to Mr White the potential danger of CTT to his position; and to persuade him that an introduction to the bank's trust company would mitigate the effect of this tax, particularly in respect of the hand-over of the business.

Should Mr White need to realise a proportion of his shareholding to provide for his retirement, the trust company will also advise on the means available to mitigate the effects of capital gains tax, particularly retirement relief available where a director in a family trading company disposes of all or part of his shareholding.

Provision for retirement

When Mr White retires from the business he will need to ensure he has adequate income for a pension. Mr White would probably gain most benefit from an individual pension scheme for directors.

(a)   Mr White could have pension provision made for him up to the maximum permissible for pension schemes for employees.
(b)   The contributions would be paid by the company and could be offset against the company's corporation tax liability.
(c)   There is no limit on the contributions the company can make and gain tax relief; and this will allow White's Engineering Ltd to build up maximum pension benefits for Mr White over a relatively short time-scale. (Obviously this is helpful as Mr White is 58 years old, and would presumably wish to retire in the not too distant future.)
(d)   Such a pension scheme would enable Mr White to build up considerable sums of money outside the company without the CGT implications of selling off a proportion of his shareholding.

The most likely ways in which the bank might assist with pension provision are:

(a)   use of an insurance-based scheme, with the bank's insurance service arranging cover; or
(b)   investment of the contributions in one of the bank's exempt unit trusts specifically designed for pension schemes.

14   The bank is faced with a new customer who has received a 'windfall' which has transformed his financial position. As an ordinary working man, it is highly likely that Mr Brown has no notion of the problems of managing such a large sum of money, and of coping with the related problems it generates, notably those of taxation. The bank has the chance to forge a valuable new connection here by helping Mr Brown, and at the same time can develop some profitable business for itself.

Investment of funds

(a)   *Short-term*   The immediate priority is to invest the cheque, since the opportunity cost of not employing such a large amount of money even for a short time is considerable. As soon as the cheque is cleared, the funds should be placed on a money market deposit with the bank.
    (i)   This will provide Mr Brown with a rate of return on his funds highly competitive with rates obtainable elsewhere on large short-term deposits

(ii) The funds remain sufficiently liquid so that, when a longer-term investment strategy has been devised, they will be available more or less immediately.

(b) *Longer-term* Given the size of Mr Brown's 'windfall', an introduction to the bank's investment management service would be appropriate. They would be able to establish, with Mr Brown, what his investment needs were, and to devise a suitable investment strategy to meet those needs.

(i) The bank's service would relieve Mr Brown of the problems involved in managing investments himself.

(ii) With a discretionary appointment, the bank would manage his investments and make any adjustments in the portfolio as market conditions change.

(iii) The customer can be assured that his funds will be managed by a professional team of investment managers.

(iv) Should Mr Brown subsequently need to use part of his investments to purchase a house or other assets this can readily be arranged by selling some of his investments.

Taxation advice

Mr Brown is going to move from an ordinary PAYE employee status, to the status of someone with a substantial investment income and substantial assets. He is certainly likely to need professional advice, and this could be provided through the bank's taxation advice service. Mr Brown is going to need help with mitigating the effects of taxation on investment income, capital gains tax and capital transfer tax.

(a) The bank's taxation service will complete Mr Brown's tax return.

(b) They will also negotiate with Mr Brown's inspector of taxes to minimise his liability.

(c) They will advise Mr Brown on ways of making best use of the various allowances and exemptions in order to reduce his liability both for income and capital gains tax.

(d) The bank can also help him to plan ahead to mitigate the effect of capital transfer tax when his estate is passed on, whether by lifetime gift or at death.

Other services

(a) An introduction to the executor and trustee subsidiary would be useful. They would advise him of the desirability of making a will and the value of appointing the bank to act as executor:

(i) Continuity – the bank, unlike a personal executor, 'never dies'.

(ii) Impartiality – the bank can be relied on to administer the estate fairly, and is above family disagreements.

(iii) Expertise – the bank has 'in-house' expertise in the winding up of estates.

(iv) Knowledge of customer's affairs – the bank is in a position to wind up the estate quickly given its intimate knowledge of the customer's affairs.

(b) The executor and trustee subsidiary would also advise on ways of planning ahead to maximise use of exemptions, and to minimise the effect of capital transfer tax on Mr Brown's estate.

(c)   Even if he does not buy a house, Mr Brown is likely to purchase other assets. The bank's insurance service could help in the insurance of these assets. Also, if part of the investment strategy involves purchasing an annuity to ensure future income, insurance services could again arrange a suitable contract.

15   The 'changing financial circumstances' referred to in the question are that Mr and Mrs Jones are moving from a position where they have had to struggle to finance the setting up of their business, to a position in which they are likely to have appreciable cash surpluses. In particular, the medium-term loan which has required annual payments of £4,000 to service it will shortly be repaid, while the hire purchase debt (£1,500 p.a.) will also be cleared shortly. The following services might usefully be drawn to Mr and Mrs Jones' attention at the forthcoming interview, though to prevent 'swamping' them with too much information, some of the services might be held over to be mentioned at a convenient later date.

(a)   *Savings facilities*   As the expected cash flow surplus begins to accumulate, it will be advisable for Mr and Mrs Jones to place these funds on an interest-bearing account until they decide how to use them. This might be a conventional deposit account, or it could be one of the higher interest regular savings schemes, perhaps linked to subsequent provision of a house mortgage (see point (c) below).
    (i)   They would receive a reasonable rate of interest rather than no interest where the funds simply accumulated on current account.
    (ii)   The money would be readily accessible when required, and transfer to current account could be easily made.

(b)   *Personal pension plan*   As self-employed people, Mr and Mrs Jones should consider making adequate provision now for a retirement income. The bank's insurance service would provide information on and arrange personal pension plan policies for them. These would be particularly beneficial as a way of using part of the cash surplus:
    (i)   The customers will have provided a retirement income for themselves.
    (ii)   Personal pension plans are very tax-efficient, allowing them to place up to 17½% of their pre-tax earnings into a plan with full tax relief on the premiums.
    (iii)   There is a wide diversity of schemes available, so that there should be a scheme which suits their requirements.

(c)   *House finance*   Mr and Mrs Jones currently live in a flat attached to one of their leasehold salons. An excellent longer-term use of their cash surplus would be to purchase their own house. As well as accumulating a suitable deposit in a bank savings scheme (see (a) above), the bank could help through the provision of a house mortgage.
    (i)   Mr and Mrs Jones would have the benefits of home ownership, including the likely rising value of their property.
    (ii)   The bank's house mortgage scheme would provide finance at a very competitive rate.

(d)   *Insurance requirements*   In both a business and personal context, Mr and Mrs Jones have a wide variety of insurance needs. Although some of these are likely to be covered already, the bank would welcome the opportunity for arranging quotations through its insurance service for:
    (i)   insurance of fixtures and fittings;
    (ii)   public liability insurance;

(iii)   motor vehicle insurance;

(iv)   life assurance cover;

(v)   personal accident and loss of earnings insurance;

(vi)   employers' insurance;

(vii)   if they do decide to buy a house:

    —   house and contents insurance;

    —   mortgage protection;

    —   endowment life assurance in connection with an endowment mortgage.

(e)   *Making a will*   The customers should be advised as to the desirability of making a will. The bank's executor and trustee department would advise; and the bank would also be prepared to act as executor for the customers.

(f)   *Finance*   The customers have clearly made use of outside finance (hire purchase) in the past. The bank could probably offer similar assistance in the purchase of cars and other assets in the future by way of a loan facility. Such facilities would have the advantages of:

(i)   minimum formality; and

(ii)   low cost.

16

Analysis of problem

Mr Williams is buying one property and selling another. The bank can help him in two distinct ways:

(a)   By providing bridging finance to cover the time-lag between completion on the purchase (end of May), and completion on the sale (3 August).

(b)   By providing a house mortgage to help him finance the purchase of the new property.

Bank's reply

Although contracts have not been exchanged on the sale at this point in time, the bank would certainly wish to assist Mr Williams with bridging finance.

(a)   The transaction is self-liquidating:

	£
Sale	
Agreed selling price	65,000
Less: Outstanding mortgage	8,000
Equity	57,000
Purchase	
Buying price	75,000
Less: Equity	57,000
Minimum funding need from house mortgage	18,000

(b)　Mr Williams is clearly a man of means, and would be able to finance interest charges on the facility.

The bank could also suggest that Mr Williams finance the purchase of his new property by using a bank mortgage rather than using building society finance.

(a)　The loan would be in the order of £20,000-£25,000 to allow margin to cover his costs.
(b)　The loan would need to be repaid by the time he retires in five years; but on a net salary of £1,400 per month, this should present no problems.
(c)　Mr Williams would be assured that the new facility could be speedily arranged, and at a rate of interest competitive with a building society mortgage.

Security arrangements

In respect of the bridging finance, this would almost certainly be arranged against a suitable solicitors' undertaking to account to the bank with the net sale proceeds on the existing property.

(a)　Unless Mr Williams' solicitor is already known to the bank, a status enquiry should be carried out on him.
(b)　The details of the transaction and outstanding mortgage should be confirmed with the solicitor.
(c)　The new property must be adequately insured as soon as contracts are exchanged, and cover would be arranged by the bank. The old property must continue to be insured until it is sold.

In respect of the house mortgage advance to purchase the new property, the bank would require a first legal mortgage.

17 Though a recent account, the Smiths show every sign of developing into worthwhile customers of the bank. They have shown a capacity to save both through the accumulation of funds on the current account in a relatively short time, and the National Savings Bank balance. Moreover, they have a useful joint income, and the clearance of the hire purchase commitment suggests they are trustworthy.

The Smiths could usefully consider a number of bank services. However, it would be important not to overwhelm them with too many services. Rather a few services, clearly geared to their particular needs, is more likely to produce results.

(a)　Services associated with their current account:
 (i)　If not already issued, there is a clear case for providing them with cheque cards. This will enhance the usefulness of their cheque books as a means of payment; and they have established themselves as suitable customers.
 (ii)　Cash cards, unless already issued, would enable the Smiths to use the bank's ATM system to access their account.
(b)　Credit facilities:
 (i)　The bank has already agreed to a loan facility for the purchase of a new car.

(ii) The Smiths could also be issued with a credit card by the bank's credit card subsidiary:
  — This would provide a source of revolving credit useful for meeting temporary peaks of expenditure.
  — It also provides an alternative means of effecting payment.

(c) Savings:
  (i) The Smiths might consider opening a deposit account, since it would be better to accumulate any surplus income on an interest-bearing account.
  (ii) Alternatively, they may consider a higher interest regular savings plan; or one designed to accumulate a deposit for a house, and offering a guaranteed house mortgage.

(d) House purchase:
The Smiths are likely, in the future, to consider buying rather than renting their home. The bank may well be able to assist with a house mortgage facility.

(e) Insurance:
  (i) The purchase of the new car gives the manager the opportunity to suggest the bank's insurance service quote for their motor insurance.
  (ii) It may also be possible to lead on to their other insurance needs such as household contents and life assurance.

18 The help which the bank could provide to the student working abroad falls into two broad categories:

(a) the general benefits which follow from being a current account holder with the bank;

(b) the specific bank services associated with his working abroad.

Benefits of a bank account

(a) Although it is a precondition of his employment, the student will gain the benefit of safety in having his pay and expenses credited to a bank account, rather than receiving substantial sums of cash.

(b) His pay will be readily accessible:
  (i) by drawing cheques on his account; or
  (ii) by use of the bank's ATM network (he would be issued with a cash dispenser card).

(c) His cheque book will provide him with a convenient alternative means of making payments; and it is very likely that the bank would in this case make a cheque card available, allowing his cheques to be widely accepted as an alternative to cash.

(d) Regular statements will allow him to keep track of his income and expenditure..

(e) Provided he was accepted by the credit card subsidiary, he could be issued with a credit card which would provide:
  (i) a source of revolving credit; and
  (ii) an alternative means of payment.
The availability of this credit facility might be especially useful where he claimed his expenses in arrears.

Services associated with working abroad

(a)   The bank would provide currency for his journeys abroad. A currency float would be essential to meet smaller out-of-pocket expenses while travelling abroad.

(b)   For large sums, the bank would provide him with travellers cheques:
        (i)   These offer greater security than cash.
        (ii)   Should the cheques be lost or stolen, he will receive a prompt refund.
        (iii) The cheques are widely accepted in other countries.

(c)   He will also be able to use his own cheque book in conjunction with a Euro-cheque card.

(d)   His credit card can be used to pay bills at a wide range of outlets abroad.

(e)   Should he need funds in an emergency, for example to cover a breakdown, the bank will make a 'telegraphic transfer' to a bank convenient to where he is at the time.

(f)   Unless he will be adequately covered by his employer, he should take out accident and medical insurance, especially in view of the work on which he will be involved. The bank would arrange suitable cover for him.

9 Bank services for business customers

INTRODUCTION

This chapter deals primarily with services for business customers, though here as in the real world the needs of personal customers may be inextricably interwoven with those of the businesses they own or control. Services for business customers are a complex subject, in that not only do they make use of many of the basic banking services used by personal customers, but also there is a wide array of services specifically designed to meet the requirements of business customers.

Amongst the array of services available to businesses, the following groups can be identified:

(a) Finance:
    (i)   overdraft facilities;
    (ii) various types of loan facility;
    (iii) acceptance credits;
    (iv) leasing;
    (v) hire-purchase.
(b) Equity capital:
    (i)   merchant banking subsidiary:
         —   direct investment;
         —   Unlisted Securities Market;
    (ii) Investors in Industry (3i's Group).
(c) Factoring.
(d) Advisory services:
    (i)   business advisory services (small firms);
    (ii) merchant banking subsidiary (large firms).
(e) Corporate trustee work, especially pension funds.
(f) International division:
    (i)   services for exporters;
    (ii) bank guarantees;
    (iii) services for importers.
(g) Miscellaneous business services including:
    (i)   computer services (payroll, accounting);
    (ii) company registrars service;
    (iii) point of sale credit facilities;
    (iv) company credit cards.

The questions which follow fall into two broad categories. Questions 1-13 are more straightforward and descriptive, requiring an answer in which a particular service (or services) is described and its main advantages to customers elucidated. The remaining questions are typically of the 'problem' type.

(a) It is necessary to analyse the material in the question to ascertain what the customer's needs are.
(b) One or more services have to be identified which fulfil the needs of the customer.
(c) The services have to be marketed to the customer by explaining the advantages to be derived by using them.

Many of these 'problem' type questions are taken from past examination papers. There does tend to be some variability in what is required: some questions simply require discussion of a single service, while others require a range of services to be covered, ostensibly in the same time. It is, however, possible to reduce the amount of writing required in answers by tabulation of points. In the answers provided, a tabulated approach is taken; but it would be possible to condense these answers further by writing in note form.

The bulk of questions in Section B of the syllabus are on services for business customers. It is particularly important, therefore, that you try the questions yourself *before* consulting the answers.

QUESTIONS

1 Outline the various ways in which a branch bank may provide financial assistance to business customers, *without* reference to the specialist financial services of the bank's various subsidiaries.

20 marks

2 XYZ Ltd is a manufacturer of chemical plant and equipment. The company was incorporated over 25 years ago. During its history it has made reasonable progress and its capital base at the latest balance sheet date (31 December 1982) was over £5 million.

There is an agreed overdraft limit at your branch of £1 million, secured by a first charge over the company's freehold factory valued at £¾ million. The account works very comfortably within this limit.

Arnold Young, the financial director of the company, calls to see you by appointment. He explains that he has recently attended a seminar organised by the local Chamber of Industry. At the seminar, one of the presentations was by a senior representative of one of your competitor banks. During his talk, he referred to acceptance credits. Although Mr Young had heard of this term, he did not fully understand it.

Explain to him:

(a) what acceptance credits are and how they work;

12 marks

(b) whether acceptance credits would be appropriate to his company—what are the benefits, etc;

6 marks

(c) whether your bank offers the facility and, if so, through which division. If not, to whom could you refer him?

2 marks

9/83 Total 20 marks

3 What are the particular advantages to a business of using industrial hire-purchase to finance the purchase of business assets?

20 marks

4 Mr Brown, managing director of XYZ Engineering Ltd, has called to see you. In 1981, the bank's leasing division assisted the company when it needed to acquire new machinery. The company is now contemplating a further expansion and had thought of again leasing the necessary additional machinery; but Mr Brown is concerned that he has read in the newspapers that leasing is not so advantageous as previously. He asks you to explain the changes which have occurred since 1981 and to tell him how they will affect the company.

15 marks

5 Mr Jones is the finance director of AB Electronics Ltd. The company is a family concern, but it has grown and prospered and has a capitalisation of just under £1 million. Continued expansion of the company is being restricted, in Mr Jones' opinion, by a lack of additional capital for further investment. Mr Jones wonders whether it would be possible to raise additional capital through the Unlisted Securities Market, and whether there is any way in which the bank could assist them to raise funds on the USM.

20 marks

6 The merchant banking subsidiaries of the clearing banks offer advice as well as finance to companies. Examine the main types of advice which they offer.

20 marks

7 Examine the role of ICFC (Industrial Commercial Finance Corporation) in the financing of small and medium sized companies.

15 marks

8 In view of its topicality, your local junior chamber of trade and commerce is holding a one-day seminar on 'Management buy-outs'. You have been asked to give a talk and lead a discussion session on the subject of 'Banks and management buy-outs'.

Tabulate the main points which you will wish to see covered in your talk and the subsequent discussion.

20 marks

9 Briefly outline the major sources of venture capital for a small business which requires an injection of additional capital to finance expansion.

20 marks

10 Maurice Hammer is a director and majority shareholder of your customer, Hammer Repairs Ltd. This company was incorporated eight years ago and is involved in motor body repairs.

During the company's history, progress has been erratic but the company now employs 15 men, and sales turnover last year was £300,000. With this increasing activity, you have become concerned at the lack of obvious management controls in the company.

You discuss this concern with Mr Hammer. He agrees that his controls are now inadequate but maintains that he does not have the experience to introduce new techniques.

Your bank operates a comprehensive business advisory service and you mention this service to Mr Hammer. He is interested but, before committing himself, asks if you would explain the service to him in more detail.

Required:
An outline of your response, noting the various areas covered by the service.

(4\84) *20 marks*

11 'So each of the major banks now has an interest, direct or indirect, in substantial factoring activity' (Hanson: *Service Banking*).

Outline the service offered to customers through these factoring subsidiaries.

20 marks

12 You have been asked to give a talk to a local business club. The theme of your talk is 'New systems of money transfer and management for corporate customers'.

Identify which bank services you would wish to cover in your talk, and outline the main features of each.

20 marks

13 Outline the main trustee services which banks offer to their corporate customers.

20 marks

14 The local Chamber of Industry and Commerce is organising a seminar entitled 'Starting your own business'. Talks are to be given by:

APRIL 82

(i)   an accountant on legal and taxation matters;
(ii)   a local businessman, who started his company five years ago, recounting his experience;
(iii)   an estate agent and the local Chief Planning Officer on property development and opportunities; and
(iv)   a business consultant, who will talk on marketing.

The secretary of the Chamber has asked you, as a local bank manager, to cover the subject of finance. Your session is to be one hour long, followed by a question and answer period involving the participants. The title of your session is: 'The various sources of finance, including the banks, and where to get the money to start your business'.

Required:
A summary of the points you will include in your presentation. (A list of sources with a brief explanation of the facilities available will be sufficient.)

20 marks

(4/82)

15 You are interviewing a Mr Marsh, who has called to discuss his future plans. He has been known to your bank for the last 15 years and during that time has been employed by a local plant contractor, mostly driving heavy earth-moving equipment. You see from your bank files that Mr Marsh is married and has two young children. He has recently moved house with the aid of an increased mortgage of £15,000.

Mr Marsh tells you that he recently inherited money from his late father's estate and, using this and certain hire-purchase facilities (which—for the present, at least—he does not wish to disturb), he has bought two machines and intends to start his own firm, Marsh Contracting Company. He will be driving one machine and will employ one other person.

As financial adviser you are the first person to whom Mr Marsh has turned in setting up his business, although he has been given the name of local accountants who will be willing to advise on book-keeping systems and to act as auditors.

You are required:
a)   to identify the matters on which Mr Marsh needs financial advice, both as a personal and as a business customer, both now and in the longer term;

12 marks

(b)   to outline the services which your bank can provide to meet his requirements.

8 marks

Total 20 marks

16 You have been asked by Mr Brown, a customer of many years' standing, whether he can come to see you, together with Mr Cotton, who is another of your customers.

Mr Brown is a registered insurance/mortgage broker. Mr Cotton was, until recently, sales director of a subsidiary company of a major UK textile company. You have heard that Mr Cotton is setting up a new company, and you surmise that the purpose of the meeting will be to ask if you will take on the company's account. The only information you have been able to obtain is as follows:

(i)   Mr Brown has attended to all Mr Cotton's insurance/pension requirements.
(ii)   From your files you know that Mr Cotton's previous work involved importing raw materials from the Far East which were processed to foreign designs to produce decorating materials for use in major high street department stores. It is said that the new venture will compete with Mr Cotton's previous company.
(iii) Mr Cotton will have £30,000 from redundancy payments and savings to start the new company.
(iv)   It is believed that the new company would be looking to borrow about £20,000 from the bank.
(v)   It is estimated that turnover in the first year's trading will be £750,000.

Required:
Identify the bank services which are most likely to be of interest/value to Mr Cotton's company, and give full reasons for your suggestions.

Note: Assume that there are no restrictions which would prevent Mr Cotton from setting up in competition with his previous employer.

20 marks

17 Arthur Carefree has run his own manufacturing company, Carefree Manufacturing Ltd, for 10 years, during which time reasonable profits have been retained each year and the latest audited balance sheet you have seen — 30 September 1980 — showed a healthy position, with a capital base approaching £100,000. You are aware that Mr Carefree relies entirely on the audited accounts, normally produced six months after the year-end, to assess the performance of the company. In June last year, when renewing the company's overdraft facility of £30,000, you tactfully suggested that there would be some advantage in introducing financial controls into the business but Mr Carefree was unimpressed and you decided not to press the matter.

Mr Carefree calls to see you today by appointment. He brings the audited accounts for the year to 30 September 1981. These show a loss of £15,000 even after Mr Carefree had halved his remuneration from £20,000.

He is particularly concerned since the bank statements have shown the account solidly overdrawn for the past five months, and at the end of last month the balance slightly exceeded the limit. Additionally, he explains that two major customers are demanding a 5% reduction in price when he was hoping for a 5% increase and three customers have just failed, leaving him with bad debts totalling £8,000, all in respect of work carried out during the last financial year. In the meantime, the Inland Revenue is pressing him to bring the company's PAYE payments up to date.

Mr Carefree also mentions that he has spoken to his accountant but could not really understand the advice he was given. However, he recalls the comments you made last time and asks if you could explain the controls you had in mind.

How would you respond to this request?

(4/82) *20 marks*

18 You agree to hold an 'Open Day' at your branch for the upper sixth form of a local school. The students, all aged 18, are to arrive at 4.00 p.m. They will be escorted round the office by the office manager, after which you have agreed to answer their questions.

Various questions have been submitted to you in advance of the visit, including the following:

I have heard that a future development in banking is a point-of-sale payments system. What does this mean and how will the system work? Will I be able to use it?

Outline your response to the question.

7 marks

19 As branch manager you have recently received the following letter from one of your bank's overseas correspondents:

Dear Sirs,

Messrs A. B. Smith & C. D. Brown

We are writing to introduce our above-named customers to you in anticipation of their arrival in the United Kingdom and should be grateful if you would kindly offer them the usual banking facilities. We are pleased to confirm that they have been known to us for a number of years and that their business transactions have always been satisfactorily conducted.

Arrangements have already been made for the purchase of a retail shop in your area from which they will be selling cameras, binoculars and hi-fi equipment to satisfy the more expensive tastes. Messrs Smith and Brown are well versed in modern business techniques and control systems and have built up an appreciable knowledge of this type of business in this country. Whilst it is not expected that any financial assistance will be required from your bank, Messrs Smith and Brown have expressed a wish to be introduced to your subsidiary company or specialist department which would be able to discuss with them facilities which are intended to encourage sales.

Yours faithfully,
J. Peterson
(Manager)

Identify and describe the service(s) which you consider will satisfy the customers' requirements and indicate the benefits which the customers would receive if they were to make use of the service(s) available.

20 marks

20 Harry Morris is managing director of TIN AUS Engineering Ltd, a successful machine tool engineering company which has banked at your branch for nearly fifty years. Notwithstanding the recession, the business is still prospering with turnover currently averaging £½million per month and this year's pre-tax profit expected to reach at least £½million. Over recent years there has been considerable capital expenditure on new machinery, all of which has been funded out of cash flow. You have agreed an overdraft limit of £300,000 at the fine rate of 1½% over base rate, but no borrowing has occurred for over six months.

Substantial credit balances—up to £½million— are now being seen on the current account. Over the past five years or so, surplus funds have been invested with you on seven days' notice deposit account, but this has at times resulted in some overdraft on the current account pending the expiry of the seven days' notice. This charging of overdraft interest has irritated Mr Morris.

Harry Morris approaches you to see if an improved scheme could be offered particularly as he has been told that higher rates of interest can be obtained than those available on deposit account. How can you help?

(4/82) *20 marks*

21 At a recent meeting with Mr Smith, managing director of your valued customers AB Engineering Ltd, during which you discussed the company's borrowing facilities, Mr Smith expressed his concern for the future. His worry was not the lack of work, but rather the competition for labour resulting from the movement of companies into the area. A substantial new office block has been completed in the town and a large United Kingdom insurance company has already announced its plans to move its main administrative work-force into these premises.

AB Engineering Ltd has a turnover in excess of £5 million p.a., it employs 100 skilled and semi-skilled engineers and fitters, and a further 40 administrative staff dealing with invoicing, general book-keeping, salaries and other clerical duties. The company also has a small accounting department dealing exclusively with preparation and monitoring of the company's cash flow projections and the costing of contracts.

Mr Smith feels that the higher office salary structure of the insurance company will entice some of his administrative staff, particularly as the insurance company's recruitment drive will start shortly. AB Engineering feels unable to raise the salaries and fringe benefits of its office staff because of the effects on the other sections of the work-force, and Mr Smith is resigned to disruption through loss of staff and the repercussions on the general efficiency of his company.

Required:
What opportunities do you see for introducing Mr Smith to specialised bank services which might be used to counter-balance the feared loss of staff and which at the

same time will develop the bank's overall business? Having identified the appropriate services, show briefly why they are relevant to the company's needs.

20 marks

22 Pressnice Ltd is involved in pressings for a wide range of UK customers. The company has banked with you for seven years and you have agreed various borrowing facilities for them. Over the past two years, trading has been difficult and losses totalling £70,000 have been incurred. You have been unwilling to increase the present limit of £150,000 which is secured by a first charge over the company's freehold factory, valued 12 months ago at £200,000 but which you feel is now worth less than this figure.

Six months ago, cheques were presented which took the borrowing to £165,000. You threatened to dishonour the cheques but reluctantly agreed to pay them. Within one week, funds were paid into the account to correct the position, since when the account has worked within the agreed limit. However, you know that this has resulted in slower payments to creditors and there is now some pressure from certain suppliers.

Arthur Solvet, the financial director, calls to discuss the present position of the company, since he is worried by the pressure from creditors, including the Inland Revenue in respect of PAYE. Sales have increased to £650,000 for the past six months and the company is back into profit. However, current debtors total £265,000.

Mr Solvet understands your unwillingness to increase the overdraft limit, but says he has heard that there are two facilities available to raise cash specifically against sales. He asks if you would explain the two facilities to him.

What advice would you give him? How would your bank be able to help him, and what conditions would probably be attached to any facility? (9/82) *20 marks*

23 Stay Bright Holdings Ltd is a holding company with six subsidiary companies involved in general engineering. By careful planning and control the group has continued to remain profitable. The record over the past three years has been as follows:

Year to 31 April	1982	1983	1984
	£	£	£
Sales	6.14 million	7.26 million	8.40 million
Net profit	200,000	175,000	225,000

The capital base of the business is now standing at £1.85 million.

The business has banked with you since it was incorporated in 1936 and the accounts of all the subsidiary companies have been transferred to you on acquisition. Overdraft facilities of £½ million have been agreed. However, in March 1983, as they were purchasing their last subsidiary company, the directors were introduced to an American bank, which agreed to provide a loan of £¼ million at a better rate than you were prepared to offer. This offer was taken up.

The directors are John and Harold Bright, sons of the late founder, and Anthony Cash, management accountant, who was appointed 17 years ago as the first subsidiary company was acquired.

The shareholding is split as follows: 40% to John Bright and his family; 40% to Harold Bright and his family; 20% to Anthony Cash.

The three men are now in their mid/late fifties. Other than their homes, all of their personal financial resources are in the business. They have become concerned at this and would prefer to correct this imbalance without, of course, losing control of the company.

They approach you at this early stage for general guidance on the options available to them. They explain that in due course they will need to discuss matters with their accountant and solicitor, and possibly with the American bank, but they feel that as their banker you are better able to help them.

What advice would you give them? How could your bank help them?

20 marks

24 Henry Barker-Hind is the sales director of Clear Lamp Ltd, a company manufacturing road lighting equipment. The accounts of both the company and Mr Barker-Hind are maintained at your branch.

Mr Barker-Hind calls to see you to explain a decision he and his co-directors have just reached. Up to now sales have been confined to the home market; in the past two years, this market has been very difficult and their sales have declined. They realise that they must try to export.

To this end, Mr Barker-Hind is to depart for Jeddah in three weeks' time with the intention of spending three months in Saudi Arabia and the Gulf States, developing sales.

Since this is the first time his company has undertaken this exercise, he discussed the matter with his brother-in-law, who is the financial director of another local company. His brother-in-law's company had undertaken a similar venture two years ago involving a visit to Canada and he recalled that his bank had been able to assist them.

Mr Barker-Hind wondered whether you would be able to help him and his company.

Describe the assistance and advice you could give Mr Barker-Hind.

20 marks

25 Two days ago you received a telephone call from Mr Stevens, a director of one of your customers, Reproduction Sales Ltd. You had recently returned some of the company's cheques to its suppliers and the purpose of Mr Steven's call was to arrange an appointment to discuss the matter.

The file shows that very recently your area office raised the company's limit to £55,000 but made it clear that this was not to be exceeded. As a result of these firm guidelines, you have felt compelled to return the cheques in question to keep the overdraft within the limit prescribed.

Also on record is the company's history which shows that it started in business four years ago selling high quality reproduction antique furniture to UK retail outlets. During the last two years or so, more and more of the company's sales have been to overseas customers, and Mr Stevens has admitted that this side of the business has developed on a rather haphazard basis. The company ships furniture against orders but it has to wait until the overseas agents have made their sales before proceeds are received in the UK. You know from previous discussions that substantial discounts are received for prompt payment to suppliers and Mr Stevens does not wish to disturb this arrangement. Mr Stevens also mentioned that it was the company's practice to give 'long lines of credit', but he did not go into detail.

Required:
In the light of your knowledge of the company's present trading arrangements and the extract of the trading figures given below, prepare notes for the next interview. These notes should outline the company's problems and indicate which specialist banking services are likely to be of assistance to the customer.

	1982 £	1983 £	1984 £
UK sales	250,000	220,000	275,000
UK debtors	60,000	60,000	80,000
Overseas sales	–	115,000	200,000
Overseas debtors	–	40,000	60,000

20 marks

26 You have recently been appointed manager of one of your bank's branches in the Midlands. Following a recent discussion with the managing director of Alpha Engineering Ltd, you have been invited to tour the company's factory. At the original meeting, the managing director mentioned that his company hoped to secure a substantial overseas contract to supply and install a number of generators for a new electricity complex in Australia. Because of the specialised nature of the contract, it was expected that funding would be required over a minimum period of eight years. You are told that the company's negotiating team expects to fly out to meet the Australian representatives within the next two months and that members of this team will wish to meet you on your forthcoming visit. They will be interested to hear what specialised services your bank has to offer which will help them in their negotiations. You have been told the contract will be worth approximately £2 million, that settlement is expected to be in sterling but that in any case no exchange risks will be incurred.

In preparation for your visit, you have looked through your branch files on this company customer, and have discovered that it is a substantial private company with a first class record and that its management is regarded as being very able. You also note that Alpha Engineering has experience of export business and carries ECGD cover.

Required:
Tabulate the specialised bank services that are likely to be relevant to the company's

needs in connection with this specific contract and give a brief explanation as to how these services might help the company's negotiators.

20 marks

27 Your customer, Bandage Ltd, is a manufacturer of medical supplies. For many years, the company has traded only in the UK, mainly supplying National Health Service hospitals. However, the directors have decided recently that they need to increase sales by exporting.

The managing director, Eric Lasto, has just received the first export enquiry. It involves supplying a government in the Middle East. The order requires an initial delivery of goods worth about £75,000, followed by six deliveries of about £25,000 each at monthly intervals. Mr Lasto is particularly keen to win this first order since 75% of the supplies could be bought in at very good prices from two other UK manufacturers.

In the documents, Mr Lasto notices various requirements with which he is unfamiliar, including:

(i)   a tender guarantee for 10% of the total price;
(ii)   a performance bond; and
(iii)   an advance payment guarantee.

He asks if you could explain these requirements and indicate to him from where he could obtain the necessary facilities.

From your records, you are aware that the company has a capital base of about £¼ million and sales last year exceeded £1 million. You have provided an overdraft facility of £100,000 secured by a debenture, incorporating a fixed and floating charge.

Required:

(a)   An explanation of the terms *tender guarantee, performance bond* and *advance payment guarantee,* noting any special factors in this particular case.

10 marks

(b)   Where could Bandage Ltd obtain these facilities, and what special factors, if any, would the provider consider in this case?

10 marks

Total 20 marks

28 Rivendell Packaging Ltd is a small private company which has had an account with the bank for five years. Mr Proudfoot, the managing director, has called by appointment to see you today. Previously the company has bought in its materials from a UK supplier, but Mr Proudfoot believes the company could acquire the same materials abroad at a lower cost. He asks you to explain what assistance the bank might provide to help the company import these materials.

Identify those bank services which you would wish to discuss with Mr Proudfoot, and explain what advantages they would offer to the company.

20 marks

29 Henry Black is the financial director of Southdown Electronics Ltd. The company, which was incorporated six years ago, is involved in the manufacture of electronic components. Three years ago you were concerned for the company's future; however, over the past 18 months trading seems to have been more successful and there has been no pressure on the bank overdraft facility.

On reviewing the annual statistics, you notice that the turnover through the bank account in 1983 for Southtown Electronics Ltd comfortably exceeded £1 million. This was the first time the company's turnover had reached this figure and you wrote a letter of congratulation to Henry Black.

Mr Black calls to see you today. He explains that the company consists of a small management team of six people who control the production, sales and admin-istration staff. The team—three directors and three senior staff—have worked for the company since its incorporation. During the first four years it was a hard struggle developing the products but the company is now reaping rewards for the effort, and good profits are beginning to appear. The budgets suggest that these profits should increase significantly over the next few years.

Over the past six years, staff benefits, including salaries, have necessarily been restricted. However, salaries have recently been increased substantially and six company cars have been issued. There are no other significant staff benefits. The directors wish to offer other benefits to the team but have been unable to agree on any one specific benefit, although they have agreed on one requirement: that the scheme needs to be tax-efficient for the company and for the member of staff.

Mr Black asks if you could help them by recommending an appropriate benefit.

Required:

(a)   Your recommendation as to a suitable scheme for Southtown Electronics, noting the various forms in which it could operate and giving details of the benefits.

14 marks

(b)   An outline of the functions which the bank would perform in the operation of such a scheme, indicating the section/department of the bank to which you would refer Mr Black.

6 marks
(4|84) *Total 20 marks*

30 Mr Arthur Penny is company secretary of Two Cents plc, a public company banking with a competitor bank. Mr Penny, who is in his early fifties, has maintained his personal account with you for many years. You notice him standing in the banking-hall and, since he looks very tired and worried, you enquire after his well-being.

He explains that he is under considerable pressure of work. His two clerks, who normally deal with shareholders, were tragically killed in a motor accident six weeks ago. The despatch of half-yearly dividends should have been made today but had yet to be balanced; work on the recent rights issue was still outstanding;

and, following a bid last week by Kwik Buck plc, his directors want him to send out defence notices early next week even though they own over 50% of the shares and have rejected the bid.

With holiday commitments finally completed, this morning he has been able to recruit staff from the general office but, with the cut-back in staff generally, inevitably this will result in delays elsewhere.

Indicate the service you would recommend to assist Two Cents plc and outline its operation.

(9|83) *20 marks*

31 Mr Thornton is the financial director and company secretary of your customers, XYZ Ltd, distributors of frozen foods. During general discussions with you, Mr Thornton mentions an administrative difficulty he is encountering. This involves the control and payment of expenses, including petrol, of the sales force.

Apparently there are 20 sales representatives covering the whole of England and Wales. Each representative settles his own expenses and then claims reimbursement from head office, supporting the claim with appropriate invoices. In the past, claims were normally submitted monthly, but with the increased cost of petrol and entertaining, the frequency of reimbursement has increased, with many weekly claims.

Although the company's book-keeping is computerised, Mr Thornton feels that he has less control of these expenses than in the past and additionally is having to issue up to 100 cheques per month.

Identify the bank service which is most likely to assist Mr Thornton. Give full reasons for your suggestion and indicate any conditions that may have to be specified.

(4|83) *20 marks*

32 You have been approached by the secretary of the local Young Farmers' Club to give a talk to members on 'Sources of finance for farmers'. The secretary mentions to you that two months ago the manager of a competitor bank had addressed members on conventional bank finance for farmers and discussed overdrafts, loans and medium-term loans from the bank in detail. For that reason, it was hoped that you would concentrate on sources of finance other than conventional bank facilities.

Required:

Prepare outline notes for your talk, listing the various sources of finance, with brief comments on each facility. If a clearing bank is involved, either directly or through a subsidiary company, this fact should be recorded in your notes.

(9|83) *20 marks*

214

ANSWERS

1 There are a variety of packages which a bank may offer directly to meet the financing needs of businesses. These packages may be made up of one or more of the following types of finance.

Overdrafts

(a) These represent an agreed 'line of credit': the business may overdraw its account up to a pre-agreed limit.
(b) Overdrafts are repayable on demand or the facility must be regularly re-negotiated. Thus, overdrafts are best suited to meet the working capital requirements of a business.
(c) Overdrafts offer a number of positive advantages to a business:
    (i) Flexibility — the business may draw as little or as much of its facility as it needs, so long as it remains within its agreed limit. This is very useful where temporary peaks of expenditure must be financed, for example, tax payments, seasonal inventories.
    (ii) Low cost — interest is only charged on the amount of the facility used on a day-to-day basis.

Loan facilities

All loan facilities offer two characteristics which distinguish them from overdrafts:

(a) Certainty: the amount of the facility and the terms on which it is granted are fixed at the outset. Once established, the facility is not subject to review, and provided the borrower complies with the terms on which the facility was granted, it cannot be revoked.
(b) Discipline: the loan facility is granted subject to a pre-defined repayment programme. Maintaining these repayments imposes a degree of financial discipline and budgetary control on the business which is absent from an overdraft facility.

Loan facilities are available for a variety of time periods:

(a) Short-term loans.
(b) Medium-term loans: This has been a major growth area in recent years. For example, over 40% of bank finance to manufacturing now takes the form of medium-term loans.
(c) Long-term loans (over 10 years). These are only likely to be available to established businesses with good growth prospects; and they may well be made available by the bank's merchant banking subsidiary.

The banks have developed a number of special loan schemes, particularly those orientated towards business start-ups and business expansion. For example, Barclays Bank in recent years has offered the following loan packages to business customers:

a) Business expansion loans:
    (i) Purpose — capital investment in small to medium sized businesses.

(ii)   Term — must not be greater than the life of the asset purchased, but might be up to 20 years.

(iii)   Amount — up to £500,000.

(iv)   Interest — may be either fixed rate or variable rate.

(v)   Repayments — repayment of capital may be deferred for up to two years, though interest must be serviced.

(b) Business start loans:

(i)   Purpose — financing the establishment of a new business or the expansion of an existing business with a new product.

(ii)   Term — five years.

(iii)   Amount — up to £50,000.

(iv)   Interest — no interest is charged. The cost of the loan is expressed as a percentage royalty on the borrower's sales.

(v)   Repayments — no capital is repaid until the end of the five-year period.

2

(a) An acceptance credit is a facility with a bank whereby short-term finance may be raised.

(i)   The bank agrees an acceptance credit facility with a business customer.

(ii)   The customer is permitted to draw bills of exchange on the bank up to an agreed limit.

(iii)   The bills are tenor bills usually payable at 60 or 90 days.

(iv)   When the bank has accepted the bill, it can be sold, normally through the discount market, and cash raised against it.

(v)   The customer will realise less than the face value when the bill is sold, the difference being the discount rate.

(vi)   However, because the bank is an undoubted name ('eligible bank') the bill will be discounted at the finest possible rate.

(vii) The customer will pay a commission to the bank for the privilege of using the acceptance credit.

(viii) When the bill matures, it will be paid by the bank debiting the customer.

(ix)   In practice, it is perfectly permissible for the facility to be 'rolled over' by the customer drawing a new bill on the bank and selling it to repay the original bill.

(b) The benefits of an acceptance credit facility are as follows:

(i)   An acceptance credit is an alternative source of short-term finance to an overdraft facility.

(ii)   Unlike an overdraft, the cost of the finance is known in advance. While base rate and hence overdraft rates are subject to variation, the discount rate at which the funds are borrowed is fixed when the bill is sold.

(iii)   The discount rate on an eligible bank bill (a bill accepted by an eligible bank) is very fine. It may be cheaper to raise short-term finance through an acceptance credit than on overdraft.

(iv)   The customer is not restricted to raising funds in sterling. It is also possible to draw bills in currency.

Whether an acceptance credit would be suitable for XYZ Ltd depends very much on the nature of the company and its needs:

(i) Acceptance credits are only available to 'good risk' companies, since the bank undertakes a significant contingent liability in making such a facility available. If the customer is not in funds when the bill matures the bank as acceptor is still legally bound to pay it.

(ii) For this reason, the bank may well insist on holding security for the contingent liability.

(iii) As the minimum facility is around half-a-million pounds, acceptance credits are only suited for larger companies with a significant short-term financing requirement.

XYZ Ltd would appear to suit these criteria, though the bank would almost certainly want to see a reduction in the marked overdraft limit if it was providing an alternative acceptance credit facility.

(c) Acceptance of bills of exchange is a traditional merchant banking function. However, the clearing banks also offer the facility through their merchant bank subsidiaries.

3 Industrial hire-purchase facilities are provided by the banks through their finance house subsidiaries.

(a) The business customer 'hires' the asset in return for a contractual obligation to make monthly or quarterly rental payments.

(b) At the completion of the hire-purchase contract, title to the asset is transferred to the customer.

(c) The payments include an element of interest on the funds advanced by the finance house to purchase the asset. The interest rate may be fixed at the outset of the contract or may vary with the finance houses' base rate.

Industrial hire-purchase offers the business customer a number of advantages:

(a) Use of industrial hire-purchase relieves pressure on:
(i) the customer's own capital resources; and
(ii) the bank accommodation available to the customer.
The customer's own capital and banking facilities are left free to finance other aspects of the business.

(b) Assistance to budgeting
Regular contractual payments of the hire-purchase rentals forces a degree of budgetary discipline on the business, as well as allowing for a planned pattern of expenditure on business assets.

(c) Self-financing
Since the business has the use of the asset, it should normally 'earn its own keep'.

(d) Simplicity and flexibility
Hire-purchase contracts are straightforward and easy to understand, even for a new or financially naive businessman. Moreover, the terms of the package can usually be adapted to meet the needs of a particular business.

(e) Industrial hire-purchase will probably be more expensive than a bank term loan as a means of acquiring a business asset. Against this higher cost, however, there are several offsetting advantages:
(i) A finance house may well be prepared to help in situations where bank finance would not be forthcoming (for example, because of lack of security).

(ii)   Using hire-purchase leaves the business's other 'lines of credit' intact. Bank accommodation may be used for other purposes.

4 Mr Brown may be told that many of the basic advantages of leasing remain as they always were:

(a)   Pressure is relieved on:
 (i)   the company's own capital resources; and
 (ii)   bank sources of finance which remain available for other purposes.
(b)   Budgeting is assisted since fixed and regular rental payments must be made for the use of the asset.
(c)   The use of leasing should be self-financing, since the company has the asset and may pay rentals out of the income it earns.
(d)   The 'deposit', if any, required in the form of advance rental payments is likely to be less than on comparable sources of finance such as industrial hire-purchase.
(e)   Leasing facilities are fairly flexible and can be largely tailored to the needs of the company.

However, in two major respects, leasing has changed markedly.

Taxation

Up to the Finance Act 1984, leasing had important tax advantages to many companies:

(a)   Purchases of plant and machinery were eligible for 100% capital allowances against taxation in the first year of ownership.
(b)   However, to be able to make full use of these capital allowances, it was necessary for a company purchasing an asset to be earning sufficient profits to generate a tax liability against which the capital allowance could be offset.
(c)   Companies making a loss or making only modest profits would not be able to take advantage of the first year capital allowances.
(d)   However, with leasing, the leasor (the bank leasing subsidiary) owns the asset and hence claims the capital allowances. The lessor gains the advantage of these indirectly through reduced rental payments.

However, with the Finance Act 1984, the capital allowances on investment in plant and machinery are to be progressively reduced to:

75%	1984/85
50%	1985/86
Zero	1986/87

Instead, the first year allowance will be replaced by a 25% p.a. writing-down allowance on the purchased asset.

In the transitional period up to the end of the tax year 1985/86, leasing continue to have reasonable taxation advantages. After this, however, the lessor will onl be able to write down the leased asset at 25% p.a. against its tax liability. Con sequently, the lessee is unlikely to see much benefit in reduced rental payments.

Treatment in the lessee's accounts

Leasing has also, traditionally, enjoyed the benefit of being an 'off-balance-sheet' item. This has meant that:

(a) neither the asset nor the rental liability appeared in the lessee's balance sheet;
(b) the annual rental payment was simply a charge against the lessee's profit and loss account.

This was advantageous because it was a way of acquiring the use of assets without disturbing the lessee's gearing (the ratio of loan finance to capital in the business).

However, as a result of SSAP 21 (Statement of Standard Accounting Practice) 'Accounting for Leases', finance leases will cease to be off-balance-sheet transactions. Finance leases (which is the type of leasing the banks are involved with) will have to be recorded in the lessee's balance sheet:

(a) showing the value of the asset; and
(b) as a liability, the present value of the obligation to pay future rental payments.

Thus, as a result of this accounting standard, leasing of assets will have a broadly similar effect on the gearing of the business to the hire-purchase of the same assets.

5 The Unlisted Securities Market (USM) was set up in November 1980, with the objective of allowing small and medium-sized companies to raise capital through the London Stock Exchange.

On the face of it, AB Electronics Ltd could be a suitable company to make use of the USM:

(a) Companies with capitalisations as small as £½ million have raised capital on the USM.
(b) The USM is particularly useful for raising outside capital to permit the expansion of the company.

Provided the company is prepared to see wider ownership of its shares, there are a number of significant advantages in going to the USM:

a) The company will be able to tap into a wholly new source of external capital.
b) The USM provides a way of giving a regular and independent valuation of the company's shares which makes them more attractive to hold.
c) The USM also provides a way for the family to liquidate part of its holding in the company, if cash is needed for other purposes (e.g. to meet taxation liabilities such as capital transfer tax).
d) A USM quotation is likely to bring favourable publicity: it is an indication of the success of the business.
e) As compared to a full Stock Exchange listing, use of the USM has several advantages to the smaller company:
    (i) Use of the USM is much cheaper than a full Stock Exchange listing.

(ii)   Less documentation and formality is required.

(iii)   The proprietors of the company need only offer a minimum of 10% of the equity to the public, as compared with 25% with a full listing. This is advantageous where a family wish to see only a small dilution of their ownership.

A company can come to the USM in one of three ways:

(a)   *An introduction*   This is the cheapest way of coming to the USM since no marketing of the shares is required. However, it is only suitable where the company already has 10% at least of its shares in public hands, and is looking for a wider market for its shares.

(b)   *A placing*   This is appropriate where the company does not have the 10% minimum of its equity in public hands. The sponsoring broker or merchant bank buys the shares being offered by the company, and sells them on at a higher price.

    (i)   The majority will go to clients of the broker or bank.

    (ii)   However, 25% of the offered shares must be offered to jobbers who make them available to the general public.

(c)   *Offer for sale*   This is a general offer to the public to subscribe for shares. It is less popular since it is considerably more expensive than a placing; but where the company wishes to raise large amounts of additional capital, an offer for sale is obligatory.

Mr Jones should be told that the bank would be able to help his company with the proposed USM capitalisation in two main ways:

(a)   The bank's merchant banking subsidiary will be able to provide detailed advice on when and how to come to the market, and at what price.

(b)   The merchant banking subsidiary would act on behalf of the company whether it chose:

    (i)   a placing; or

    (ii)   an offer for sale.

(**Note**: a listing would not be appropriate for AB Electonics Ltd as it would seem likely none of their shares are presently publicly owned.)

6 The merchant banking subsidiaries of the clearing banks offer broadly the same range of services as the more traditional merchant banks. In terms of their advisory role to companies, there are two main areas in which this has particular importance

(a)   advice on the issue of shares on the Stock Exchange or on the Unlisted Securities Market (USM); and

(b)   advice on mergers and take-overs.

Issue of shares

The merchant banking subsidiaries will provide advice in two distinct situations:

(a)   where the company is coming to the market for the first time to raise capital

(b)   where the company is already listed on the Stock Exchange or participating under the USM, but wishes to raise further capital by way of a rights issue.

Where the bank's subsidiary acts as the 'issuing house' on behalf of a company, it fulfils a number of functions:

(a) It will advise the company on important aspects of the issue such as the offer price.
(b) It will ensure the correct information is supplied to support the issue, as laid down under Stock Exchange Rules.
(c) Where a public issue is involved, the merchant bank will administer the applications and the allotment of shares for the company.
(d) Where shares are subject to a 'placing', the merchant bank will place the shares with their clients, typically pension funds, insurance companies, etc.
(e) The merchant bank will arrange for the issue to be underwritten: any shares not taken up at the offer price by the public will be taken up by the underwriters.

Advice on mergers and take-overs

The merchant banks, including the clearing bank subsidiaries, have come to play a very prominent role as advisers in take-over and merger situations.

(a) Where a company wishes to take over another company, it will employ a merchant bank to advise on such strategic issues as:
    (i) the bid price for the other company;
    (ii) the nature of the bid, cash or shares or a combination of both;
    (iii) if and when to increase the bid price.
(b) Equally, where a company is the subject of a take-over bid, it will consult its merchant bank on such issues as:
    (i) whether to recommend acceptance or rejection of the bid;
    (ii) how to defend against the take-over bid.

7 ICFC (Industrial and Commercial Finance Corporation) is the largest subsidiary of the '3i's Group' (Investors in Industry). In turn, the '3i's Group' is 85% owned by the English and Scottish clearing banks and 15% owned by the Bank of England.

ICFC operates by raising wholesale deposits and employing them in the provision of tailor-made financing packages for small to medium sized companies. ICFC is prepared to help in a range of circumstances:

(a) start-up finance for new businesses;
(b) finance for the expansion of established companies;
(c) taking an equity stake in a company, in order to release some of the proprietor's capital;
(d) assistance with management buy-outs.

The financing package for each company is tailored to the specific needs of that company; but it will draw on one or more of the following elements:

( ) Term loan:
    (i) 5-20 years term;
    (ii) capital repayments may be scheduled to coincide with the company's cash flow;

  (iii) the interest rate is fixed at the outset of the loan for its duration;

  (iv) amounts from £5,000 to over £2 million are available (though over 50% of loans are for £50,000 or less).

(b) Venture capital: ICFC is prepared to take an equity stake in companies, taking up:

  (i) preference shares; and/or

  (ii) ordinary shares.

  ICFC will take only a minority stake (usually 10-30% of the equity) and does not intervene in the running of the company.

Additionally, ICFC offices are able to offer other sources of financing:

(a) Technical Development Capital Ltd (TDC) is a sister company which specialises in finance for companies in high technology industries, in which conventional financial institutions have always found difficulty in helping because of the problem of risk assessment.

(b) Estate Duties Investment Trust plc (EDITH) is an investment company managed by ICFC. It specialises in taking minority stakes in unlisted companies, allowing existing shareholders to raise cash to meet taxation liabilities or for other purposes.

(c) ICFC Leasing Ltd provides both leasing and hire-purchase facilities to companies.

8 The primary role of banks in relation to management buy-outs will be financing. The role of the banks in financing a management buy-out may be classified under three headings:

(a) Assisting the 'managers' to raise personal finance in order to buy a share in the business being taken over.

(b) Provision of direct financial assistance to finance the purchase of the business from its previous owners.

(c) Provision of continuing financial support to allow the business to continue to trade after its acquisition.

Assistance to managers

The managers and other employees who intend to take over the business will obviously need to finance the purchase of a significant stake in the business, yet it is unlikely that many of them will have large amounts of free cash available for investment. The bank may be able to assist them in one of two ways:

(a) The bank may be prepared to make term loans directly to the managers secured against their personal assets, for example, second mortgages on their homes.

(b) Alternatively, if the bank itself cannot help, it should be able to introduce the managers to other institutions, for example, insurance companies, which are prepared to lend to them.

Direct financial assistance

The bank's merchant banking subsidiary or venture capital subsidiary may be prepared to provide financial assistance to enable the managers to take over the business. This assistance may include one or both of the following:

(a)   term loans;
(b)   taking an equity stake in the business.

If the bank cannot help directly, it should be able to put the managers in touch with other venture capital organisations, such as ICFC, which may be able to help.

Continuing financial assistance

It is not enough for the managers to be able to finance the acquisition of the business. They must also be able to finance the continued running of the business. The bank may help in several ways:

(a)   *Overdraft facility* This would be appropriate to assist the company in meeting its working capital requirements.
(b)   *Financing asset acquisition* When the business needs, from time to time, to acquire new business assets, the bank may help:
    (i)   directly with a term loan facility; or
    (ii)   indirectly through leasing or hire-purchase finance provided by its finance house subsidiary.

An example of how such a financial package might work is shown below.

Proposition The purchase of ABC Ltd for £500,000 with the provision of a further £100,000 for working capital.

Package

		£000
Managers	'A' ordinary shares	90
Institution (e.g. merchant banking subsidiary)	'B' preferred ordinary shares	40
	Voting equity	130
Institution	Redeemable preference shares	240
	Capital	370
Institution	Loan	130
		500
Clearing bank	Overdraft	100
		600

The buy-out team has acquired 70% of the voting equity, but has put in only 18% of the buy-out price and only 15% of the overall funding requirement.

Venture capital may be defined as money invested in a business from external sources (i.e. not by the proprietors themselves) in return for an equity stake in the business. Many small businesses, as they expand, will find:

(a)   that their gearing will not allow them to raise more loan finance; while
(b)   the proprietors cannot afford to increase their own equity stake.

In these circumstances, a banker could well find himself called upon to provide advice on alternative sources of additional venture capital.

With the growth of interest in small firms, there has been a growth in the number of institutions prepared to put up venture capital for appropriate businesses. This growth was reflected in the formation of the British Venture Capital Association in 1983. The major sources of venture capital are considered below.

The banks

Both the traditional merchant banks and clearing bank subsidiaries are able to assist with venture capital provision.

All the clearing banks have venture capital schemes. These are provided either:

(a)   through their merchant banking subsidiaries (e.g. the County Bank subsidiary of National Westminster); or
(b)   through specialist subsidiaries, e.g.
      Pegasus Holdings – Lloyds Barclays Development Capital
      Midland VC $\Big\}$ Midland
      Moracrest

As the business continues to grow and prosper, the merchant banking subsidiaries may again be able to help. When the company has reached a sufficient size, it will be appropriate to look for further capital through the Unlisted Securities Market. Merchant banks will be able to help either:

(a)   by arranging a placing; or
(b)   by arranging an offer for sale.

(**Note**: see question 5 for further details.)

3i's Group

The Investors in Industry (3i's) Group is 85% owned by the English and Scottish clearing banks, and 15% owned by the Bank of England.

(a)   It is prepared to provide tailor-made financial packages including equity as well as loan finance.
(b)   One of its main features is that it does not ask for a say in how the company is run through a seat on the Board of Directors.

(**Note**: see question 7 for more detail on the financial packages offered by the 3i's Group.)

Specialist venture capital organisations

A number of other venture capital organisations have grown up which are unconnected with the banks. They have been described as more 'pro-active organisations'; that is, they are not simply involved in making an investment in suitable companies, but become closely involved in the management of the companies which they back.

Business expansion scheme

This scheme was introduced in April 1983 by the government to encourage people with investment funds available to use them to take an equity stake in expanding businesses.

To qualify under the BES, the investment must be in a qualifying company engaged in a qualifying trade:

(a)   The company must not be quoted on the Stock Exchange or Unlisted Securities Market.
(b)   It must be a UK resident company.
(c)   It must be a UK trading company or holding company for a group of wholly owned UK trading companies.
(d)   Qualifying trades exclude companies engaged in finance, leasing, legal and accountancy services, and since March 1984, farming.

Provided the investor takes up new ordinary shares issued by the company, up to £40,000 invested in any one financial year will enjoy tax relief at the full marginal rate of tax of the investor.

For example:

	£
Cost of shares	10,000
Less: Tax relief (at 60%)	6,000
Net cost of shares	4,000

However, to gain these tax benefits, the investor must fulfil certain criteria:

a)   He must be a UK resident.
b)   He must not be 'connected with' the company.
c)   The shares must be held for a minimum of five years to gain full tax relief.
d)   Capital gains tax will be payable when the holding is realised, but the buying price will be the cost of the shares before tax relief.

A business looking for venture capital can take advantage of the BES in two ways:

)   The business may know of someone who is not a 'connected' person, and who is prepared to make an equity investment in the company. In practice, such individual investments are more likely to come about as a result of an introduction by a professional adviser, for example, an accountant, who has

225

a client who is looking for tax avoidance opportunities.

(b) Business Expansion Scheme funds: a number of professionally managed BES funds have emerged. High rate taxpayers gain the same tax reliefs by investing in the fund which in turn invests in eligible companies. From the investor's point of view there are two advantages:

   (i)   Assessment of suitable investments in small companies is a skilled and time-consuming business. The investor effectively off-loads this problem on to the fund managers.

   (ii) Normally, a BES investment in a company must be at least £500. This limits the investor's ability to spread risks. However, where investment is made through a BES fund, this minimum does not apply, enabling the investor to obtain a better spread of risk.

If the company needing to raise venture capital is assessed as having good growth prospects, it may attract an investment from one of the BES funds.

10 Many of the clearing banks now operate a business advisory service.

(a) The bank second experienced managerial staff into their business advisory units.

(b) The staff collect information about the business:
   (i)   from the firm's accounts and records; and
   (ii) by visiting the business and interviewing the management.

(c) Subsequently a report is prepared and presented to the proprietors of the business:
   (i)   analysing the strengths and weaknesses of the firm; and
   (ii) suggesting possible improvements.

(d) The initial report is normally free of charge to the businesses which are bank customers, though any follow-up visits may be charged.

The business advisory service is prepared to investigate a diverse range of areas connected with the business. These include the following:

(a) *Objectives of the business* This involves helping the business to define what it is in business to achieve, since all the other planning and control of the business follows from this. Having established the basic objectives being pursued, it will be necessary:
   (i)   to convert these objectives into operational targets;
   (ii)   to devise a long-term plan to achieve these targets;
   (iii) to communicate the targets and the plans to employees responsible for their fulfilment;
   (iv)   to devise effective criteria for measuring how well the business is meeting its planned targets.

(b) *Budgeting* This involves explanation of the importance of budgeting to the successful running of a business. From this follows:
   (i)   advice on how to prepare effective budgets; and
   (ii) advice on how to use budgets, particularly as a means of monitoring actual performance.

(c) *Costing* The business must have an effective system for costing its activities. In particular, the firm needs to be able to identify the costs associated with different aspects of its operations. The business advisory service will help with information on different costing systems, and advice on which system might be appropriate for the particular firm.

(d) *Pricing* A firm's pricing policy clearly affects its revenue. The advisory unit will wish to analyse and advise on:
 (i) how prices are fixed in the business;
 (ii) whether mark-ups used by the firm are comparable with those used by other firms in the same industry;
 (iii) how sensitive demand is to price changes (demand elasticity).

(e) *Cash flow* Cash flow is crucial to the working capital requirement of the business:
 (i) Advice will be offered on effective cash flow forecasting methods.
 (ii) The need to compare forecast and actual cash flow with the budget will be explained.

(f) *Credit control* Effective credit control is an essential ingredient in avoiding cash flow strain. The business advisory unit will analyse and advise on:
 (i) the effectiveness of the firm's credit control system;
 (ii) the efficiency of the firm's debt collection system;
 (iii) whether the firm has a worse bad debt experience than similar firms in the same industry.

(g) *Stock control* Poor stock control can be both disruptive to the smooth operation of the business if inadequate stocks are held and expensive where working capital is tied up in holding excessive stocks.
 (i) The firm will need to have an efficient and accurate system for recording stock levels.
 (ii) Effective liaison is needed between the production and sales sides of the business.

(h) *Management accounting information* Effective control and management of the business, so that it achieves its objectives, requires accurate and up-to-date information on the performance of the business.
 (i) The firm may well need advice on introducing appropriate systems for producing management accounting reports.
 (ii) Also, help in the interpretation and use of such reports may also be needed.

Given the erratic progress of Hammer Repairs Ltd and the concern expressed about the lack of management controls, this is likely to be an area which receives particular attention from the business advisory service.

(i) *Book-keeping and financial records* The precondition of good management accounting reports is that the firm should have a sound system of keeping up to date and accurate financial records. The business advisory unit will analyse the present systems, and advise on whether and how they might be improved.

(j) *Capital investment appraisal* In the development and expansion of the business, scarce capital resources must be deployed as effectively as possible.
 (i) The advisory unit will analyse whether the firm uses any system for appraisal of its investment decisions.
 (ii) The unit will also advise on which investment appraisal technique is likely to be most helpful to the company.

(k) *Finance* Where additional finance is required, the business advisory unit can suggest less obvious alternative sources of finance to the firm.

11 First of all, the quotation in the question should be corrected since Barclays Bank sold off its factoring interests in 1983. However, all the other major clearing banks retain their factoring interests.

In describing the service offered by factoring to business customers, it is necessary to realise that factoring consists of three distinct services:

(a) debt administration;
(b) credit protection;
(c) finance.

Debt administration

This is essentially a computer-based service.

(a) The factor will maintain the sales ledger for the client company.
(b) Invoices will be despatched to customers of the client company.
(c) Debts owed to the client company will be collected.
(d) The factor provides a measure of credit control by ensuring prompt invoicing and chasing slow payers.

The service is charged for by the factor. It is usually offered with credit protection as a combined package, and charged for on the basis of turnover of the book debts. However, despite the charge there can be several advantages to the client company in making use of the debt administration service.

(a) *Savings on administrative costs* There are savings in clerical staff since the client has effectively subcontracted its debtor administration to the factor. There should also be savings in managerial and supervisory time which no longer needs to be devoted to this task.
(b) *Prompt payment of debts* The more professional invoicing and debt collection service should lead to prompter payment of debts owed to the client company. This improves the productivity of the working capital since it turns over more quickly.
(c) *Management savings* Management time is released from the problems associated with control and management of the company's debtors: they can devote all their energies to production and sales.

These advantages are particularly beneficial to small to medium sized companies, since they could not provide such a quality of debt administration service for themselves at a comparable cost.

Credit protection

This involves protection of the client company against the risk of bad debts.

(a) *Credit information* Factoring companies have an unrivalled information base on the credit-standing of UK and overseas companies. Thus, they are well placed to advise client companies on the degree of credit risk associated with a particular customer.

(b) *Credit insurance* The client company, to all intents and purposes, replaces its many trade debtors with a single debtor, the factor. The factor collects payment on the invoices and hands it on to the client company. However, if one of the client company's customers defaults, the factor undertakes to pay the client company.

Obviously, the factor will not be prepared to provide the credit protection service to a client company which has customers which are assessed as a bad risk. But, assuming they are assessed as a reasonable risk by the factor, the client company is relieved of all worries about bad debts.

Finance

In addition to debt administration/credit protection, the client company can also turn to the factor as a source of finance.

(a) A factor may be prepared to advance up to 80% of the face value to a client company as soon as the invoices are issued.
(b) In due course, when the trade debtor pays, the factor will gain repayment with the balance being handed over to the client company.
(c) The factor will charge interest on the funds advanced against the invoices until payment is received, usually somewhere in the range of 2–4% over base rate.

Factoring as a source of finance offers a number of advantages to client companies. Traditionally, it has been seen as a last resort for a financially troubled company. But increasingly it is being seen as a sensible strategy for an expanding company to convert its trade debtors into cash.

(a) Factoring advances are an alternative source of short-term finance to bank overdrafts. However, they have several advantages over an overdraft:
    (i) A factoring advance may be available to a client company which is unable to negotiate a comparable overdraft facility.
    (ii) Factoring finance expands in line with the client company's business. Overdraft facilities tend to be based on audited accounts which may give a very conservative picture of the present financial state of an expanding company.
    (iii) Whereas an overdraft facility will appear in the client company's balance sheet, factoring advances are an off-balance-sheet item. Thus, they do not adversely affect the company's gearing.
(b) A factoring advance effectively increases the productivity of the client company's working capital. Instead of the working capital having to finance a period of credit for buyers, 80% of the client's sales are immediately converted to cash, and are available for redeployment in the business. This means either:
    (i) the firm is able to finance an expansion of its trading activities from the same working capital base; or
    (ii) the firm can finance the same volume of trading activity from a smaller working capital base.

(c)   The greater efficiency with which working capital is deployed is particularly useful in the export trade, where time taken by buyers to pay can be very much longer than in domestic trade.

Target market

It is important to realise that many companies are, for one reason or another, unsuitable for factoring services. A company which falls down on one or more of the following criteria will tend to be an unsuitable subject for factoring:

(a)   Turnover or sales:
    (i)   not under £100,000 p.a.;
    (ii)   ideally not less than £250,000 p.a.
(b)   There must not be a large number of debtors for small amounts.
(c)   The company must not be involved in either:
    (i)   a speculative business; or
    (ii)   an unusual or specialist business where assessment of credit risk is difficult.
(d)   There must not be one or a small number of debtors since this provides too concentrated a risk.
(e)   Companies selling a large range of low-priced products to the general public are most unsuitable.
(f)   Companies with a high bad debt record are unacceptable.

12 It would seem sensible to restrict the talk to the main developments in money transfer and management for corporate customers of the banks. Accordingly, the following services would be covered.

Bankers Automated Clearing Services Ltd (BACS)

This system of money transfer is based on the well established Bank Giro credit payments mechanism. However, rather than payments being cleared manually between the banks, they are settled automatically by an exchange of computer data.

A corporate customer who wishes to make use of the BACS system must be sponsored by his bank.

(a)   The BACS system can be used by companies for a variety of payment purposes:
    (i)   For making payments to third parties, such as trade creditors, whether on a regular basis by means of standing order/direct debit or on an irregular basis.
    (ii)   For payment of wages and salaries direct to the bank accounts of employees.
(b)   Corporate customers wishing to make use of the BACS system must submit the necessary payments data to the BACS computer centre:
    (i)   This may take the form of data on magnetic tape, floppy disk or cassette.
    (ii)   From January 1984, BACS users have been able to transmit their payments data to the BACS computer centre by a telecommunication

link, rather than having physically to deliver the data on a tape, etc. This new extension of the service is known as BACSTEL.

There are several reasons why corporate customers may find the BACS system advantageous.

(a) Though charges are negotiated between the company user and its bank, they should be appreciably lower than for payments made manually.
(b) Once the corporate customer is geared up to use the BACS system, it is much more simple and convenient than manual payment:
   (i) The output of the company's own computer system can be used directly as the input to the BACS payment system, without any intervening paperwork on the part of the company.
   (ii) Payments data can be originated at any time, but with instructions that payments should only be effected on a specified date. This enables the company to process payments at its convenience, and to spread the work-load more evenly.

Clearing House Automated Payments System (CHAPS)

This is a much more recent innovation in the payments system, coming into operation in February 1984. However, like BACS, it is based on an earlier payments system: the Town Clearing system.

Like the Town Clearing, CHAPS is designed to achieve same day inter-bank settlement on high value payments. However, there are important differences:

(a) Like the Town Clearing, the minimum size of payment which CHAPS deals with is £10,000.
(b) However, CHAPS is a computer-based payments system, whereas the Town Clearing is a manual system.
   (i) There are twelve settlement banks, each with its own 'gateway' computer which gives it access into the CHAPS system.
   (ii) Each settlement bank transmits and receives payment instructions through its gateway computer to other settlement banks.
   (iii) Once accepted, payments made by CHAPS are irrevocable, and represent guaranteed cleared funds.
   (iv) Settlement between the banks is on a same day basis.
(c) Since CHAPS is a computer-based system, it can be accessed countrywide by the telecommunications network. This stands in marked contrast to Town Clearing which is only available on cheques drawn on bank branches within the City of London.

Corporate customers cannot use the CHAPS systems directly. But provided the company invests in the appropriate office computer terminal, it will be able to gain access to the CHAPS system via its own bank's gateway computer.

The CHAPS system has advantages for corporate customers:

(a) It can be a convenient and simple way of effecting payment to or receiving payment from other companies.

(b) The payments are guaranteed: once the payment has been received from the originating settlement bank, it cannot be revoked.

(c) The company gains same day value: the recipient of the funds will obtain value on the payment on the same day that it is originated.

(d) The CHAPS system allows these advantages to be enjoyed by companies outside the City of London, and without the cumbersome procedures of conventional 'telegraphic transfers'.

It is important to remember, however, that corporate customers wishing to use the CHAPS system must:

(a) be originating payments which are individually at least £10,000; and

(b) invest in the necessary computer interface which allows them to make use of their own bank's gateway computer.

Cash management services

One of the fastest growing professional specialisms in medium to large companies is that of the corporate treasurer. The corporate treasurer will typically have a number of functions to perform for his company:

(a) cash flow forecasting and management;

(b) management of foreign exchange rate risk;

(c) management of interest rate risk;

(d) advice on the raising of capital for the company.

The banks are increasingly developing a range of services to assist the corporate treasury manager:

(a) Cash management services: these are being developed by the banks, to allow the corporate treasurer to use computer terminals to access information on important aspects of the company's financial position, for example:
    (i) cleared balances;
    (ii) cash flow forecasting.

(b) Linked with this, the systems of funds transfer already examined (BACS and CHAPS) can be used to manage the company's day-to-day position as efficiently as possible.

(c) The banks also offer corporate treasurers access to various financial markets:
    (i) Money markets — for the development of short-term cash surpluses at market rates of interest.
    (ii) Foreign exchange market — for hedging exchange rate risks.
    (iii) London International Financial Futures Exchange (LIFFE) — which offers a variety of futures contracts which can be used to hedge exchange rate and interest rate risk.

13 Corporate trusteeship refers to trusts set up by corporate bodies for the purposes of their own business. There are a number of examples of corporate trusteeship performed by the banks. It is proposed here to examine only the more important ones:

(a) pension fund trusteeship;

(b)   debenture trusteeship;
(c)   unit trust trusteeship;
(d)   consortium trusteeship.

Pension fund trusteeship

The most popular form of occupational pension scheme is that based on the pension fund; that is, the contributions of the employees and the company are invested in a portfolio of assets, and these provide the income from which pension benefits are paid.

All pension funds require a trustee and a manager for the fund's assets; and the bank is prepared to provide these services.

(a)   *Trustee to the fund*   This will involve the bank being formally appointed as trustee to the fund.
    (i)   The bank will hold the assets in which the fund is invested.
    (ii)   The bank will collect together the contributions of both the employees and employer.
    (iii) Maintenance of contributions records for each employee will be undertaken.
    (iv)   The bank will oversee the investment of the funds in accordance with the pension fund trust deed.
    (v)   Arrangements will be made for the payment of pensions to retired employees.
(b)   *Investment management*   The bank is also prepared to manage the assets in which the pension fund is invested. The service is based on the bank's investment management service.

Appointment of the bank to act on behalf of a company pension fund offers a number of advantages:

(a)   Pension fund trustee:
    (i)   Release of staff — company employees are released from the administrative work involved in running the pension fund.
    (ii)   Independence and integrity — the bank is independent from the company, and its reputation for financial probity should mean it enjoys the fullest confidence of the employees.
    (iii) Continuity — the bank can act as trustee indefinitely. This avoids the dislocation which can arise where an individual trustee leaves the company or dies.
(b)   Investment management:
    (i)   Release of staff — company staff are released from the problems of managing the investments of the fund. This can often be an onerous duty for the company secretary.
    (ii)   Professional service — the bank has 'in-house' expertise in the management of investments.
    (iii) Cost savings — the bank's service is competive with similar professional investment management services. For small to medium sized companies, the bank's service will be cheaper than employing its own investment manager.

(iv) Ease of removal − as a 'subcontract' investment manager, the bank can readily be removed. At first sight this may seem an odd advantage to mention, but a company may be more disposed to give the bank a chance as pension fund trustee when it knows the bank can be removed if it is not successful.

Debenture trusteeship

A debenture trustee is required whenever a company issues debenture stock to the general public. The debenture trustee acts in general to safeguard the interests of the debenture stockholders.

(a) The trustee holds the documents of title to the assets which have been charged as security by the company in favour of the debenture stockholders.
(b) The trustee oversees the conditions imposed on the company in the trust deed, and ensures these are not breached.
(c) If the company is in default under the terms of the debenture deed the trustee initiates action on behalf of the stockholders, for example, calling in a receiver for the company.

Banks (along with insurance companies) are the natural debenture trustees:

(a) They have the necessary skills in financial problems and asset management to enable them to act effectively on behalf of the debenture stockholders.
(b) They have a reputation for integrity and honesty which is essential in a debenture trustee.

That said, the market for debenture trusteeship has contracted, as companies have issued less and less debenture stock. However, should the market in long-term corporate debt stage a resurgence, as some commentators have suggested, this could again become a buoyant area of corporate trusteeship.

Unit trust trusteeship

Banks are involved in unit trusts in two distinct ways:

(a) as managers of their own unit trusts;
(b) as trustees for unit trusts managed by other organisations.

Note: the bank cannot be, at the same time, both manager and trustee of its own unit trust, or of a unit trust managed by an associate or subsidiary. Usually bank unit trusts use an insurance company as trustee.

The role of unit trust trustee is both responsible and fairly onerous.

(a) A unit trust is administered under the terms of a trust deed. The trustee has overall responsibility for ensuring that the terms of the trust deed are observed, notably by the trust managers.
(b) The trustee must also ensure Department of Trade regulations are observed, particularly that the funds of an *authorised unit trust* are correctly invested.

(c) The trustee is responsible for:
  (i)   holding the title documents to the assets in which the trust is invested;
  (ii)   holding the cash subscriptions of unit-holders pending their investment;
  (iii) collecting and distributing income from the trust assets;
  (iv)   issuing unit trust certificates;
  (v)   maintaining the unit-holders' register.
(d) Overall, the unit trust trustee is responsible for safeguarding the interests of the unit-holders.

As with debenture trusteeship, the combination of financial expertise with the standing of the clearing banks makes them natural unit trust trustees. Over 80% of authorised unit trusts have a UK clearing bank as trustee.

Consortium trusteeship

This is a relatively recent area of corporate trusteeship. The bank acts as 'holding trustee' for a consortium of companies sharing in some major project (e.g. North Sea oil development). The detailed duties of a consortium trustee will vary from one trust to another, but in broad terms will include the following:

(a) The trustee handles the day-to-day financial arrangements of the project, for example, stage payments, currency risk management, performance bonds, etc.
(b) The trustee is the focus for legal, accountancy and administrative aspects of the project.

14 Given the strong emphasis which has been placed on small businesses over the last decade, there is a confusing array of sources to which a new business might consider looking for start-up finance. To attempt to order the various sources, and make them more comprehensible, it would seem sensible to classify them into broad headings:

(a) bank sources;
(b) bank-related sources;
(c) non-bank sources;
(d) governmental sources.

Bank sources

(a) *Overdraft facilities*   These represent a short-term source of finance suitable to meet the working capital requirements of the new business.
(b) *Loan facilities*   These represent an advance of funds to the business for a specified time period, with a regular repayments programme usually. They are well suited to covering setting-up costs, investment in business assets, acquisition costs of licences, franchises, etc.
  (i)   Most of the banks have special business loan schemes which are purpose-designed for new businesses or which are capable of being applied for business start-up purposes.
  (ii) Some of the schemes have special features which can be helpful to a new business, for example, a capital repayment holiday of up to two years.

(c) *Government loan guarantee scheme* Where a bank is not able to lend money to a business on ordinary commercial grounds, it may still be able to lend the necessary finance under the government loan guarantee scheme:
   (i) Up to £75,000 may be available.
   (ii) The term is up to seven years.
   (iii) 70% of the borrowing is secured by a government guarantee, for which a commission is charged to the borrower.
   The scheme was renewed in May 1984 (at which time the amount of the guarantee was reduced from 80% to 70% of the borrowing). At the end of 1984 the scheme was renewed for a further 12 months to the end of 1985.

Bank-related sources

(a) *Merchant banking or venture capital subsidiary* It may be possible to raise either a long-term venture capital loan or even equity capital from the merchant banking/venture capital subsidiary.
(b) *Industrial hire-purchase* The acquisition of business assets could be financed with a hire-purchase facility from the bank's finance house subsidiary.
(c) *Leasing* Alternatively, the assets could be leased, again through the finance house subsidiary.

In the cases of (b) and (c), the business will obtain the use of the assets; and they should pay for themselves out of the income they earn. In the case of hire-purchase, the asset will ultimately be owned by the business, whereas with leasing the leasing company will continue to own the asset.

Other sources

(a) *The proprietor himself and/or his family* It would be expected that the proprietor would put money into the new business.
(b) *Business expansion scheme* An unconnected individual may be prepared to put money into the business as equity capital:
   (i) It must be an incorporated business.
   (ii) The business must be in a qualifying activity.
   (iii) The investor must subscribe for new ordinary shares.
   The investor gains the advantage that up to £40,000 invested in an unquoted company would be eligible for tax relief at his full marginal rate. For this reason, an accountant or other professional adviser may be able to introduce the new business to one of his clients who is looking for tax avoidance investments.
(c) *Specialist institutions* Specialist institutions, notably the 3i's Group (Investors in Industry), may be prepared to help in the financing of the new business. In the case of the 3i's Group, this would involve a tailor-made financial package involving:
   (i) term loans at a fixed rate of interest; and/or
   (ii) an equity stake.
(d) *Other institutions* It may be possible to tap into institutions such as insurance companies; for example, an insurance company may be prepared to make a term loan for the purchase of premises.

(e) *Trade creditors* These are a significant source of working capital for many businesses. By taking longer to settle its debts, the business has the funds available to use in the business. However, a new business should be cautious in using this method of financing. Creditors will obviously be wary of a new business until its payment record is established; and taking time to pay may give the new business a bad name and make credit difficult to come by.

Governmental sources

A wide range of governmental sources is available. The following is no more than a selection of the more important ones.

(a) *Regional assistance* Cash grants may be available on investments in new buildings and plant and machinery in the assisted areas.
(b) *Local authorities* Loans, improvements grants and rating concessions may be available depending on the authority area in which the business locates.
(c) *Rural areas* Loans on concessionary terms may be available to approved projects which create jobs in rural areas, from COSIRA (Council for Small Industries in Rural Areas).
(d) *European Community assistance* A number of schemes, through which finance is available, are offered through the European Community. For example:
    (i) European Investment Bank loans at concessionary interest rates.
    (ii) Loans and grants to businesses from the European Coal and Steel Community Fund. These may be available when jobs are created in areas where jobs have been lost in these two industries.

15 Mr Marsh's changed circumstances have created a number of matters on which he needs financial advice and at the same time, an opportunity for the bank to market some of its services.

Personal customer needs

(a) *Immediate needs* Mr Marsh has an immediate need for insurance cover to protect himself and his family:
    (i) Mortgage protection:
    In view of his new mortgage commitment, it would be sensible for him to take out a mortgage protection policy to safeguard his family in the event of his death.
    (ii) Life cover:
    A term life policy would create a cash lump sum, or a family income benefit policy would provide a continuing income in the event of Mr Marsh's death.
    (iii) Personal accident and sickness:
    Given Mr Marsh's position as a self-employed person, it would be very important to protect his income against accidents or sickness which prevented him working.
The bank's insurance service would be able to advise Mr Marsh on suitable insurance cover to meet his requirements. They would also be able to obtain competitive quotations and effect cover on his behalf.

237

(b) *Longer-term needs*
    (i)   Pension provision:
        As a self-employed person, Mr Marsh should give some thought to providing for his ultimate retirement from the business. He should be advised to take out a personal pension plan.
        (i)   This would allow him to pay premiums during his working life, and be able to purchase an annuity on his retirement from which his pension would be provided.
        (ii)   Personal pension plans are particularly attractive because they are highly tax-efficient. Mr Marsh will be able to place up to 17½% of his net earnings before tax into a pension plan, and claim full tax relief on these payments.
        Again, the bank's insurance service will be able to advise him and will also be able to obtain quotations and effect cover on his behalf.
    (ii)   Making a will:
        As a result of his inheritance, and particularly if his new business is successful, Mr Marsh is likely to leave a substantial estate. He would therefore be well advised to make a will.

        The bank's executor and trustee subsidiary would be prepared to advise on making a will; and he would obviously be a very suitable case for the bank to be appointed as his executor.
    (iii) Taxation advice:
        Mr Marsh's taxation affairs are likely to become much more involved.
        (1)   He will have a self-employed income from his business, and this offers him the possibility of mitigating his tax liability by making full use of the allowances available.
        (2)   He could well face the problem of capital transfer tax when his estate is handed on at death or when the business is passed to his children on retirement.
        This is a sensitive area, and Mr Marsh clearly already has an accountant. But if he is not already professionally advised on his tax affairs, the bank's taxation advisory service would be prepared to act.

Business customer needs

(a) *Immediate needs*   The new business will create a whole series of risks for Mr Marsh which could occasion him a loss. He would therefore be sensible to insure against these risks.
    (i)   Public liability insurance:
        Particularly in relation to the nature of his business, Mr Marsh may be subject to claims from third parties in respect of damage to property or injury to persons. He therefore needs suitable public liability insurance cover to protect against these risks.
    (ii)   Employer liability insurance:
        Mr Marsh is initially intending to employ one person, and his payroll may increase as the business grows. He therefore needs insurance cover for any claims by his employees that arise from their employment.
    (iii) Vehicle insurance:
        Mr Marsh is clearly intending to operate vehicles. He will therefore need insurance cover for these.

In each case, the bank's insurance service will be able to advise on appropriate cover, obtain competitive quotations and effect cover for the business.

(b) *Longer-term needs* As the business expands there are likely to be additional financing requirements.

    (i) There may be an increased working capital requirement. The bank may be prepared to assist with an overdraft facility.

    (ii) Further machinery will need to be purchased, either to replace the existing machines or to purchase additional ones as the business expands. The bank would wish to assist here, and might do so in any of the following ways:

        (1) term loan;

        (2) hire-purchase facility;

        (3) leasing.

Additionally, as Mr Marsh has not run a business before, it can be anticipated that he will find some difficulties arising. He has a need for effective advice, and a visit and subsequent report from the bank's business advisory service may well prove beneficial.

16 The primary need which Mr Cotton has is to launch his new company successfully.

(a) Mr Cotton clearly has experience of the business in which his new company will operate. But, at least latterly, this experience has lain on the sales side of the business.

(b) In his new company, Mr Cotton will have to be able to manage the business efficiently and to control it effectively.

For this reason, an early introduction to the bank's business advisory service would seem to be desirable. This service will be able to assist Mr Cotton to introduce effective systems of management and control particularly in those areas where he lacks previous experience.

(a) *Budgeting* In order to run the new business successfully and to achieve his objectives, Mr Cotton must ensure the company employs budgeting techniques. In broad terms, a budget is a financial plan for the next year of operation, covering expected sales income, costs and profit. If Mr Cotton has been largely involved on the sales side of the business, he may have little familiarity with the preparation of budgets. This is therefore an important area in which the business advisory service could help.

(b) *Cash flow forecasting* Proper knowledge of and control of cash flow is essential if the new business is to avoid liquidity problems. The business advisory service will advise on the preparation of cash flow forecasts, and how to monitor cash flow in relation to the budget. Again, this is an area where Mr Cotton may not have had prior practical experience.

(c) *Costing* If the new business is to be successful, it must ensure it has a system for accurately costing different units of output. On the one hand, excessive costs are likely to render the business uncompetitive; but on the other hand, underestimating costs of a particular output could inflict a loss. The business advisory unit will again assist Mr Cotton to set up a costing system appropriate to his business.

(d) *Pricing* Equally, a successful pricing policy is critical to the competitiveness and profitability of the new company. This may well be an area in which Mr Cotton feels more familiar given his 'sales' background. But even here, the business advisory unit can help him to institute a sound pricing policy.

(e) *Credit control* It is not sufficient to sell the new company's products — payment must be obtained. If customers take an unreasonable time to pay, this may throw a strain on the company's working capital. If the company experiences a significant bad debt problem, this can inflict a significant loss on the company. The business advisory service can help in several ways.

    (i) Advice on how to set up an efficient system for prompt invoicing and debt chasing.

    (ii) Advice on credit risk assessment, and particularly the specialised services available to gain credit information including the bank's own status opinion service.

(f) *Stock control* As a former sales director, Mr Cotton may well be inclined to place a high priority on holding good stocks of finished goods to be able to supply customers from stock at all times. What he will need to realise is that, while this may be desirable, holding excessive stocks is expensive to the business in terms of the working capital (in this case the bank overdraft) tied up in the stocks. The business advisory service will assist in the implementation of stock control systems to ensure customers can largely be supplied from stock without the cost of excessive inventories.

(g) *Management information* Conventional accounting statements portray how well the business was doing in the past, rather than how well it is doing now. The company needs an effective management accounting system to ensure that Mr Cotton can obtain the necessary information on current performance to be able to manage the business effectively. Assistance in the development of effective management information systems is likely to be one of the most important areas of help which the business advisory service could offer.

(h) *Book-keeping and financial accounts* The company must have an effective system for recording the basic data from which the account statements about the company's position will be drawn. The advisory unit will help Mr Cotton to identify a suitable system for his company.

(i) *Finance* The bank is already helping Mr Cotton, and he is putting in his own funds. However, the business advisory service may well be able to help by alerting Mr Cotton to the various less obvious sources of finance which he might in future make use of:

    (i) For the acquisition of additional business assets, leasing or industrial hire-purchase.

    (ii) Factoring, and especially advances against invoices, would be particularly beneficial in a business which is likely to have a reasonable spread of customers, where average invoice size is likely to be significant, and where there may be delays in obtaining payment through customers taking extended credit.

    (iii) Sources of venture capital, when the business needs to expand.

(j) *International trade* The new company will be importing raw materials. I Mr Cotton's experience has been mainly on the sales side, he may have littl experience of the administrative and financial problems involved in importin goods. The advisory unit could help here, and an introduction to the bank' overseas department may also be beneficial.

17 Carefree Manufacturing Ltd clearly faces a number of problems.

(a) *Cash flow problem* This is reflected in the solid bank overdraft, in the problem over payments from customers, and in the pressure from the Inland Revenue.

(b) *Debtor control problem* This is apparent both:
   (i)   from the long delay in collecting payments from customers (the customers who have failed incurred their debts in the previous financial year); and
   (ii) from the incidence of bad debts which suggest that credit control is not all it should be.

(c) *Management control* The criticism levelled at the company by the manager when the overdraft facility was renewed remains pertinent. Mr Carefree is relying wholly on historical accounting data and has no information on the current trading position of the company.

The bank can respond to Mr Carefree's request in several ways.

Business advice

Mr Carefree clearly is looking for some immediate help. A branch manager should be able to provide general advice on how to introduce some basic techniques of managerial control.

(a) Advice on the introduction of procedures for effective:
   (i)   budgeting;
   (ii)   cash flow forecasting;
   (iii) costing;
   (iv)   pricing.

(b) Advice on the calculation of simple indicators of the financial position of the company, for example, ratio analysis:
   (i)   profit to sales;
   (ii)   debtors to sales;
   (iii) cost to sales;
   (iv)   stock to turnover;
   (v)   return on capital.

In the longer term, the company would benefit from an introduction to the bank's business advisory service. The service would almost certainly be free to Mr Carefree and would involve a report being prepared covering the key problems faced by the company.

(a) *Budgeting* Advice on the preparation of budgets for the coming year, which will cover expected sales income, costs and profits. Effective budgeting would help the company, in various ways, to overcome its present problems.
   (i)   The company will have a working plan on which to base its operations.
   (ii)   As a longer-term plan, the budget will force the company to look beyond day-to-day issues towards the crucial areas for success, such as cash flow, costs and profitability.
   (iii) The budget is an instrument of control over the business, setting targets for costs and sales and providing a measure of actual performance

against budgeted performance.

(b) *Cash flow* The advisory unit would also give help on setting up effective systems of cash flow forecasting. Forecasting will not solve the company's cash flow problem but it will give warning of impending difficulties, and give the company a chance to take corrective action.

(c) *Credit control* The business advisory service would also help the company to improve its credit control systems:

    (i)   More effective credit assessment methods may be helpful, particularly in view of the recent bad debt history.

    (ii)   Greater efficiency on invoicing and debt collection may also be possible.

(An introduction to the bank's factoring subsidiary may also be advised — see below).

(d) *Management control* The key to the more successful running of the business lies in the development of a management information system. It is essential that Mr Carefree should have accurate and up-to-date information on the company's performance now and not how well it was performing up to 18 months previously. The business advisory unit will help the company to adopt suitable management accounting systems.

Factoring

The types of problem encountered by Carefree Manufacturing Ltd could be alleviated by making use of the bank's factoring subsidiary, with the proviso that the company is a suitable client for factoring.

(a) *Debt administration service* There is some evidence of slowness to collect debts owed to the company. If the factoring subsidiary acted for the customer, it would arrange:

    (i)   prompt invoicing; and

    (ii)   efficient debt collection.

(b) *Credit protection* The factoring subsidiary has first-rate credit intelligence, and the company would be able to obtain highly reliable advice on the credit standing of its potential customers. Provided these customers were acceptable to the factor, the credit insurance aspect of factoring would ensure that the company would not suffer a loss as a result of bad debts in the future.

(c) *Finance* Clearly, the company has come under cash flow pressure. Raising finance by arranging advances of up to 80% of the value of invoices, as soon as they are issued, would improve the company's cash flow position.

18 The system which the student has heard about is known as EFTPoS (Electronic Funds Transfer at Point of Sale).

(a) EFTPoS means that, when a consumer purchases a good, the retailer will obtain payment by the direct debiting of the consumer's bank account.

    (i)   At the time the sale is made, the retailer will electronically debit the consumer's account; and

    (ii)   credit his own account.

EFTPoS is thus an alternative to cash or a cheque as a means of payment.

(b) The EFTPoS system works as follows:

    (i)   A bank customer is issued with a card which is magnetically encoded.

    (ii)   The retailer 'wipes' this card through his terminal which is on-line wit the bank's computer.

    (iii)   The customer then keys in his PIN (personal identification number).

    (iv)   The bank's computer will either authorise the transaction or reject it.

    (v)   If the transaction is authorised, the customer's account is debited either immediately, or after some predetermined time lag.

(c)   As far as use of EFTPoS by the customer goes, the system is still largely experimental. A well documented example is the scheme between BP and Clydesdale Bank at certain Scottish garages. However, for EFTPoS to be of any significance amongst bank customers, it needs to gain the acceptance of both retailers who are prepared to use it, and consumers who are prepared to allow their accounts to be debited.

19 The new customers' requirements are to be introduced to bank services which will enhance their retail sales of expensive camera and hi-fi equipment. This type of service will almost certainly be one which allows the equipment to be purchased on credit terms. Expensive equipment of this nature is the sort of consumer item which is likely to be purchased with the assistance of credit facilities; and if Messrs Smith and Brown could offer such facilities to their customers, this should increase their sales.

Point of sale credit

Consumers who wished to buy goods on credit would be able to complete an application form for a credit facility to enable the equipment to be purchased. The application would be arranged by the retailer, but it would be addressed to the bank's hire-purchase subsidiary which would provide the finance if the application were agreed.

There would be a number of advantages in Messrs Smith and Brown arranging a point-of-sale credit facility with the bank's hire-purchase subsidiary:

(a)   Most obviously, the consumer is able to make a purchase which he might not otherwise have made for lack of cash.

(b)   Sizeable credit facilities can be available to approved borrowers, and this will be especially advantageous given the expensive nature of the equipment being sold.

(c)   If credit is not available via the retail outlet, the consumer must borrow from another source. This could be disadvantageous, since the sale might be lost as a result of the consumer changing his mind about buying the good, or going to another retailer.

(d)   It would be possible for Messrs Smith and Brown to set up their own credit provision subsidiary. But by using the bank's hire-purchase subsidiary instead, they avoid the complications arising from:

    (i)   credit appraisal;

    (ii)   administration of the outstanding finance;

    (iii)   chasing debtors in arrears;

    (iv)   carrying bad debts.

Credit card

A second way in which credit sales could be stimulated is by Messrs Smith and

Brown agreeing to accept the bank's credit card in payment for goods. Transactions involving credit cards must be conducted in accordance with the following principles:

(a) The card-holder must sign a voucher for payment of the good, and the signature must correspond to that on the card.
(b) The value of the transaction must not exceed the limit agreed between the retailer and the credit card company. If it does, authorisation for the transaction must be obtained from the credit card company first.
(c) The card must be in date and not have been circulated as a stolen card.

The vouchers are paid in and the retailer's account credited.

Acceptance of the bank's credit card offers a number of advantages to Messrs Smith and Brown:

(a) Primarily, consumers are able to make purchases on credit. This should increase the level of demand for the goods being sold.
(b) The transactions are more secure in several ways:
  (i) Payment is guaranteed, providing the conditions mentioned above are fulfilled. This avoids the danger of dishonoured cheques and bad debts.
  (ii) By avoiding cash payments, the retailer avoids the security problems which arise from handling large volumes of cash.
(c) Payment can be quickly and easily obtained from the credit card company.

20 The 'problem' faced by Mr Morris is one of how to manage substantial cash surpluses for the benefit of the company. These cash surpluses are evidenced in:

(a) the substantial credit balances on current account; and
(b) the fact that, in the recent past, the company has been able to finance considerable capital investment out of cash flow.

The cash surplus management creates problems in two separate time horizons:

(a) Short-term — allowing surplus cash to accumulate on current account has a cost to the company in terms of the interest forgone in temporarily investing it in some interest-bearing form.
(b) Long-term — if the cash surpluses are not all to be reinvested in developing the company's business, it will be necessary to develop a long-term investment strategy for the surplus funds.

Short-term employment of surplus funds

The bank's treasurer's department would be able to place the cash surpluses at money market rates of interest. This would have several advantages to Mr Morris and the company:

(a) The rates of interest received would be highly competitive, and certainly far more attractive than a conventional seven-day deposit.
(b) The funds could be placed at various maturities to suit the cash flow requirements of the company.

(c)   The problem of overdraft interest in respect of temporary company borrowing could be overcome by holding a proportion of the surplus at call. This would allow the company to recall a proportion of its money market deposits to meet a temporary cash shortage.

It should be emphasised to Mr Morris that the bank will only be able to place cleared funds on behalf of the company.

Longer-term employment of surplus funds

If the company does not intend to use all or a proportion of the cash surpluses by re-investing them in the business, then it will be necessary to develop a strategy for the long-term deployment of these funds.

An introduction to the bank's investment management service would be helpful in this respect:

(a)   They would assist the company to define its investment objectives.
(b)   They would advise on suitable investments in which the surplus should be invested to achieve these objectives.
(c)   They would be prepared to act on a discretionary basis, and manage the investments on the company's behalf.
(d)   If the directors/shareholders wish to 'siphon off' some of the cash surplus from the company, they would advise on tax-efficient ways of doing this, for example, directors' pension plans.

21   AB Engineering Ltd faces the problem of losing administrative and clerical staff to a higher wage employer. The effect of this is likely to be a loss of efficiency in key areas such as invoicing and debtor control.

Clearly the bank cannot replace the lost staff. But it may be able to provide services which allow the company to subcontract some of its administrative functions to the bank, and thereby accommodate to a reduced level of administrative staffing.

Factoring

An introduction to the factoring subsidiary, and more specifically to the debt administration service, would be beneficial. This is a computer-based debt management service, and its use could have several advantages to the company:

a)   The factor would provide basic debt management services:
  (i)   maintenance of the company's sales ledger;
  (ii)   issue of invoices;
  (iii)   collection of payment from debtors.
  Thus the company would be relieved of much of the routine work of debt management and would be able to operate on a much reduced level of administrative staff.
)   The quality of the bank's service is probably higher than AB Engineering Ltd could provide for itself at a comparable cost.
)   Prompt invoicing and efficient debt collection may well improve the cash flow position of the company. It should certainly prevent the deterioration

245

which would otherwise arise from delays over invoicing resulting from reduced levels of administrative staff.

(d)   There should also be savings in management time. Time which would have had to be devoted to supervising the worsening debt management position of the company, can now be devoted to managing production and sales.

The factor will charge a commission on turnover of debtors. This will include credit protection as well as debt administration. Thus, as a bonus, the company will be relieved of any bad debt problems.

Computer services

The bank's computer bureau offers a number of computer-based services which could help the company to accommodate to the loss of administrative staff:

(a)   *Payroll service*   The bank's computer service would prepare wage or salary advices, having calculated the correct deductions for PAYE and National Insurance.
      (i)   Though the company must provide raw data on wages and salaries, administrative staff will be saved on the detailed preparation of the wage/salary advices.
      (ii)   If payment is made by BGC or by the BACS system, rather than in cash, the company will make savings on the clerical labour needed for cash wage preparation.
(b)   *Computer-aided accounting*   The computer bureau could assist the company to maintain its basic financial records, for example, the purchases ledger (and sales ledger where the factor is not used). Again this will ensure savings in administrative staff.

22   The two facilities whereby cash may be raised against sales, which Mr Solvet has heard of, are:

(a)   factoring; and
(b)   invoice discounting.

Both of these means of financing are provided by the bank's factoring subsidiary; but there are important differences between them.

Factoring

(a)   Factoring is a source of finance in that the factor is prepared to advance up to 80% of the face value of trade debts as soon as they are invoiced by the client.
      (i)   The factor is repaid when the trade debtor pays.
      (ii)   For the duration of the advance, the client company will pay interest typically in the range of 2-4% over base rate.
(b)   The factor thus provides a means whereby the client company may shorten its working capital cycle, and thereby increase the volume of trading which can be supported on a given level of working capital.
(c)   Factoring is usually an ongoing facility whereby the factor makes advances against the whole sales ledger of the client.

246

(d) In addition to financing, factoring offers two other associated services:
   (i) Debt administration:
       The factor takes over the administration of the client's debtors, covering such things as invoicing, sales ledger maintenance, and debt collection.
   (ii) Credit protection:
       Provided the factor is satisfied that the client's trade debtors represent an acceptable risk, insurance against bad debts is also available.
   These two additional services are usually offered as a package, with the client being charged a commission on debtor turnover, typically in the range 0.5-2.5% depending on the size of the business and the degree of risk.
(e) Not every company is a suitable client for factoring. Where the full range of factoring services is offered, the client will ideally have the following attributes:
   (i) A turnover of £250,000 minimum (though exceptionally figures as low as £100,000 may occur).
   (ii) Neither a few dominant customers nor many small customers (ideally 20-100 customers, none constituting more than 15% of turnover).
   (iii) A reasonable number of fairly large invoices (say around £500), not many small invoices.
   (iv) The client company will not be involved in either a speculative or high risk business; and it will not have an above average bad debt record.

Invoice discounting

(a) Like factoring, invoice discounting involves an advance against sales. It thus has the same effect of shortening the working capital cycle.
(b) However, there are important detail differences:
   (i) Typically, the whole sales ledger of the client is not taken over as it is with factoring. The client selectively discounts some of his trade debts.
   (ii) Invoice discounting may be a 'one-off' operation where occasionally the client raises money against sales at need. Factoring is normally a regular ongoing relationship between client and factor.
(c) Invoice discounting is simply a means of raising finance:
   (i) It does not offer additional services such as debt administration. The client company does its own invoicing, sales ledger maintenance and debt collection, remitting the proceeds to the discounter to clear the advance.
   (ii) If a trade debtor turns into a bad debt, the loss is borne by the client. There is no credit protection.

Conditions attached to a factoring or invoice discounting facility

Both factoring and invoice discounting have the effect of shortening the working capital cycle. This should mean the same volume of trading can be supported on a smaller working capital base.

For this reason, it may be appropriate to link the use of this supplementary source of finance with a downward revision of the company's overdraft facility.

The directors of Stay Bright Holdings Ltd face two principal problems:

(a) succession in the company;
(b) the financial situation of the directors.

Both of these problems are linked to the age of the directors and their future retirement from the company.

Succession in the company

The directors must decide on what they wish to happen to the company when they retire, since this has a major bearing on what strategies they should adopt, and on how the bank can help them:

(a) Do they wish total control of the company to remain with their families?
(b) Are they prepared to allow a proportion of the equity to pass to outsiders, but with the family retaining a controlling interest?
(c) Are they prepared to sell off the company to another company in a take-over? This seems unlikely here.

Sale of an equity stake

If the directors are prepared to sell a minority equity stake in the business, this could be beneficial in several ways:

(a) The directors, by realising a proportion of their stake in the company, will provide capital for their retirement.
(b) Control of the company will, nevertheless, remain with the family.

There are several ways in which the bank could assist the directors and the company.

Merchant banking subsidiary

The bank's merchant banking subsidiary could be of assistance in two main ways:

(a) *Equity stake* The merchant bank may be prepared to take up a minority equity stake itself in Stay Bright Holdings Ltd.
(b) *Unlisted Securities Market* As an alternative, the company could be introduced on the Unlisted Securities Market:
  (i) The merchant banking subsidiary would assist:
    – by arranging a placement of the company's shares;
    – by arranging an offer for sale.
  (ii) Since the company is not obliged to offer more than 10% of its shares to the public, the family would retain control.

Other sources of equity finance

Alternatively, the bank could arrange an introduction to an institutional investor prepared to take an equity stake in the company.

(a) Investors in Industry Group (3i's Group):
  The Industrial Commercial and Finance Corporation (ICFC) or Estate Duty Investment Trust plc (EDITH) may be prepared to help:

(i) They will take an equity stake in appropriate companies to allow family shareholders to realise a proportion of their stake in the company.

(ii) They have the particular attraction of not wishing to participate in running the company, and not requiring a seat on the board.

(b) Insurance company or pension fund.

Take-over of the company

Should the directors wish to sell the company, the bank could help through its merchant bank subsidiary. The latter may well know of companies looking to make take-over bids, and would effect an introduction.

Directors' financial position

The directors must provide financially for when they retire from the company:

(a) *Sale of shares* Where the directors have sold some or all their shareholding in the company, they will have a capital lump sum. The bank's specialist subsidiaries could provide advice on the various investment options open to the directors.

(b) *Pension provision* The directors will need to make provision to ensure their future income. Where they are retaining all or the majority of the equity, probably their most sensible course of action is for the company to invest in a directors' pension plan on their behalf:

(i) There is no limit on the contributions the company can pay in on their behalf. Thus pension benefits can be built up very quickly, an important point given their ages.

(ii) Contributions made by the company can be offset against its corporation tax liability.

(iii) Such a pension plan is a useful way of taking money out of the company without the problems of capital gains tax.

The bank could provide advice on directors' pension plans, and assist in identifying an appropriate plan (for example, through its insurance subsidiary).

(c) *Taxation* Whatever action the directors take, they will face a considerable tax planning problem:

(i) capital gains tax (CGT) on the sale of shares in the company;

(ii) capital transfer tax (CTT) when the shareholding is handed on to the next generation whether by life-time gift or at death.

The bank's trust company will help the directors to arrange their affairs in such a way as to take maximum advantage of exemptions and reliefs, and to minimise their tax liability.

(d) *Will* It would be appropriate for the bank to ensure:

(i) that the directors have made wills; and

(ii) that their present wills adequately deal with the complexity of their financial position.

If new wills need to be drawn up, the bank could arrange this with the possibility also of a bank appointment as executor.

4 There are a number of ways in which the bank can assist Mr Barker-Hind and the company with the sales trip to the Middle East:

(a) information;
(b) financial services for Mr Barker-Hind's trip abroad;
(c) back-up facilities to assist the company in winning contracts;
(d) assistance with Mr Barker-Hind's personal affairs while he is abroad.

Information

As this is the first time the company has entered into the export market, it will require as much help and guidance as possible.

(a) *Economic intelligence* The bank's economic intelligence department produces reports on economic prospects, political stability and commercial customs in specific areas of the world. This will be useful background information to Mr Barker-Hind in preparing for his visit.
(b) *Letters of introduction* The bank can furnish Mr Barker-Hind with letters of introduction which will give him access to a useful range of contacts, banks, agents, overseas trade associations, etc.
(c) Advice on exchange control and documentation regulations on the prospective export markets.
(d) Advice on sources of official aid to exporters, for example, Department of Trade help such as the Market Entry Guarantee Scheme. Mr Barker-Hind may be able to obtain financial assistance towards his trip abroad and in the promotion of sales.
(e) It would be useful for Mr Barker-Hind to go equipped with a general appreciation of settlement methods in overseas trade and of problems of exchange rate risk. The bank's international division will help here.

Financial services for trip abroad

Mr Barker-Hind will be travelling and living abroad for an extended period of time. There are a number of ways the bank can help:

(a) *Foreign currency* Mr Barker-Hind will require a cash float to meet out of pocket expenses when he arrives. The bank will obtain the currency for him.
(b) *Travellers cheques* The bulk of the money he takes with him will be in the form of travellers cheques:
 (i) They are readily encashable at a wide variety of outlets.
 (ii) They offer safety in that, if they are lost or stolen, he will be reimbursed.
(c) *Credit card* Mr Barker-Hind will be able to use either his personal credit card or a company credit card to pay bills and to obtain cash while he is abroad.
(d) *Open credits* Facilities can be arranged for him to be able to draw cash from specified banks abroad. This would be useful where he is operating in the same place for any length of time.
(e) *Telegraphic transfers* Where Mr Barker-Hind needs additional funds, whether to meet unforeseen expenditure or otherwise, the bank will transfer funds abroad to him.
(f) *Travel and medical insurance* Clearly an extended trip abroad involves significant risk of illness, personal injury and loss of property. The bank would arrange suitable cover for these risks.

Back-up facilities

Mr Barker-Hind is travelling abroad in order to secure orders. It would be useful for him to know what facilities the bank offers which would help him secure contracts abroad.

(a) *ECGD* The bank would arrange an introduction to the Export Credit Guarantee Department prior to his departure.

    (i) ECGD provide insurance against loss occasioned by default on the part of the overseas buyer or for political reasons.

    (ii) The bank would be prepared to provide financial assistance to the company at preferential rates to assist with the export orders, provided the company had taken out an ECGD guarantee.

(b) *Tender and performance bonds* As a supplier of street lighting, it is possible the company may become involved in public works contracts. If it does, it may need to provide tender and performance bonds to secure contracts, and the bank can provide these.

Personal assistance to Mr Barker-Hind

Mr Barker-Hind will be away for an extended period of time. The bank can help to ensure his absence causes minimal financial problems for his family.

(a) If not already attended to, a joint account facility or at least signing authority for his wife will ensure the family continue to have access to his account.

(b) Problems of meeting regular payments could be solved by a greater use of standing order and direct debit payments.

(c) Mr Barker-Hind could receive advice on the taxation consequences of his extended working trip abroad.

(d) It would be sensible for him to make a will before leaving, if this has not already been done.

25 Reproduction Sales Ltd appear to be facing two principal problems:

(a) A cash flow problem brought about by the 'long lines of credit' offered by the company to both domestic and overseas customers.

(b) A lack of effective control over the export side of the business. On Mr Stevens' own admission, the overseas side of the business has grown haphazardly, yet the potential risks from such overseas sales are markedly greater than with domestic sales.

Overseas sales

At present the company is supplying goods on an *open account* basis. Furniture is shipped abroad on credit terms, with settlement after the overseas agent has sold the item. The fairly lengthy time-lag before payment is received is being financed from the company's working capital.

What is required is advice on how the company can raise finance against its overseas sales, and thereby improve its strained cash flow position. There are several possibilities.

(a) *Documentary letters of credit*   This is the most secure way for the company to obtain payment for the goods it exports.
  (i)   The overseas importer instructs his bank to open a letter of credit in favour of Reproduction Sales Ltd.
  (ii) Reproduction Sales Ltd would ship the goods and present the shipping documents to a bank in the UK representing the overseas importer's bank.
  (iii) Provided the documents are in order and the conditions laid down in the letter of credit have been fulfilled, the bank will accept, on behalf of the importer, a bill of exchange drawn on it in payment for the goods.
  (iv) Reproduction Sales Ltd can then discount (sell) this bill to raise immediate finance against its export sales. With a bank acceptance on the bill it can be discounted at a very fine rate.

The bank can advise its customer on how to arrange for a documentary letter of credit to be set up, and the importance of ensuring it is irrevocable (cannot be amended without the company's consent).

Note: Given that Reproduction Sales Ltd have previously traded on open account terms, it is likely to encounter resistance from existing overseas customers to use of documentary credits. However, new customers may be more amenable.

(b) *Use of bills of exchange*   As an alternative Reproduction Sales Ltd could arrange with its importers to draw bills of exchange on the importers in payment for the furniture. These bills could be either:
  (i)   clean − a simple bill of exchange drawn on the importer, with the documents of title to the goods sent separately to the importer;
  (ii) documentary − the documents of title are only handed over to the importer after he has paid or accepted the bill.

The use of bills of exchange has two major advantages to the company:
  (i)   It puts payment on a regular footing. The company will know when the bills it draws mature and payment will be received. With open account dealings, there is no certainty as to when payment will be received.
  (ii) If the company wishes to raise finance in advance of the bills' maturing, they could be discounted.

The bank might assist the company to obtain the benefit of both of these advantages.
  (i)   The bank will collect the proceeds of the bills for the company (and prior to this obtain acceptance of the bills on behalf of the company).
  (ii) The bank may be prepared either:
    −   to negotiate (discount) the bill; or
    −   to make an advance to the company against the security of the bill.

In both cases, the bank would need to be satisfied that the company was good for the contingent liability if the bills were dishonoured by non-payment.

(c) *ECGD guarantees*   The company would be well advised to take out an ECGD *comprehensive short-term policy*.
  (i)   This would cover export contracts where credit of up to six months is extended to importers. Reproduction Sales Ltd would be insured for 90% of the loss where an importer defaults over payment.
  (ii) Where ECGD insurance cover has been held for 12 months, the com

pany could then benefit from an ECGD guarantee. This would take the form of a *short-term supplier credit guarantee* which would cover export sales on credit terms of up to six months either on open account or covered by bills of exchange.

The bank could help the company, here, in two ways:

(i)   by introducing it to the services of the ECGD:

(ii) once an ECGD guarantee had been arranged, the bank would advance finance for the export sales and at a very fine rate of interest.

(d)   *Export factoring*   The bank might effect an introduction of the company to its factoring subsidiary. It could assist the company to resolve its cash flow problem by advancing up to 80% of the face value of invoices for export sales as soon as they were issued.

(i)   The pressure on the company's cash flow would be reduced by shortening the working capital cycle.

(ii) However, there are certain drawbacks:

 –   The facility is likely to be more expensive than an ECGD guarantee facility.

 –   The factor would need to be satisfied that the company was good for the contingent liability if any of the overseas importers defaulted.

By the use of one or more of these techniques, it should be possible to help Reproduction Sales Ltd:

(a)   to ease its cash flow by raising finance against its overseas sales; and

(b)   to gain greater control over its overseas sales.

Domestic sales

Again, the company needs to raise finance against its sales in order to ease cash flow pressures. An introduction to the bank's factoring subsidiary would appear to be the most appropriate solution.

(a)   The factor would advance up to 80% of the face value of sales as soon as they were invoiced.

(b)   The working capital cycle of the company would be reduced, easing pressure on the overdraft and accelerating the cash flow from sales.

26   The bank can assist the negotiating team of Alpha Engineering Ltd to win the Australian contract in two principal ways:

(a)   providing bank guarantees;

(b)   provision of a financing package for the Australian buyer, linked to acceptance of Alpha Engineering's tender.

Bank guarantees

With large overseas contracts such as this, it is usual for the buyer to look for a guarantee that this is a serious tender for the contract; and that the tendering company will be able to complete the contract in accordance with the terms of its offer. These guarantees will usually be provided by the tendering company's bankers.

(a) *Bid or tender guarantee* This is a guarantee given by the bank that the company will enter into a contract with the buyer, based on the terms of its tender.

    (i)   If the company's tender is accepted, and it fails to sign a contract based on the tender, the guarantee will financially compensate the buyer.

    (ii)   Thus, a tender guarantee will help Alpha Engineering Ltd by giving credibility to its tender for the contract.

(b) *Performance guarantee* This is a guarantee given by the bank to the buyer, guaranteeing that the company will fulfil the contract within the terms and conditions laid down in it.

    (i)   If the company fails to complete the contract, or is in breach of one of its conditions (e.g. date of completion) the buyer will be financially compensated by the bank.

    (ii)   The performance guarantee is an expression of the bank's confidence in the ability of the company to complete the contract. As such, it will again enhance the chances of the company's securing the contract.

(c) *Maintenance guarantee* Given the nature of the contract (supply of electricity generating plant) the performance guarantee will incorporate a maintenance guarantee also.

    (i)   This guarantees that, for a specified period, the company will ensure that the equipment continues to function and that necessary spare parts are made available.

    (ii)   Again, the bank's undertaking lends credibility to the company's bid.

Thus, the negotiating team will be able to tell the Australian buyers that their bankers are backing their tender; and that they are prepared to provide suitable guarantees in support of their bid.

Finance

A second selling point which the negotiating team could take with them is a financing package. This would take the form of finance to the Australian buyers to allow them to purchase the equipment from Alpha Engineering Ltd, the finance being provided under an *ECGD buyer credit* facility by the bank.

(a) The contract, worth £2 million, would be eligible for a single contract buyer credit facility.

(b) The company already holds an ECGD policy, and so would be eligible to take advantage of ECGD guarantees.

(c) The bank would be prepared to advance up to 85% of the contract price to the Australian buyer.

(d) The bank's security would be an ECGD guarantee in its favour.

(e) The normal term of ECGD buyer credit is 5 years; but it could be extended to 8–10 years.

Clearly, it will be highly advantageous for the team from Alpha Engineering to be able to take along not only an attractively priced contract for a technically sound product but also to be able to offer financial facilities to the buyer as part of the deal.

Ancillary services

(a) Though the company has exported before, if it is not familiar with conditions in the Australian market, the bank's economic intelligence unit may be able to assist with reports and other information.

(b) The negotiating team will be travelling to Australia to negotiate the deal. The bank will help them with the usual travel services:

  (i)   currency;
  (ii) travellers cheques;
  (iii) travel insurance.

27 Tender guarantee

This is a guarantee given by the bank.

(a) The bank guarantees that Bandage Ltd will enter into a contract of supply based on its tender.

(b) If Bandage Ltd were to win the contract, but refuse to sign a contract consistent with its tender, the buyer would receive financial compensation from the bank.

Performance bond

This, too, is a guarantee given by the bank.

(a) The bank guarantees that the company will fulfil the contract within the terms and conditions in the agreement.

(b) Should Bandage Ltd fail to do so, the buyer will be financially compensated by the bank.

Advance payment guarantee

Where the buyer makes payment in advance of delivery of goods or where progress payments are made during the course of the contract, there is always a risk that the supplier will default and not complete the contract. An advance payments guarantee provides for repayment of any advance payments, by the bank, in the event of Bandage Ltd not completing the contract.

Special conditions in providing guarantees to Bandage Ltd

Clearly, the company could look to its bankers to provide the necessary guarantees to enable it to secure the contract. However, before the bank would be prepared to grant such a facility to Bandage Ltd, there are a number of points to consider.

(a) Around 75% of the supplies which Bandage Ltd will be using to complete the contract will be bought in from two other companies. The bank will need to be satisfied that not only can Bandage Ltd fulfil the contract, but also that these other two companies will be able to supply on time goods of the correct quality.

(b) Should the bank have to pay out on any of the guarantees it gives to the Middle Eastern buyer, it will look to Bandage Ltd to indemnify it for its loss.

Thus, an important part of the bank's considerations in granting the guarantees is whether the company is good for the contingent liability. This assessment will be influenced by a number of factors including the following:

(i)   the company's capital base;
(ii) the profitability of the company;
(iii) the extent of other liabilities of the company to the bank;
(iv) the value of any security held by the bank from the company;
(v)   the financial viability of the contract: does it appear to be a profitable venture?
(vi) the duration of the guarantee.

28   If Rivendell Packaging Ltd go ahead and import materials from abroad, they will be faced with a number of *additional* problems, as compared to procuring their materials within the UK.

Payment overseas

Achieving settlement with the overseas supplier for the materials received is somewhat more complex than with a UK supplier. There are several possible means of settlement, and the bank will be able to advise Mr Proudfoot about each, though the exporter will obviously be a major determinant of which payment method is used.

(a) *Open account*   A large proportion of overseas trade is conducted on open account terms: the importer receives the goods, and either pays for them on delivery or after he has taken a period of credit. If Rivendell Packaging Ltd negotiate a contract of supply on open account terms, they will have to arrange to make payment overseas. These arrangements would be made through the bank, and would take one of the following forms:
     (i)   telegraphic transfer or urgent SWIFT message;
     (ii) mail transfer or SWIFT message;
     (iii) banker's draft;
     (iv) international money order.
     The advantage to the company of this means of payment is that it would be able to operate on broadly the same terms of credit as with domestic suppliers, while the additional costs of making the payments abroad would be low.
(b) *Bills of exchange*   As an alternative, Rivendell Packaging Ltd may agree to allow their overseas supplier to draw bills of exchange on the company in order to achieve settlement. These bills may take two forms:
     (i)   Clean bills — payment would be effected by a bill drawn by the importer on Rivendell Packaging; but the company would obtain the documents of title to the goods independent of their acceptance of and payment of the bill.
     (ii) Documentary bills — payment would again be effected by a bill drawn on the company; but they would not obtain the documents of title and hence control of the goods until they had either accepted the bill or paid it.
     In either case, it is almost certain that the bills will be domiciled at the bank (drawn payable at the bank). Settlement by bill of exchange still allows the possibility of the materials being supplied on credit terms, depending on how the bills are to be drawn. But the date for payment has now been fixed by the

date of maturity of the bill: it is outside the discretion of Rivendell Packaging.

(c) *Documentary credits* The overseas supplier may insist on payment by means of documentary credit, since this is the safest form of payment from an exporter's point of view.

  (i)   Rivendell Packaging would ask the bank to open a letter of credit in favour of the overseas exporter.

  (ii) The letter would detail the amount of the facility, and conditions which must be fulfilled before payment is made.

  (iii) When the exporter ships the goods he presents the documents relevant to the shipment to a correspondent bank of the UK bank which has opened the credit.

  (iv) If the documents are in order, the exporter will be paid. Typically, this payment will take the form of acceptance by the bank of a bill of exchange drawn on it which the importer will then be able to discount.

This method of payment, from Rivendell Packaging's point of view, is more formal and likely to be more expensive. However, until the company has established itself with overseas suppliers, they may require the additional safety of documentary credit settlement.

Finance

If the company has to settle earlier for its imported supplies than on UK supplies, this may place additional pressure on its working capital. The bank may be prepared to assist in several ways:

(a) Overdraft facility.

(b) Produce loan — whereby an advance is given against the security of the imported goods, repayment coming from their sale. However, given that Rivendell Packaging are likely to be using the materials in some sort of manufacturing process, a produce loan may not be appropriate.

(c) Acceptance credit — the company would draw bills on the bank up to an agreed limit, and discount these to raise working capital. This type of facility will only be available to larger companies since the minimum acceptance credit facility is usually £½ million. It is likely that Rivendell Packaging are too small to take advantage of it.

Foreign exchange

Unless payment for the imported supplies is to be in sterling, Rivendell Packaging will encounter problems in the area of foreign exchange.

(a) *Payments in foreign currency* Where the company is required to make payment in currency, the bank will be able to procure the necessary currency for the company.

(b) *Exchange rate risk* Where payments are to be made in currency at a future date, there is always the danger that a depreciation of the sterling exchange rate would leave the company paying appreciably more in terms of sterling for its materials than anticipated. The company can safeguard itself by buying the currencies it needs under a forward exchange contract through the bank. This would fix the sterling cost of the contract to the company, irrespective of what subsequently happened to the sterling exchange rate.

Miscellaneous problems

There are a number of problems of detail which the company will face in importing for the first time. The bank can help to smooth away these problems.

(a)   *References*   Overseas exporters will not know the status and creditworthiness of Rivendell Packaging Ltd. The bank can assist by supplying references on the company's behalf (equivalent to domestic bankers' opinions).
(b)   *Insurance*   If the exporter is not insuring the consignment (FOB contract), the bank will arrange for suitable cover on behalf of the company.
(c)   *Travel facilities*   If Mr Proudfoot needs to travel abroad to arrange contracts of supply, the bank will provide the usual travel facilities.
(d)   *Overseas agents*   If the company wishes to appoint an overseas agent to represent its interests, the bank's international division or overseas correspondent bank may be able to provide lists of suitable agents.

29   The most obvious scheme for the company to adopt, which would give worthwhile benefits to the senior staff while also being tax-efficient, is an executive pension scheme. Such a scheme would offer a number of advantages if it were adopted:

(a)   The company can make unlimited payments into a pension scheme for its executives, and such payments can be set off against the company's corporation tax liability.
(b)   It is thus possible for the company to build up substantial pension benefits for its executives very quickly. However, it should be remembered that the maximum pension benefits for tax purposes are the same as those for any occupational pension scheme.
(c)   The schemes are normally flexible, allowing the company to step up its payments in profitable years to maximise the corporation tax offset while making lower payments in less successful years.
(d)   Such pension schemes would be particularly attractive if the executors are major shareholders, since it is a way of withdrawing funds out of the company without any of the capital gains tax problems which might arise where shares were realised.

If the company should decide to go ahead with a pension scheme for executives, there are three alternative ways of achieving this.

Insured schemes

Here, the pension benefits would be underwritten by an insurance company, the level of benefit being related to the level of premium paid by the company.

(a)   Insured schemes offer guaranteed minimum pension benefits to the beneficiaries.
(b)   There will usually be integral life cover to cover death before the pension becomes payable.

Should the company wish to know more about insured schemes, the bank's insurance subsidiary will be able to provide advice.

(a) The insurance subsidiary would arrange for a range of quotations to be obtained from insurance companies.

(b) If the company went ahead with an insured scheme, the insurance subsidiary would arrange the requisite cover with the chosen insurance company.

Managed pension funds

These again usually involve a scheme offered by an insurance company; but there are important differences.

(a) The pension premiums paid by the company will be used to buy 'units' in one of the insurance company's managed funds.

(b) There would be no guaranteed pension benefits under the scheme.

(c) When the pension becomes payable, the 'units' bought with the premiums are used to purchase an annuity and to create any other pension benefits. Clearly the scale of the annuity and of the pension benefits depends on the performance of the investments in which the fund was invested, and hence the value of the 'units'.

(d) Such schemes have the benefit that pension premiums are invested in a specific fund; and if the fund performs satisfactorily, the pension benefits may be better than with an insured scheme.

Again, the bank's insurance subsidiary would advise the company on the various unit-linked pension schemes offered by the insurance companies and arrange a contract with one of the life offices if required.

Self-administered schemes

This is a pension scheme in which the pension contributions made by the company are invested in a portfolio of assets, the pension fund. Pension benefits are paid from the income or sale of these assets.

(a) Self-administered schemes give the company maximum control over its own pension scheme.

(b) The schemes also give the company greatest flexibility to vary its contributions according to its trading performance.

If the company did decide to provide its executive pension scheme on a self-administered basis, the bank's Trust Company could help in several ways:

(a) Advice on how to set up such a scheme and its pros and cons.

(b) Self-administered pension schemes must have a trustee whose job it is to hold the title documents to the assets and to ensure the fund is properly administered. The company could appoint the bank to act as trustee to its pension fund. Appointment of the bank would be beneficial in a number of ways:

    (i) The bank would look after the administrative tasks associated with running a pension fund:
        — maintenance of contributions records;
        — payment of pensions to retired members.

    (ii) The continuity of the bank (as a corporate trustee the bank 'never dies') would be beneficial. It avoids the need to transfer the assets into the name of new trustees as existing trustees die or retire.

(iii) The independence and integrity of the bank will give all the members of the scheme confidence in it.

(c) A self-administered scheme is based on a portfolio of assets which must be managed against changing market conditions. The bank Trust Company would be prepared to offer the services of its investment management service.

(i) This would relieve the company and its officials of the onerous task of managing the investments.

(ii) The Trust Company has 'in-house' expertise in the effective management of assets, and so offers a highly professional service.

30 Mr Penny's and the company's problem stems from the pressure of work on the registrar's function within the company. The service which the bank might recommend to ease this problem is the bank's own Company Registrars Service. The service is available to the company even though it is not a customer of the bank.

Effectively, the company subcontracts its company registrar function to a specialist department of the bank. The main features of the service are as follows:

(a) Maintenance of the company's register of shareholders:

(i) The bank maintains the company's records of shareholders' holdings and their names and addresses.

(ii) The bank processes any changes in the register brought about by sales or other transfers.

(b) Preparation and issue of share certificates.

(c) Payment of dividends: the bank arranges preparation, printing and distribution of dividends. This is clearly an aspect of the service which the company would have found of benefit in its present situation.

(d) Reconcilation of the dividend account: full responsibility is taken for maintaining the company's dividend account, including reconciliation of the account and reminders to shareholders who have not presented their warrants for payment.

(e) Redemption and conversion of share capital or loan stock on behalf of the company.

(f) Despatch of annual reports and accounts to shareholders.

(g) Despatch of other company communications to shareholders. This would have been particularly valuable in ensuring the prompt distribution of the directors' defence to the Kwik Buck plc take-over bid.

(h) Checking of proxies: the bank processes postal proxy votes on resolutions in company general meetings.

(i) Preparation of statutory returns.

(j) Enquiries from shareholders: the bank handles all the enquiries from shareholders and from stockbrokers, etc., relating to shareholdings, transfers of shares and dividends.

Adoption of the bank's company registrar service would bring a number of advantages for the company:

(a) *Cost savings* Though the bank obviously charges a commission for the service related to the volume of work, the company should be able to make offsetting cost savings:

  (i)   Staff — a reduction in clerical staff may be possible; and certainly there will be savings on staff overtime at the critical peak periods of work.
  (ii)   Overheads — there will be savings in office overheads.

(b) *Freeing of staff* Mr Penny and his staff will be freed to carry out their principal duties more effectively.

(c) *Efficiency* The bank should be able to offer a more efficient and professional service than the company could provide for itself for an equivalent cost. Moreover, the bank's service has the capacity to absorb sudden problems in a way which clearly is not possible for Mr Penny and his staff.

(d) *Security* Company registrar's work is a confidential and sensitive area of its operation for a company to devolve. The bank's reputation for confidentiality and integrity are obviously reassuring to all concerned.

(Note: there is a slight chance that the manager might also successfully introduce Two Cents plc to its merchant banking subsidiary. They would be prepared to advise the company in relation to the take-over. However, it is almost certain the company already has such advice.)

31 The company is facing two interrelated problems:

(a) Mr Thornton believes that there has been a loss of control in respect of expenses paid to sales representatives.

(b) With up to 100 expenses cheques being debited to the company's account each month, its commission charges will be significantly higher.

The service which the bank could offer to the company to overcome these problems would be a company credit card facility. Adoption of this service would be beneficial both to the company and to its employees.

Benefits to company

(a) The company can arrange for cards to be issued to as many of its employees as it wishes, giving the company complete flexibility in the use of the service.

(b) Use of company credit cards should considerably improve the degree of information about, and control of, expenses by the sales representatives.

  (i)   Each card will have its own individual credit limit, so the company can tailor each representative's facility to his particular needs.
  (ii)   The company is free to impose its own internal conditions on the use of the card by employees;
  (iii) A monthly statement is produced for each card-holder. By showing the nature, place and amount of each transaction, the company is better able to control the expenses paid to representatives.
  (iv)   The company will also receive a monthly summary statement showing the total due from the company. This will help the company to monitor the overall position on expenses.

(c) Use of company credit cards should also work out cheaper than the present arrangement of drawing cheques to reimburse the sales representatives.

  (i)   There will be an annual fee charged by the credit card company for the service. No interest will be paid as the company will pay the account each month.

(ii) The one hundred expenses cheques debited to the company's account each month will be replaced by a single direct debit to settle the monthly account with the credit card company, effecting a significant saving in commission.

(d) Payment of the expenses account once a month in arrears, rather than on a weekly basis, should improve the company's cash flow position.

(e) The credit available is of a revolving nature: as the montly account is paid off, the full credit limit on each card is renewed.

(f) The major bank credit cards are accepted at a very wide range of garages and other retail outlets across England and Wales. The company's sales force should have no difficulty in settling their expenses using a company credit card.

Benefits to staff

It is important that the new scheme should also benefit the staff who will have to use it. If there are staff benefits, the company will find it easier to persuade its employees to cooperate with the new system for expenses.

(a) The availability of a company credit card will save the employees from the problems of carrying a cash float and from the problem of having to meet their expenses from their own pockets pending reimbursement.

(b) The monthly statement for each card-holder, produced by the credit card company, will save the employees the chore of having to write up and submit detailed claims for expenses.

(c) Employees who are trusted with a company credit card gain a psychological benefit, an increase of status.

Conditions on issue of company credit cards

The company will have to agree to be bound by the usual card-holder's agreement. However, the principal consideration is that the company is considered good for the monthly credit facility which it will enjoy. The account-holding branch will need to confirm this to the credit card company.

32 As with any business, farmers can look to their bankers for finance in the form of overdrafts and loans. However, farmers also have a number of alternative sources of finance available to them, both from the banks and from other sources.

Short-term finance

Other than a conventional bank overdraft, there are two other readily available sources of working capital available to farmers (other than their own resources):

(a) *Trade credit* This has been a traditional source of working capital to the farming industry:
  (i) Agricultural merchants have been prepared to supply seed, fertiliser, feedstuffs, etc., on credit terms.
  (ii) Payment would be made, often considerably later, out of harvest sale proceeds.

262

Trade credit is looked on with less favour by agricultural merchants today because of the pressure it places on their own cash flow, while from the farmer's point of view, he is tied to the supplier and unable either to 'shop around' or to take advantage of possible discounts.

(b) *Point of sale credit*   Again, agricultural inputs (seeds, fertiliser, etc.) are purchased from an agricultural merchant on credit terms. However, there are important differences compared to trade credit:

(i) Finance for the purchase is arranged at the time the goods are purchased, and through the agricultural merchant (point of sale).

(ii) The finance is not, however, provided by the merchant, but by a subsidiary of the bank for whom the merchant acts as an agent.

Point of sale credit is convenient to the farmer because he can simultaneously arrange both the purchase of his inputs and finance in one transaction. Also, some merchants may be prepared to subsidise the interest rate charged by the bank to encourage custom.

Medium-term finance

Apart from bank loans, there are a number of alternative sources of medium-term finance available, both from the banks and from other sources.

(a) *Leasing and hire-purchase*   Both leasing and hire-purchase of farming assets (machinery, equipment, etc.) can be arranged through the finance house subsidiary of the bank. Both leasing and hire-purchase offer a number of common advantages to the farmer:

(i) The cost of acquiring the use of farming assets is spread, thus easing pressure on the farmer's cash flow.

(ii) As an external source of finance, both leasing and hire-purchase leave the farmer free to use his own capital resources for other purposes.

(iii) The arrangement should be largely self-financing, since the farmer has the use of the assets, and can meet the rental payments from income (though with arable farming especially, income flow will be irregular and thus this is less of an advantage than with, say, manufacturing).

The tax advantages of leasing over hire-purchase are being phased out under the terms of the Finance Act 1984, which has abolished capital allowances, and by 1986/87 leasing and hire-purchase will be on the same footing in terms of taxation. One difference does remain in that under financial leases, ownership of the asset always remains with the leasor, whereas with hire-purchase, the ownership of the asset passes to the farmer at the completion of payments under the contract.

(b) *Syndicate credit*   In recent years, there has been a tendency for syndicates of farmers in a particular locality to come together to purchase farm machinery. The development of syndicates makes good economic sense:

(i) The cost of acquisition is spread over a number of farmers, rather than being borne by an individual farmer.

(ii) Particularly with expensive machinery it makes little sense for each farmer to buy the same machine which is considerably under-utilised in relation to the work available on the farm when several farms could share the same machine which has sufficient capacity to meet all their needs.

Syndication has been encouraged by the NFU (National Farmers Union).

263

Where application is made via the local branch of the NFU, the banks are prepared to put up a large part of the purchase cost of the machinery with syndicate loans repayable on terms of up to seven years.

Long-term finance

Agricultural land is a basic resource in any society and its value has consistently risen. For this reason, there is no shortage of lenders prepared to make long-term finance available to farmers, usually secured against the land.

(a) *Agricultural Mortgage Corporation (AMC)* AMC is wholly owned by the Bank of England and the clearing banks. It lends money to farmers, primarily for the purchase of land or for investment in land improvement, security being provided by a first legal mortgage over the property. There are two types of facility available to farmers:
- (i) Repayment loans:
  - term: 10 to 40 years;
  - maximum facility limited to two thirds of the valuation of the farmland;
  - interest can be fixed or variable;
  - repayments of interest and capital are made half-yearly.
- (ii) Interest only loans:
  - term: 5 to 10 years;
  - maximum facility is limited to 50% of the farm valuation;
  - interest may be fixed or variable;
  - interest is paid during the period of the loan but capital repayment is deferred to the end of the loan period.

(b) *Private loans* It may be possible for the farmer to raise long-term finance from private sources, for example, from other members of his family. The advantage here is that the facility may well be at a lower rate of interest than a commercial facility (the family member's assessment of interest will tend to be in terms of rates received by depositors rather than those charged by lenders).

(c) *Sale and leaseback* Here, the farmer would sell all or a part of the farm to an institutional investor (insurance company, pension fund); and the land is then leased back to the farmer at a rental. Such arrangements are something of a mixed blessing:
- (i) The farmer surrenders ownership of all or part of his farm, and becomes a tenant.
- (ii) The farmer becomes liable for rental payments.
- (iii) Against this, substantial capital is released which should enable him to farm more profitably.

(d) *Insurance companies* Insurance companies may be prepared to make long-term loans to farmers secured by a mortgage over the farm. Usually, the loan is cleared by an endowment policy written by the company on the farmer's life.

Government grants

Apart from borrowing money, farmers may be able to raise finance from a variety of government grants available to different types of farmer. The farmer will be able to obtain up-to-date details through the local office of the Ministry of Agriculture.

Agricultural Credit Corporation (ACC)

The ACC is not a source of finance. Rather it provides guarantees on behalf of farmers, which enable them to borrow on term loan from their bankers.

(a)   The borrowing propositions must be viable. The guarantee is typically needed because the farmer cannot provide alternative security.

(b)   The farmer must pay an annual fee for the guarantee, in addition to interest on the loan.

(c)   ACC guarantees are particularly helpful to new farmers where a bank may be concerned about the lack of 'proven track record' and tenant farmers who are unable to offer the land they farm as security.

Index

Page numbers in **bold** type refer to the introductory sections of each chapter; those in roman type are to questions, and those in *italics* are to answers.